For Sara, for everything

DUDEVILLE

A Novel by J.D. Kleinke

Bayamet Books / Portland, Oregon

ALSO BY J.D. KLEINKE

FICTION
Catching Babies

NON-FICTION
Oxymorons: The Myth of a US Health Care System
Bleeding Edge: The Business of Health Care in the New Century

Dudeville is a work of fiction. Excluding references to public or historical figures and events, the names, characters, and incidents portrayed in this book are drawn from the author's imagination and used fictitiously. Any resemblance to events or persons, living or dead, is coincidental.

Bayamet Books
www.bayametbooks.com
Portland, Oregon

Cover design by Mindee Thyrring
Cover photograph by Author
Author photograph by Rob Bodner

ISBN: 978-0-692-97776-7

Bayamet Books Edition: November 2017
10 9 8 7 6 5 4 3 2 1

AUTHOR'S NOTE

Dudeville is a work of fiction. The characters portrayed and incidents described in this novel are products of my research, imagination, self-indulgence, and spiritual attachment to several extraordinary places in the American West. Any resemblance between one of these characters and any person living or dead – aside from explicit references to public figures, mountaineering accidents, or acts of violence known to the general public – is purely coincidental. (All dogs portrayed in *Dudeville*, however, are based on real dogs. To honor their superhuman levels of physical stamina and personal loyalty, I have used their actual names.)

The dates of origin of the known universe as expressed by *Dudeville*'s narrator are based on generally accepted knowledge in 2001. These dates have been and will continue to be subject to revision, based on evolving scientific and political conditions.

I have attempted to align my descriptions of mountaineering, skiing, snowboarding and hang-gliding techniques in *Dudeville* with what were best practices in the late 1990s and early 2000s. Before proceeding into any Rocky Mountain, Sonora Desert, or Sierra Nevada wilderness area, you should understand the risks, know how to use your equipment, and be prepared for dangerous conditions. You should also use the same precautions before proceeding into a locals' bar in any small town adjacent to those areas.

J.D. Kleinke
Half Moon Bay, California
October 4, 2017

I reckon I got to light out for the Territory ahead of the rest, because Aunt Sally she's going to adopt me and sivilize me and I can't stand it. I been there before.

Mark Twain
The Adventures of Huckleberry Finn

Colorado
Summer, 2001

Summit Fever

Those kids shouldn't have been up here alone, summit-drunk and dancing around on an unstable boulder field above treeline, any more than I should have been up here alone to rescue them. But they were and I did, even if it spooked me from coming back for so many months to what had become a routine training run – an up-and-down solo climb with my snowboard and packful of emergency gear – onto the roof of the Rocky Mountains.

I probably shouldn't be back up here alone today either. But they were tourists, and I know what I'm doing. Danny and Aaron are both working, like they were a year ago. And Jill is gone again, finally and forever this time, not that I really care. I will always have these trees to keep me company, the glowing blue spruces and towering lodgepole pines and red-orange ponderosas, reaching up into a patchwork canopy of snow-bent boughs and blue sky. On this warm morning, they are shaking off big wet clumps of snow, and ripening sweet and spicy with the belated spring that is May at 10,000 feet.

They urge me up the mountain, my chest heaving against packstraps pulled tight with the weight of my board and gear, a cage for lungs scratching like dried paper for more parched air.

Slow down and stay in the box, the aerobic box, I remind myself as the first glimpse of snowfield and summit pull at me. *Breathe in, breathe out, look down at the trail, breathe in again.*

It is easy to get ahead of my own pace when I'm climbing solo; but otherwise, the solitude way up here suits me just fine. Right after Tom and Becky sold the company and I was finally able to run west, most of my big days up here in the mountains or down in the desert were exactly that: solo. No wife, no job, no kids, no worries, just me, the earth, the sky, and time.

When I look up again, the last of the snow is dropping in crusty clumps from the wind-sculpted trees, into piles across the trail, along old drifts and banks of it, spiked with cones and dusted with pine debris.

I climb up and over each snow bench with my load, into my own private sanctuary, these old trees a congregation of druid-priests in robes of glittering snowmelt. John Muir – who also started out as an engineer Back East before he too found the Presence up here – wrote love letters to the hushed anthropomorphic huddle of these old trees at altitude. But so far today, no Presence, not yet, nor any wind, just scattered birdsong, and the scratch of pikas, and the random clop of snow off a sagging limb.

Maybe the Presence is late to the mountain this morning because of the nagging memory, the lingering presence of those kids: I'm not here today so much as I'm still here last spring, when this sanctuary was pierced by a girl's scream somewhere up ahead, then more screams and a frantic flash of color through the green and gray and snow-rimmed trees.

"Help us! Please!!!" she shrieked, bounding over the ridge of snow up the trail, all spindly legs and big brown hiking boots, her dirty blond hair poking out of a blue bandana. She was maybe 25 years old and no more than a hundred pounds, her thin white arms, streaked with what looked like blood, waving at me, "Please help us!"

She almost knocked me over, winded, and when she grabbed my packstraps, I saw that it *was* blood, dried streaks of it down her arms and all over her hands. "Please! Now!!!"

I don't remember what I said or she said next, only what I felt pulling at my entire body and can feel right now: the maniacal tug of those little bloody hands on my packstraps, trying to drag me up the trail. I also remember feeling, in that same instant, myself going into shitstorm mode, something deep inside me reaching up and holding her and me in place, something rooted and solid and steady as one of these tough old trees.

Then my own voice, as if from faraway, in the eye of that shitstorm: "Yes, I'm here, and I will help you. But first," I watched myself holding and rotating her arms, scanning them for the source of the blood. "Where are you hurt?"

"I'm fine!" she screamed and pulled her arms away and bent over on her knees, gulping for air. "This is just – from that rock. I cut myself – trying to move it."

I dropped my pack and pulled out a water bottle for her, but she kept sucking for air and then collapsed onto her knees. "But you're bleeding," I pulled my snowboard off my pack, wondering what other weight I could shed before we ran up the trail. "Are you sure you're ok?"

"It's from – trying to move – that damn rock! But my boyfriend! He's trapped!"

And then I heard Aaron's voice, also from the eye of the shitstorm: *Always get their names,* he has told me a dozen times, *because communication and trust are critical.*

"What's your name?" I asked and handed her the water bottle.

"Angie –" she gulped at the water through breaths. Her face was streaked with the mud of tears, sweat, and dust. "Please! You have to help us!"

"Ok, Angie," I said, propping my snowboard and camera into the crook of a tree next to the trail, wishing I had more weight to shed but knowing all my other gear – of varying necessity in normal circumstances – might be critical in a rescue. "Take a deep breath, ok?" I cinched my pack down tight around my ax, shovel, and rope, and took the water bottle from her. "And tell me where we're headed."

"On the rocks! Up near the top! My boyfriend – his leg is trapped! Please hurry!"

"Toward the summit?" I pulled on my pack, now half the weight without my snowboard. "Up on the boulderfield?"

"Yes! Those damn boulders!" She took another gulp of water and coughed it back up. "His leg is caught – and I think it's broken! I tried to move the rock," she held up her bloody hands, "and it – I – I think I made it worse. Please come now!"

She sprinted back up the trail, and I hurried after her, jumping right out of the aerobic box, instantly winded, my breath gone and legs turning to dumb stumps.

But I caught her soon enough: she was actually trying to run, still frantic and wiped out by the altitude but driven by bad adrenaline, the worst way to get anywhere up here.

A few minutes up the trail, the last of the shriveled druid-pines gave way to a sweep of rock and snow, a terminal moraine cascading like a great river of rock, tumbling down at us and what was left of the treeline. She scrambled up the brown snowpack of trail zigzagging through the moraine, clawing at loose boulders for balance. I ran after her as fast as I could, trying not to post-hole in the snow or lose my balance with my pack pulling at me, flushed with my own bad adrenaline, time slowing, an odd metallic taste welling in my mouth.

"Hurry!" she turned and screamed at me from the top. "Please!" And then she was gone.

I crested the moraine, onto the long, jagged lip of the boulder field spilling off the summit of Sunrise Peak. Reverberating through the rock I could hear and feel her frantic route before I could see her on it. She wasn't following the trail, marked by cairns if you know to look for them, that switchbacks up shelves of relatively stabilized boulders; she was scrambling straight up the middle, two and three hundred pound rocks shifting and clacking and clattering in her wake like giant bowling balls. As I started up the field and tested my own weight against each sharp, jagged, loose rock – splashed with lime-green and burnt-orange lichen on one side, worn and broken off on the others – I heard Aaron's voice again: *Panicking during a rescue will create a second rescue. Don't turn yourself into another victim. Watch your step, keep breathing, and stay calm.*

I picked my way quickly but carefully up the slope, over the top of that torrent of sharp, angular, loose rock spilled down through giant round boulders, fighting the weight of my pack and hot rasp of my lungs. I'd helped people with minor stuff on trails, and I'd been doing first responder and mountain rescue training with Aaron for more than a year now. But this would be my first real rescue, and my first one solo, as these kids' especially shitty luck would have it.

My mind raced with the possibilities, all of them until that moment textbook-diagram, clinic-demo, roadtrip-story stuff, and all of them horrific: a trapped leg, maybe a fracture, and if so, maybe open and bloody; if not, maybe closed but unstable, the fracture pinching shut a major artery, the leg dying right in front of you. But beyond all those images, lessons, stories, there was an odd, intense, inner trance of perfect calm at the center of everything.

You can lever the rock off his leg with your ice ax, I remember hearing my own voice, in eye-of-the-shitstorm mode – a voice I hadn't heard since a very bad day at work several years ago – as my body struggled its way up those rattling shifting rocks. *Assess first: how bad a fracture? If open, will it be bleeding? Or is the rock working like a tourniquet, compressing the femoral artery – and when you lever the rock off, will he bleed out? Or even if closed, what if it's an unstable fracture, the tibia and fibula jammed into the neurovascular bundle, his foot gone numb, and without blood, his lower leg already dead or dying, and sure to be dead before you can get him off this mountain? What's the acronym to check for that? CSM? Yes, that's it: circulation, sensation, movement.*

I had only ever heard Aaron talk about CSM, or seen it in the manuals, or watched Aaron demonstrate how to check for it and fix it – *another damn acronym, TIP for traction in place, right?* – on Jill's perfectly fine leg during a clinic.

As I scrambled after her, I did not look up from the rock, from each careful handhold and foothold; I saw only Aaron's still young but strong, weathered hands on Jill's tanned and muscled leg, heard only Aaron's voice, explaining over and over how to traction an unstable leg fracture. *The leg wants to go back where it belongs, but you have to give it room. You can't just force it back. You have to pull it out, gently, straight out, and hold it in line, gently but firmly, and let it find its way back. It's all feel, and a little counterintuitive, but you'll feel it.*

And I remembered thinking, back in the clinic: I don't *ever* want to feel that, the twisted rubber of someone's shattered and dying leg in my hands, and certainly not on top of some mountain with no real help and no idea how to get him down.

"We're coming, honey!" her faraway scream jarred me back from the clinic, Aaron's voice, Jill's leg. "Almost there!"

I looked up the boulder field and saw Angie bouncing from rock to rock about fifty yards ahead. Another fifty yards or so above her, halfway to the summit and splayed out in that massive pile of rock, I spotted what looked like a tangle of rags, whipping in the wind. I felt another surge of bad adrenaline, watching her jump from boulder to boulder, screaming and waving her arms.

"I found someone, honey! We're coming! He's got gear and stuff and can get you out!"

I picked my way up the boulders toward them as fast as I dared, careful to look at my feet, the pack swinging back and forth. *Don't turn yourself into a second victim; watch your step; keep breathing; stay calm.*

Another dozen handholds and footholds, gravity and the howling wind pulling at me and my pack, and I looked up again just in time to see her reach him. He was not moving. Maybe he was passed out, maybe in shock from bleeding out, maybe all but dead by now.

The odd calm at my core was flushed with more bad adrenaline and another version of my own voice, crazy with fear, broke through all that howling wind, yelling over my eye-of-the-shitstorm voice: *What the hell are you supposed to do if he's passed out or dead? You've only ever done CPR on a resuscitation dummy, all of twice, and that was in the bright lights of the clinic with Aaron and Jill standing there, watching, correcting, encouraging. Your first rescue ever, and solo? Above treeline in a screaming wind, with no route out?? Who are you kidding??? This isn't some bullshit business crisis you used to be so good at handling. These kids are counting on you, and not in the way Tom or Becky or one of your staff* *counted on you to clean up some work mess back when – or the band counted on you with a long guitar solo when Johnny was melting down on stage **way** back when. That was all corporate trivia or party noise, all status, swagger, or saving face. But this? This is life-or-death.*

I tried to ignore that other voice and shot up the steepest section of the boulder field, a three-dimensional puzzle of sharp and shifting rock, as fast as I dared.

"Here he comes, honey!" Angie shouted over the wind, as much to me as to him as I pulled myself up into the crevice below them.

He was splayed out on a 45-degree slab, hovering over the crevice at an odd angle, propped up on his elbows and grimacing, his left leg jammed down into a crack spilling off the other side. He was Angie's age, his freckled face drained of color, his red curls tied back in a blue bandana like hers, shivering and moaning.

Angie crouched over him, trying to lift his head and get water in him, and he tried to mumble something to her over the wind.

"What's his name?" I shouted to her, as I dropped my pack next to him.

"Sean!"

"How you doing, Sean?" I shouted over the wind. "I'm Jack."

He mumbled something, and tried to make eye contact, but he was shivering and shaking, and going in and out.

I searched the crack, the gap above, alongside, and below his leg. No blood, good; the shiny black treads of a mostly new hiking boot along the seam at an odd angle, not so good. I scrambled back onto the slab next to him and saw the culprit: a round boulder no bigger than a very large watermelon had rolled down and wedged into the crack alongside the slab, grabbing and clamping down on his leg just below the knee.

A howling gust of wind blasted us with grit.

First, get them warm, Aaron always says. When the blast of wind passed, I stood and dumped out my pack. I pulled out my green poncho, a $25 sheet of green plastic that has saved more lives in the backcountry in more ways – insulation, shelter, warmth, water-catcher, tourniquet – than every other piece of survival gear and technology combined.

"We're gonna get you out of here!" I said as I fitted the poncho around as much of him as I could. "Ok, buddy?"

He tried to nod, his head mostly just lolling backward.

"Can you feel your left leg?" I shouted over the wind.

"What are we going to do?" Angie shouted, her voice still edgy and panicked. "We need to move this damn rock off his leg!"

Speak calmly, Aaron always says, and look them in the eye. Take another breath, close your eyes, and you'll figure out what to do. After enough of these drills, a rescue strategy will come to you. Just take another breath.

"Yes," I shouted over the wind, my eye-of-the-shitstorm voice again. "We're going to get this rock off his leg, and then we're going to get you guys out of here. Ok?"

"Ok! But please hurry!"

The rest is a blur of execution, and Aaron was exactly right: I didn't figure out what to do so much as it just came to me, and I don't really remember how. I remember only this: seeing a flash of light out of the corner of my eye, and looking over at the glintering of the sun in the crisscross of silvery nicks and dings in the steel-blue handle of my ice ax. Then the ax was in my left hand, and a small rock just wider than Sean's leg was in my right hand, and the long handle was sliding into the slot below his knee and above where the boulder was clamped down around his leg, bulging purple, like a huge grape about to burst.

And I remember saying, as calmly as I could over the wind, "Ok, Angie, I'll lever this to get the rock off. But he's going to start sliding down when it comes off. So you hold him in place, ok?"

"Yes! Please! Do it now!"

"Ok, Sean? Are you with me? Just keep breathing, buddy, and – "

"Ok," he tried to shout back, sounding like a drunk on the edge of passing out. "I'm cool. I'll be cool. I'm cool."

"Good," I said, and forced eye contact. "And listen, man. This might hurt when the rock comes off – ok?"

Out of the corners of my eyes, I could see Angie's eyes bulge with panic and tears, so I moved in right over him, looking straight down into his dazed, nearly vacant face.

"Just keep breathing, ok? And don't look down."

"Ok, man," he panted, "ok."

"Look over there," I nodded toward Powell's Peak, the high point to the south, still wreathed in snow and ice and gleaming in the late morning sun. "Check out that awesome summit."

"Where?" he moaned, his head rolling around, eyes swimming.

"Over there," I pointed with the ax. "That's Powell's Peak. A great summit."

I probed the crack along the boulder and the slab with the tip of my ice ax, to see what else might break loose with the rock when I lifted it.

"What's it called?" he mumbled.

"Powell's Peak," I said as I inserted the levering stone into the crack just above his leg. With the slightest movement of my own weight, I could feel gravity pulling me down off that angled slab to the ledge below us.

"You – you been – up there?" He was trying to make small talk, and I knew exactly why, and would have done the same thing. "On the top of that?"

"Many times," I said as I tested the angle with my ax, the edges of the rock and where it would slip, the sharp edges wiggling and tightening around his leg. "You can see all the way down into New Mexico from up there. Amazing views."

He mumbled something, but I was absorbed in trying to project which way the boulder will move when I pushed against the levering stone. I knew it would move fast and down, as fast and down as it could go; and I knew that at the exact same moment, his leg would explode into fiery and nauseating pain – if we were lucky, and he didn't have an unstable fracture. Little or no pain would actually mean something much worse.

All bad outcomes, I thought. So my mind busied itself with the brute physics of the thing, a classical engineering problem of lever, opposite point on a curving plane, friction, weight and gravity. I would worry about the other thing after the eternity of the next few seconds.

"Ok, Angie!" I was snapped back by my own voice, straining over the wind from the eye of the shitstorm. "Let's get this done."

She looked up at me, her eyes frantic, searching mine.

"I'm going to lever this rock off his leg right here. And it's going to go fast, ok? Right down through there. So help me out by holding him up as tight as you can. All his weight, with everything you got, ok?"

"Ok! Do it!! Please!!!"

"On my count of three. And don't you look down at it either. Just look at me, ok?"

"Ok!"

I crouched down as low as I could over the slab and braced my foot against the only nub I could find.

"Ok. 1 – 2 – 3."

I held the levering stone in place with my left hand and pressed down onto the ax handle with a steady progression of force with my right hand and with almost no effort, scarcely any pressure at all...

POP! the boulder sprang from the crevice and Sean let out one short piercing shriek – a stabbing yelp, like a dog rundown by a car – and the rock rolled down onto the ledge below, landing with a thud that stopped the wind, stopped all sound, stopped the whoosh of the blood in my ears for the eternity of an instant...

And then the wind and Sean's screams rushed back with the thunder of blood rushing into my ears, and I turned to see Angie holding him fast and weeping.

I don't remember dropping the levering stone and ax, or sliding down the slab into place, only that I was there below him, bracing against the wind and holding the bottom of his new hiking boot, staring at his bulging purple lower leg. It was turned at a slightly odd – maybe five or six or seven degrees off axis – but not the grotesque angle I'd been imagining. And I remember thinking: *Yes, keep screaming and howling, buddy. Your leg is broken just above the boot top, but there are no bones sticking through. And you can feel it, which means that it's not dying.*

I knew I still had to check his leg for CSM, splint it, and figure out how to get him down off this mountain. But when I looked up and saw Angie hugging him, fiercely, her face covered in tears – yelling and crying "thank you, thank you!" to me over the wind – I realized how bad this could have been, and still might be. I looked back at his twisted leg, the skin purple and swollen near to bursting, and I felt a wave of nausea crash up into my throat.

I lowered his leg carefully onto the slab and myself into the gap where the boulder had been, trying not to look at his leg, trying to catch my breath and choke back the bile and find the eye of the shitstorm again.

"You're free, honey!" Angie yelled and held and rocked him. "The rock is off! You're free!"

He was trying to choke back the pain, writhing in a nest of muffled howls in her arms, as she wept and stroked his sweat- and mud-streaked face. She turned to shout *Thank you!* again to me but an odd *What's the matter?* look came over her face when she saw I don't know what on my face, and...

FLASH!

In the trees, just up ahead, a deer breaks from cover.

Angie's face, wet with tears and splotched with dirt and blood, is whisked away, along with that horribly broken leg.

I stop and look up the trail as another clump of snow drops from the canopy and explodes onto the trail. Sunlight flashes off a field of snow further up. The woods are eerily silent after the memory of all that screaming wind.

I follow the trail up and over a gap between two boulders, and down into a little glade flooded with sunlight, the late spring snow cupped and dusted with tiny pine needles. It seems like a scene out of a bad dream I keep having, except I'm awake and it wasn't a dream. And it's especially real, standing here on the same rise where I first heard that piercing scream, caught that flash of color through the old trees, saw the blood streaking her arms as she ran straight at me.

I stop for some water and a deep breath, and listen to the woods. No wind, the trees stilled, a cone dropping from the trees with a puff of pine dust and rolling down a tongue of snow. The skitter of a pika over a rock, a bird flitting through the canopy, the sound of my own heartbeat.

I've imagined far more gruesome things happening up here: the dozens of stories Aaron tells about rescues that didn't go as well; Danny's cataloging of every detail about his own accident – leg fracture AND a concussion – on Quandary Peak his first year out here; and all the stories in the rescue manuals, and climbing memoirs, and pages of *Outside Magazine*. And it could have gone so much worse for Sean too. He could have knocked a bigger rock loose and ended up with a nastier fracture. Or the way Angie was running around up here, she could have hurt herself too. Or if she had made it down this far in one piece, it was another couple hours back to the trailhead. Or on that particular day, I could just as easily have chosen instead to run up and snowboard off Powell's, or Prosperity, or Opal, or the left side of The Lady. Worst of all, Sean could have been up here hiking solo, like I am today, with no one around to run for help or bail him out. He would have died, eventually, from hypothermia, which wouldn't be painful, would actually have been a nice buzz on the way out, but he'd still end up dead.

I tighten my packstraps, drink more water, and look up through the last of the trees at the first long ridge of boulders, at that terminal moraine, the start of the push to the summit.

Different situation, I say to myself as I start back up the trail, *because I know what I'm doing*. I won't be up there wandering off the settled route through the boulder field, dancing around on unstable rock like two kids on vacation, drunk with altitude and summit fever. And Aaron and Danny both know where I'm headed, what route I'm taking, and the latest possible time I should be back to check in, cardinal rules of solo summiting or canyoneering. The rest, well, is luck.

As for Sean and Angie, on that day a little more than a year ago, I guess they were unlucky *and* lucky. The accident happened; but I also happened to come along at exactly the right time, on what I know is a wildly random trajectory – to this particular mountain, in the cirque above Dudeville, on a spring day in 2001, two and a half years after fleeing the steady grind of a corporate job Back East to the wild blur of the mountains Out West.

I tried explaining that to them in Ullar's, where they insisted on buying me a bunch of beers a few days after Sean was out of surgery and the hospital, hauling his leg around in a huge cast.

But Angie and Sean – good Midwestern kids to the core, and just under the grad-school hippie surface, still Presbyterian or Methodist or whatever – insisted that it wasn't a coincidence at all. Our trajectories, Sean tried to explain to me, weren't random but something cosmic, the consequences of what he called "The Really Big Math."

"It's like you were meant to be there," he kept saying, because "God" (he lowered his voice; we were in a bar, after all) was looking out for him and Angie, and teaching all three of us important lessons about ourselves.

Maybe it was all those beers – and/or maybe just a little of the odd affection I had for them because of what we'd been through and the consequent intense affection they had for me – but I copped to just a little bit of my own ongoing fascination with The Really Big Math. I knew that what Sean was saying about cosmic trajectories was equal parts wishful thinking and nonsense; but I did admit to them that I mess around with The Really Big Math myself all the time, when I'm hiking around way up here, or way down in some isolated desert canyon. But the cosmic whatever I encounter almost every time I'm alone in the wilderness, I tried to explain, is hardly benevolent, or malevolent, or either depending on the Almighty Mood Swing, as they and the rest of the believers would have it. What I find instead – what I feel, or intuit, or sense like an unseen but palpable presence in a room the size of everything – is simply that: an unseen but palpable presence. Hence my clever name for the Presence. (I was never any good at that corporate branding stuff.)

But they would have none of it. To them, my saving Sean and his leg was the sole, proximate and sufficient reason that I woke up one day at age 37, blew off my job, and moved west to snowboard in the backcountry.

So I eventually just let them believe that. It was a lot more interesting than the plain old truth: after years of daydreaming, planning, and hoarding, I blew off not just a great job but a great career, a good if dull marriage, and everything else I'd piled up and welded together from a rock bottom start to life. Or the not so plain truth: I moved west to run around up here in the mountains, sure; but I really came out here, and up here, because after twenty years of crawling out of my broken parents' small-town poverty – and then out of the self-imposed poverty of the big city music dream – I found myself right back where I started: alone, in the woods, where I was free. And not really alone, because there was always the Presence, usually somewhere just past treeline, or just below the rim of the canyon, or right up there on that summit.

How to explain this to these good kids from good families from the middle of wherever? How to explain that, after the long slow death of my marriage and another decade of seven-day workweeks, the success-rush was gone and money didn't matter anymore? Or that I had fallen not for any woman or drug or cult, but for this thing I can't name, let alone explain? Or that, in my pursuit of this thing, this Presence, I'd become preoccupied if not obsessed with snow and rock and ice, with channeling all my physical and emotional energy to the adrenaline rush of reaching the summit of something massive and dangerous, and then hurling myself off on a snowboard, or a hang-glider, or skis?

The rest of that Really Big Math is – sorry kids – completely random. I happened to end up in Dudeville, because I happened to meet Aaron when he was working on a ski patrol back in Vermont one winter, because he happened to be renting a room in Amy the Rebound Girl's ski house, whom I happened to meet in a bar in Killington after the lifts had closed. I've been learning mountain rescue not so I could and would one day end up happening to rescue Sean, but because I have to: one day I might have to rescue someone with me on a climb.

And maybe just a little bit because I like being useful. Wanting to be useful, which always used to correlate, roughly, with the cash that usefulness generates, is why I gave up on the music dream. It's why I ground my way through that early, workmanlike marriage to a woman who'd also fled poverty. And it's why I ended up in engineering school. I always wanted to do something real, even if by the mid-1990s, that meant managing a hundred other engineers who built nothing more real than software.

What is real, by contrast to all of that, is what is all around me up here. No software, no people, no money – only these old, weathered trees, and those snow-aproned boulders up ahead, tumbled all the way down here from the summit to their angles of repose, and the electric blue dream of Colorado sky bathing all of this in light so intense it makes my eyes ache.

Out finally from under the edge of the canopy, I hike up through a maze of old pines that looks, from down below or a distant ridge, like treeline. But when you are actually up here in it, you know there is no tree*line*, only a gradual falling away of the trees, bent but not broken from uncounted thrashings of snow and wind. On this warm spring day, these old priests of the mountain –dozens or maybe hundreds of years older than I am – slip off their encrusted snow robes, awaiting nothing but for me to pass by and be gone.

I thread my way through them on a trail worn brown into the snowpack, past their stooped heads and drooping arms. I pick my steps carefully, as the sun-softened crust breaks under my weight and the weight of my snowboard and gear. The last of the snowpack up here is pockmarked and pebbled with a maroon haze of late season alpine algae, melting into the climbing maze of boulders up ahead.

My breathing is off, something is off, and I realize that part of me is bracing – not for the usual post-holing, a breaking through the snowpack, which happens on this kind of snow all the time – but for the piercing of a woman's scream, somewhere up on this mountain.

I stop, laugh it off and push on. It wasn't really me who helped them anyway, just a well-programmed machine that looked like me but moved to the task like Aaron and did exactly what it had seen demonstrated in the clinic and read about a dozen times in the manual. I wasn't up there with Sean and Angie; I was up there watching me with Sean and Angie.

"His leg is pretty badly broken," I remember hearing myself say, mostly to myself, as I stood there in the crevice holding his leg in place and choking back the bile flooding my mouth, the wind howling all around the three of us.

Sean was moaning, whimpering, half out of it, and Angie was weeping silently and holding him, shivering, trying to keep him warm.

"Getting him out of here's going to be a little tricky," I shouted. "And I need to test for something first."

"Test for what?"

I looked up at him. "Are you with me, Sean?"

"Yeah," he grimaced. "I'm cool. What?"

The moldable splint in my kit looked small and flimsy next to that bent and bulging leg, and I needed the splint lined up before I could traction it – *if* I had to traction it – which I hoped I didn't. Every minute would count if the blood had stopped flowing to everything below that fracture.

I started to unlace his boot as carefully as I dared, and he screamed and writhed with the pain, and I knew that was a good thing, but still I had to check. I felt for a pulse along the inside of his ankle, and thought there might just be the slightest tap-tap under the skin.

"Can you feel that, Sean?" I asked as I scratched at the skin down around his ankle.

"Yes," he gasped for air.

"Are you sure?" I dug my fingernail in.

"Yes!"

"Ok, that's good. And can you wiggle your toes?"

"Ow! Shit! Yes!" he screamed, and I saw his big and second toe wiggle, just barely, but they did. "That hurts!"

"Good!" I said, relieved that I didn't have to think about let alone try to traction it. "Now – all we have to do is get you the hell out of here."

And it really was all mechanics after that. The machine version of me followed the general directions for a full leg splint in the rescue manual and improvised the specifics, building it from the moldable splint, the detachable handle from my avalanche shovel, and my ice-ax – his foot stabilized inside the right angle where the handle meets the head. I secured the splint with the extra snowboard strap in my kit and rescue rope.

It took three agonizing, exhausting hours, step-by-careful-step, to half-lead and half-carry Sean – propped up between Angie and me – down off the boulder field, and then down off the moraine, to just right here among the druid pines at treeline. It was the middle of the afternoon, and the days were starting to stretch out; but the nights were coming fast and cold when they did. Sean and Angie were both drunk from all the hours at this altitude, the stress and the adrenaline of the rescue. And we were out of food and nearly out of water.

It took two more slow, grinding hours to get Sean down the lower half of this trail to the junction with the fire road, where we stopped again to rest and finish the last of our water.

I was just starting to feel the trickling tug of more bad adrenaline as I thought about how far we still were to the nearest trailhead – and how it was hit or miss down there with cell phone reception – when I heard a familiar sing-song breathing coming up through the trees. It was a huffing and puffing with a tune in it, and at the very moment I thought *Tyler?*

"Hey guys!"

There was Tyler, bursting around the bend in the fire road, at a full run in a full backpack, humming some old pop song, out on his daily training route.

"What's up?" he said to Angie and me, his tanned, sculpted, always busy face bathed in sweat, as if he'd half expected to run into us there.

"Oh man, are we glad to see you," I said.

Then he noticed Sean sprawled out on the ground, half-passed out.

"Looks like it," he said, dropping his pack with a heavy thud next to Sean. "How are *you* doing, buddy?"

Tyler was one more piece of good luck for them. And for me too at that point, I suppose, because the day, the stress, all the bad adrenaline, and the five-hour crawl of a descent had wiped me out too.

Before I could finish telling Tyler what had happened, he'd dumped out his pack, which was stuffed with his laundry – or "full and consistent ballast for the workout," as he always calls it – he'd swapped out his hiking boots for trail runners tucked away in the ballast and he'd fished out all his water and emergency food for us. He told us to wait there with his pack and the pile of laundry, and sprinted down the trail the last two miles to town.

He was back within 45 minutes with Aaron, Gregor, Leese, and a stretcher.

Because Tyler is the man, I say to myself, which is how we always end our trail stories about him, and I push on past the very last of the trees.

I hike out onto the first of the flattest, biggest boulder tops, submerged into tundra and snowpack, leading up onto the moraine. I spot the first cairn up ahead, note the stitching of the switchbacks beyond, trace the thread of a trail backward from the first cairn to the snowline at my feet, and dig in.

Tyler is indeed the man, as we say when we're telling stories about other climbs to pass the time. He's indefatigable, indestructible, and just a little bit crazy – everything I'd be if I could take all the energy I waste on rumination or regret up here and put it to kinetic use. Tyler ditched a ten-year business career to run ultra-marathons (100 milers), sky marathons (marathons at altitude), ultra-sky-marathons (100 milers at altitude) and, for pleasure and relaxation, climb ice and rock. He is a wire sculpture of a man – sun-bleached hair and hard blue eyes, mahogany from the sun, his jaw always a little clenched – and impossible to catch. Aaron told me on our first climb with Tyler that, when you're sucking wind trying to keep up with him on the trail, just ask him to tell you a story.

Like the one about his first one-day solo ascent of something that normally takes three days. ("Because gear is what slows you down, man!") Or the one about his first ultra-sky-marathon ("I kinda got hypothermic because my blood sugar was messed up, so I ate a banana and puked most of it up and ate another and puked up only some of that and then I was fine.") Or the first time he broke 2:30 in the Boston ("fricking damp and cold back there in April, man – I ran that fast just to try and keep warm.")

And if getting him to talk the whole way up doesn't work, then you just ask him to sing: he knew the words to every pop song from the 70s and 80s, every word in *Jesus Christ Superstar*, and every word in "American Pie," "Alice's Restaurant," and "Bohemian Rhapsody," and he did them with all the funny voices. I usually asked him to start backwards from there, because I knew the stories and knew I would never keep up with him just talking instead of singing. And he is always the first one on top, of course, giggling at the view, that clenched jaw finally let go into the goofy smile of a big kid.

At altitude, Tyler finally goes from alpha-beast to all-boy, a sweetness and joy splashed all over his face at altitude, like he's finally breathing normally.

Which I'm finally doing again, I realize, as I pick my way up through the boulders of the moraine.

I have been revving it too much all morning – hiking outside the aerobic box, running out of breath, having to stop to catch it every few hundred feet – thanks to that awful memory of what happened with Sean and Angie the last time I was up here.

I wonder how they are. Did they did end up getting married? What do they think now about their time out here? After they tracked me down at Ullar's and we had those beers, they gave me their home number – told me they wanted me to come to their wedding – but I never did call them. Maybe I should have gotten their email addresses. I hate talking on the phone (just ask Jill), and email is how everybody keeps in touch these days anyway. I'm sure they're married by now, maybe even pregnant already, their big Colorado adventure story tucked away like an old photo album they pull out only when someone asks Sean about that scar down the front of his left leg.

I suppose I could dig up their number when I get back and just call them. "Hey you guys, guess where I was climbing today?" I'd say. But then what?

They probably don't want to hear any of that. It was a terrifying ordeal, and maybe they don't ever want to be reminded of it. Maybe hearing my voice would freak them out.

And I don't want to do that, I think, as I climb around the boulder below the crest of the moraine. The wind is picking up in my ears, a steady hum but just barely, and no wind compared to that day, or to most days up here.

The crest drops off to the northwest, opening out to the cirque and the canyon and the mountains beyond.

I thread my way up onto the ridge, into the first blast of wind off the summit, and there it is, one more time: the sweep of the ancient treeline pines into the forest below; the charcoal and red rock of the cirque; and the granite milky grays of the range beyond, all of it topped with a gleaming white as the horizon seesaws open into the searing blue sky and adolescent swagger and brawn of the Rockies.

The vastness of this continental cacophony is nothing like the old hills Back East, rounded and stooped. This is a youthful geology's arrogant challenge to gravity, the roof of the world turned upside down, mammoth formations of rock and ice the size of cities pointing upward toward forever.

Everything and nothing, eternity, infinity, home.

I turn and look back at my own private city this morning: the summit of Sunrise Peak, half a mile straight up this last boulderfield.

Breathe in, breathe out, and listen. Is it there yet?

No.

I push up into the boulderfield toward the first cairn, the weight of my board and pack pulling me back down the mountain. As always above treeline – not counting the last time I was up here, chasing Angie – I spot and place one careful step at a time, a mindful back and forth across the facial pores of a mountain awakening from a hundred-million year slumber.

Stay in the box and breathe, ten more steps, cairn, breathe, turn, ten more steps, breathe.

The route up the boulderfield runs about fifty yards uphill of where Sean had been trapped. As I pass by the spot, I stop and just stare at it.

Nothing, just the wind, in and out of a low howl. Even on a bluebird day like today, there is always an unchecked wind up here, rushing out of the canyon and across the range, cleansing the mountains, cleansing the earth, cleansing me.

But today, so far, nothing.

I pick my way up through the puzzle of the boulders, well north now of where Sean had been. One foot at a time, a great pile of jigsaw puzzle pieces, all mass and movement beneath me. Because the entire mountain is restless, temporary, perturbed by my weight and unforgiving of any mistake of balance or timing, ready to turn a simple day's climb into my own broken leg or worse, and a long night of crawling back down the mountain. If I'm lucky.

Best not to think about all of that, especially when I'm alone and this close to the top. Aaron isn't up ahead, narrating weather, route, snowpack and terrain; or recounting some trip turned weird or rescue gone wrong; or telling another story about Kit Carson or Edward Abbey or David Brower. And Danny isn't on my heels, talking about the Tao or the I Ching or Whitman or Kerouac, or recounting raunch in triple-X deets from last night's local Betty or recently heartbroken tourist he was happy to help on her road to recovery.

I stop, wait, watch, listen. At my feet are the remnants of a cairn, a pile of rock splattered and splotched with sun-bleached green and orange. One of the burnt orange growths is perfectly roundly symmetrical, with dozens of tiny brighter orange squiggles emanating from its center, like a pictograph of the sun, or a sea creature in a tide pool, stranded two miles above sea level.

And there it is: the Presence.

I stand and turn, as if to listen.

A sense beyond all sensation, turned way up when I am way up here, the Presence simply is. It's an odd feeling, just off my peripheral field of vision, that someone is here in the room with me – except the room is the size of everything and I'm all alone, but not alone at all.

I slip out of my pack and grab some water and calories for the final push to the top. The tingle of sun and wind on my face for the first time today means I must be smiling, like a kid let out of school for summer.

I look back the other way, out across the haze of brown dust cloud running east. Unlike that kid, I know this summer will end. (It does every day, for a few minutes anyway, when I check email and the market and the news and I think about when I might have to go back to work.) But right now, my body knows only the release of standing above treeline, a speck of flesh on a continent of rock, flattened by a cobalt blue sky, far, far, far above...the haze-brown dirt cloud you can see from up here, enshrouding the silly little fluorescent-gray world way, way, way down there.

Up here, none of what is so real and pressing down there is real at all. Up here, there is no technology rush, or market bubble, or corporate earnings season. The only deadlines up here are sunhit, and thunderheads moving in, and the sun going down, and missing one of those can actually kill you. Up here, no one can hide behind their market share, or their big desk, or their stupid re-org, or their fucking lawyer. Gravity is the only law and it can't be bent in on itself by somebody else's fucking lawyer to screw you. Up here, only your weakness or carelessness or cluelessness can screw you, as Sean and Angie found out.

That, and bad luck of course. Up here this morning, in this rushing river of crisp, cleansing air, I'm happy to take my chances. Because I'm *not* weak, or careless, or clueless (even if my father used to call me all that and worse during one of his benders). On top of this and every other decent mountain out here, I cannot control for luck, but I can control for me. Up here, calibrated to the scale of my own massive insignificance, I feel far more powerful than I ever did down there.

"It's a *koan*," Danny always likes to say, "the great power that comes with facing your powerlessness."

And he is exactly right. There is a glimpse of pure freedom in the tiny safety margins up here alone on top of a mountain, and the very real fact that I could screw up with the next hurried step and be dead of hypothermia by sundown. There is something that feels like – I don't know, transcendence maybe? – when the utter fragility of the human body and mind confront Earth Scale. And it should be terrifying; but it isn't, because I do sense – beyond all sensations turned way up, when way up here – that I am not alone.

I hoist my pack with its swingweight of snowboard, ice ax, avy shovel, and emergency food and gear for the final push to the top of Sunrise Peak. Technically, I am not on top of the world, but it sure feels like it.

The summit top is blown clean, more tundra and scree than boulder, maybe a hundred feet as the alpine tern flies, its feathers black in summer, white in winter. And a couple of those terns are skittering around up there right now.

One final push up through the last upthrust of boulders, and suddenly, a stubby wind-chewed stick pokes into the sky at an odd angle, and it's a few more precarious steps up, up, up and . . .

SUMMIT!

Today I Am in Love with Sunrise Peak

I have made it to the top, one more time. Just me and my gear, a little stamina, a little skill, no bad luck, and here I am.

And here too, the Presence. Unnamed and unfiltered, indescribable but unmistakable. I stand here bathing in it, just like I am standing here in the howling wind.

I have no idea what this Presence is; but I know that it is here, now, with me. I also know that it is independently verifiable, witnessed through the experience of other people. I've watched them, after getting to the top of one of these mountains for their first time, burst into tears. And I've always wondered: tears of what? joy? relief? recognition?

Sometimes they say out loud what they are feeling, but they never say directly, only compare it to what they've felt somewhere else. And it's the same short list for me: walking along a great empty beach, the sky all pastel streaks of dawn or fiery dusk; or standing at the edge of a desert canyon, the blood red earth opening up like a great womb; or stumbling out of a sweaty bar out in the country, into the sudden hush of a skyful of stars.

If I didn't know – like all rational, unsentimental, uncowed adults in 2001 – that the idea of "God" had long since been reduced from equal parts kiddie cartoon, shaming mechanism and political cudgel, I'd just call it "God." But I do know better, and so I call it the Presence, and keep it to myself.

Today, the Presence is up here on this summit, as surely as I am. Once again and always – every time I break past treeline, or drop into a maze of rock carved into the desert, or shoot out the other end of a canyon river onto calm water – the Presence is right there where the earth meets the sky, in the exactitude of a moment that is at once immediate and forever.

The Presence is here every time I come up, especially alone like today. The rock and ice colossus of any big mountain teems with it, the same way it hosts and teems with billions of adapted little lives – brown marmots, black pikas, black and white terns, green and orange lichen, maroon snow-algae – loomingly indifferent to me and the rest of humanity. And always with its hearty, eternally sarcastic greeting: *Welcome to reality, buddy, to a four-billion-year-old bundle of elements doing its little dance in a 15-billion-year old universe.*

Danny might call it a *koan*, and most of the people I knew Back East would call me crazy: but I am acutely aware of the Presence as I stand here, overwhelmed by all that is without, conjuring something that is deeply, infinitely within. And as I hover right here at the midpoint, right where they connect, I feel – like I do the rest of the time – the ultimate pointlessness of my existence. Except right here and now, it doesn't bother me one little bit.

Anywhere above treeline, but especially up here on a summit, I can look back and see that life down there really is just a silly little dance. I can see that whatever construct I might cling to back in the world turns to mush as I confront the rock bottom fact about everything: I am a twitching of human flesh on a planet that cannot wait to turn me back into dust, me and my precious little family (if I had one, I mean), and the whole rounding error that is the species and all civilization. When I gaze out across this black and gray archipelago of granite peaks, pausing for this one little geologic moment to shake off last winter's snow and ice, I realize that there is no me, nor a Colorado, nor a Back East, nor anything, just the earth and sky and time, the whole sweep of it whisking across the face of the planet and off into space and on toward forever.

A scamper of pikas, up through the rocks beneath me, look for food.

I know I shouldn't, and I wouldn't in front of Aaron, but I drop a few crumbs from my energy bar for them and stow the wrapper. There's sun and wind on my face, so I must be smiling again.

I pull the camera from my pack, not because any picture will be worth a shit compared to this view, but because I always take a picture from the summit, if only because I can.

Aaron always scoffs at the waste of weight, even with just one roll of film. ("At least get one of the new digital cameras," he always says.) But the new digital pictures are even more worthless than the pictures I take up here. Dulled, blurred, flat. Maybe this camera and a roll of film *are* a waste of weight. But the whole point of being up here is to confront the fact that I will one day be dead and gone, and the picture will be some kind of evidence that I was – on this one fleeting day – alive and here, in full raging fact.

I take half a dozen shots, down into the canyon and out across the cirque. I'll have them printed, and if there's a good one, I'll put it on my refrigerator with the others –even though most of those are shots not from the summit but from a distance of the whole mountain. My entire fridge is now covered with them, front and side, two years after moving to Dudeville for the altitude-acclimatization and ready access to powder days.

Those pictures, ha!

"There are *plenty* of women in your life!" Amy the Rebound Girl yelled at me, pointing at the collage of mountains on my refrigerator. I had just told her that I'd already done marriage, ten years of all work and no play, and that I had no interest in another commitment, and no love to give anyone.

"Oh, yes you do," she snapped back, pointing at them again. "Right there. *That's* who you love!"

I chuckle as I put away the camera and down another energy bar and more water. "Amy the Rebound Girl" – as she called herself in bitter jest the last night of her visit from Back East, hoping I would refute her – was exactly right. I was in love, but not with her or any woman. It was a very long drive all the way down to the Denver airport the next day, the last I ever saw or heard from her.

Today I am in love with Sunrise Peak, one of my favorite local booty calls. She is one of several mountains rising off the cirque that hovers over the muddy streets of Dudeville and all the way out over the far end of Prosperity, the ski resort off her outstretched left arm. Sunrise stands at 12,619 feet, almost as tall as The Lady, who towers over them all. But she's smaller and easier to access – just a long hike off the far end of the top of Prosperity – which is why she will seduce the occasional tourist couple with summit fever. Best of all, we can ski right off her top, down the snowfield spilling off the north face right over there.

Amy the Rebound Girl may have been right, but her tantrum applies maybe half the time, as Danny and Aaron and I have discussed at length, on a long approach hike or camped at a trailhead. A "she-mountain" is all long curves or heaving *zaftig* middle or wide welcoming lap; a "he-mountain" is spiky and spiny, pointed at the top, no hips. Some mountains, like some people, are a little of both and you can't tell until you're on them. And they all have their moods, hold their secrets, throw fits in bad weather.

Down in Dudeville, or from the chairlifts over at the resort, the tourists look up here in awe and take their own pictures, the lucky ones catching a glimpse of a late morning avalanche off the cirque. But when the snow stops and it consolidates like right now, Sunrise, Opal, Powell, and Prosperity (the peak itself, not the ski area below) – the whole cirque north of Dudeville and the range south – is our own personal gym, a high-altitude training circuit with mind-bending views and a little bit of everything: rock, snow, ice, glade, gully, up and down, up and down, back to town, and back again tomorrow. Because we are always training for something bigger, even if no one ever talks about why.

Lately, all of that training has been for The Lady, and in this case we do know why. People have skied off the top of everything in the Rockies; I've managed to throw myself off a few of the biggest too, on skis, with Jill. The sponsored guys and sponsored Betties, Jill crewing along with them, are skiing off the top of everything in Alaska and around the rest of the world. A few guys that Aaron patrols with are even trying to snowboard off all of Colorado's Fourteeners. But only the great Len Davies has ever actually skied down and off The Lady. And no one has ever ridden her on a snowboard.

Even in late summer, with the snowpack settled in, the only time you are safe from either type of avalanche – cold and dry, or warm and wet – you have to climb up Avalanche Peak off her right shoulder.

Then you have to work around her backside, and spend the night up top to get on the face before the sun does.

And then at dawn, you have to drop in with ropes onto the snowfield, suspended as if in mid-air, all for those fifty forbidden turns we can see and only imagine every day from town.

Except you have to start stopping, before you start falling, or you will not stop falling . . .

. . . for another thousand feet into the trees.

This could be the year we step onto that snowfield on our boards, with some good weather and good luck. Aaron and Danny and I have been talking about it since the day we met, staring up at The Lady through the mud-smudged plexiglass window of Ullar's: imagining and scheming, planning the gear, plotting the route, the drop, the ride. With some good weather and good luck.

But The Lady can wait a little longer. Because today I am in love with Sunrise Peak, and we're about to go dancing.

I gulp down more water and smear on more sunscreen, then stow my gear for the ride down. My pack is half its weight without my snowboard but still heavy enough to swing me off center with each turn down the mountain, so I cinch it down tight as I can. Then I tuck all the strap ends so they won't catch on the gnarled fingers of branches – when the vast snowfield at my feet breaks into glade at the treeline and narrows into a gully through the woods – that always seem to reach out and grab at you when you're flying past.

I hoist my pack, and strap into my snowboard, and take one last look out at the screaming firmament. Then I smile, and say *hello* again, and *goodbye*, and *thank you* to the Presence.

I stand up on the board and find my balance, shuffling back and forth on the crusty snow as my backpack finds its balance. And then, with just a slip of board edge off the earth's edge. . .

I drop in.

I shoot off the edge of the summit and across the fall-line, then turn and point straight down the snowfield spilling from the face, the adrenaline coursing through my body like cool water down a parched throat. Back and forth, time slowing and the horizon blurring, nothing but gravity; back and forth across a perfect snowpack, continuous and consolidated around this side, just a blank canvas of creamy spring snow tilted 40 degrees. I am surfing off the roof of the world, flushed clean with good adrenaline, the cool water spreading from parched throat to everywhere else, my body taut as a guitar string. Once again, I am everything and nothing, fully awake and fiercely alive, absolutely powerful and completely vulnerable, one caught edge or overthrown turn and down I go, rag-dolling into the treeline and boulders...

But not today, and not me. Today, in this terrifying ecstatic dance with gravity, this navigation between transcendent bliss and utter catastrophe, there is no me. There is only focus: on the tracing of perfect little half circles, the fury from my core channeled into arcing snowboard turns as my body mass crisscrosses the fall-line and dissolves into gravity, in perfect time to some grunge song in my head, the gritty chug-chug of a guitar and a primal scream, shooting me down the face of the mountain.

And then the spell breaks.

Always suddenly and way too soon, the first straggly tops of pine trees pop from the snow, tattered and dazed. They point not quite up at the sun, but more down the mountain, avalanche vanes worn raw by massive movements of snow, ice, mush and slush, the mountain falling off itself, down, always down.

I narrow my turns and rip my board around the knee-high pines, which I know are a good five to ten feet tall below the surface. And as the treetops straighten and thicken, the snow goes soft and collapses into their wells and around the tops of boulders, pine dust, twigs, cones and little boughs covering the last of the snowfield as it braids into the forest.

I swing around to a stop, plop down on a boulder bench, and scream out for pure joy, "Yes!"

My lone voice, small and shocking, echoes off the mountain and down into the woods, "yes, yes, yes."

I catch my breath, then scream again, "Yes!" and listen to the echo.

My face aches with sun and wind and what has to be an idiotic grin, and the Presence catches up with me. And I think – like I have so many times in these mountains – I could die right here and right now, and that would be just fine.

Sure you could, the Presence says. *But why, when you can come back up here tomorrow?*

And then the spell breaks and I know the Presence is right: I can come back and do all of this again tomorrow, or the same thing on some other peak. And of course there's The Lady – Danny and Aaron are counting on me, and the trip requires all three of us – so I'll ride it out another day.

I look down into the woods below, studying the glade as it drops into a rollercoaster of curves, in and out of the trees, a skateboard park through the wilderness. With a deep breath, I stand, point my snowboard down the gully, and drop in.

I ride back and forth on a frozen river ricocheting off its own banks and cascading into the dark, quiet forest. I slip along the slabs of fallen trees, charge up the face of waves frozen onto great boulders, cut back across the frozen creek bottom and up the other side, pop off more downed trees, and fly back across the middle. As the gully tightens and my turns quicken, the tune in my head melts from grunge into the jackhammer rhythm of a noisy surf-punk guitar. The whole of the mountain behind me narrows into one enormous, jagged half pipe, carved by gravity and snowmelt and rushing water, the inspiration behind all the imitation, the creation behind all the re-creations, behind all the surf and skate and snowboard swagger. I feel the tangled fury of it deep in my core as I run my board up the walls of the frozen creek – everything going suddenly slow-motion again – and cut back across the bottom. It is the sensation of raw, young anger, the confused fury of adolescence, and just a glimpse of the pure white light that is a moment's release from all of life's horrors, all of its limitations, boredom, uncertainty, and fear. It does not matter who I am or how old I am because in this raging and beatific moment, I – kick – ass.

And then this spell breaks too, nearly as quickly as it came, when the gully flattens out into a maze of trees, crisscrossed by cross-country or telemark ski tracks.

I ride over the tracks – five or six people have been through here – and pull up just short of where the gully breaks through to rushing creek.

With a joyous grunt, I plop down in the snow, winded, emptied but for adrenaline, and flooded with peace.

I catch my breath and look up to scan the trees in all directions. There is no way out of here but up and over. I knew this was coming; but I also knew I'd have the buzz from the adrenaline for the half mile hump.

And I do. I switch out my snowboard for the snowshoes in my pack, and find a convergence of ski and deer tracks up through a grove of aspens all greening in with spring and birdsong.

Even though all is in shadow, it's only 7,000 feet down here and well after noon, so the snow has turned into a beaded crust. With the weight of my pack, my snowshoes are breaking through and even they can't keep me from post-holing a good foot or so as I clamber up the trail.

As Aaron does on all down hikes and run outs, I go right to: what mountain next? It's especially important as we move into summer, the end of which will open up the two- or three-week window for bagging The Lady.

I hump back up over the ridge, and the broken crust of snow consolidates into one long last tongue through standing and downed trees.

Checklist for training this summer: more rope work, more bivouacs high up, more knot practice, a few big rappels. And more time at altitude, even though The Treehouse – my house just up the road from Dudeville – sits at 8,250 feet. (Simply sleeping way up here every night has done more for my stamina than the twenty hours a week I used to spend working out Back East.)

Finally, I see dry trail up ahead, running down to the fire road that serves as the boundary trail for the ski area. I walk the snow crust along the edge of the road, so I don't have to take off my snowshoes until it's time to switch back to the board.

It's a slog along the fire road from the trail crossing to the tangled orange boundary fence, but when I get to the top where the ski area starts, I'm not out of breath. Yes, sleeping at 8,250 feet has been good for me, Jill said that first night at my house – which she dubbed "The Treehouse" the next morning, when she woke up and went straight out onto my deck, perched among all those aspens and evergreens filling the side canyon.

"No wonder you're in such good shape," she said. "For an old man."

She probably thought she was joking, but I knew she was also trying to convince herself that it was ok.

"I'm sorry," she said, when I didn't laugh and she turned and saw what was no doubt a sour look on my face.

She certainly hadn't been sorry the night before, when I spent half of it hell-bent – hanging off the couch, sprawling across the living room floor, bobbing up and down in the hot tub out on the deck, and finally around the world in my bed until dawn – showing her just how old I wasn't. ("Again? Really? Wow! I don't think I can come anymore!") But by dawn, the only thing I was proving was how long it had been since Amy the Rebound Girl had fled; how rotten my luck had been with the tourists, never anything more than Danny's wingman; and how certain I was that I'd never see her again.

But I'm not thinking about Jill right now.

Nor about those long professional ski mountaineering legs. And how they wrapped around my own legs and ass in the hot tub like sinew, the hot bubbly water moving with us into bigger and bigger waves until it was all crashing over the sides. I'm not thinking about her at all, at least not until I have to deal with her. Which is soon, because I know she's back in town already.

Aside from all that, she would have loved today's climb up and ride down, and Kettle would have loved it too.

But so what? Jill may be in town today, but she will be gone tomorrow, off on another adventure, just like always. No promises, no commitments, nothing but big mountains and long romps, just the way we both want it.

And besides: today, I am in love with Sunrise Peak.

Mud Season

The run-out for this morning's climb and ride is the trail off Prosperity's upper chairlift. When I reach it, I snowshoe back up the trail, past a tangle of dirty orange netting, to a cluster of old gray shacks near the top.

This time of year – worn out from another winter, caked in mud, thrashed with weather – the summit of our little local ski area looks like one of those century-old mining camps, right after the mine played out and everyone fled.

On top, I switch back to my snowboard for the ride out, hoist my gear, and look down the long dirty snow tongue to the bottom. The big wide trail has been groomed hard and flat, and skied off and groomed, and skied off and groomed again, a hundred or so times this past winter.

I start down the trail, big sloping turns through the spring mush, flushing the day's work from my old legs. The snow is too soft so I cut left, into the shade, over near the lifeless chairlift. The roped off section running under the lift is cratered with dirt and littered with gloves, water bottles, garbage bags, tubes of sunscreen, lighters.

As I ride up and over the last crest, I can see down to the parking lot, a sprawl of mud, flat as a pancake and empty but for my truck and three snowcats. From up here, they look like some kid's toys.

I ride the rest of the beaten groomer to the bottom, shoot past the stilled chairlift works – a gawky industrial skeleton mired in blackened snow and mud – and ride right to the edge of the empty lot.

"Hey man," I hear behind me, as I'm stowing my gear in the back of my truck.

I turn around, and it's Scott, riding up on a mountain bike without pedaling, pulled by his big husky, Tashi (for Natasha). Her tongue hangs out with the work, fat and long as an elephant's trunk.

Scott's backpack is open at the top, climbing gear bulging out like antennas. He is more beard than face, his frumpy brown ski hat – worn earflaps, missing pom-pom – and frumpier purple fleece all flecked with dried grass, pine needles, lint and dog hair, the makings of a good bird's nest.

"Hey man," I call back.

He pulls up and Tashi sits back on her haunches.

"Coming off Sunrise?"

"Yeah."

"Face still clean?" he asks, in that lolling, half-stoned surfer drawl indigenous to the upper Midwest.

"Oh yeah," I say.

"Manky?"

"Nope. Still corn. Mush down in the trees, but it's still solid up top."

"Sweet."

Tashi yips in agreement with what must be doggy for *Sweet*.

I look at the gear welling up behind his head.

"Been top-roping?"

"Yeah-up. Back side of Opal."

"Butt Cracks?"

"Nah – still wet up top. Lower Windows. Dry as dust."

"Early sunhit this time of year."

"Yup," he says.

"Sweet."

Tashi yips *Sweet* in agreement.

"Yeah, buddy," he says. He climbs back onto the bike and Tashi springs up, tail wagging. "Sunrise Peak on a spring day. She's a purdy one."

"Yes she is."

"Later, man."

Tashi yips *Later* and I watch her pull him across the big wide mudflat of the parking lot, back toward Dudeville.

A few minutes later, I pass them on the road as I'm driving my truck up the canyon from Prosperity and head into the near ghost town that is Dudeville in mud season. Or Dudeville most of the rest of the year too. Old gingerbread houses, squat bungalows, and bulging logframes all lean just out of square. Half are blown by wind and grit to raw wood, the other half painted the colors of fresh fruit – cherry, lemon, orange, grape, and green apple. Every porch is cluttered with a tangle of rusted bikes and whatever old skis and snowboards haven't yet been turned into picket fences or hammered into the gaps in the plain board fences lining the streets. Ragged lines of rainbow prayer flags hang from everything.

The half dozen Victorian storefront blocks of Main Street are empty, but for Deputy Dog, Tyler's old bloodhound, waddling down the middle of the street on patrol, and two tourists looking in the windows of t-shirt shops closed between the end of ski season and start of summer.

Dudeville is actually "Columbine" on all the maps, on my mail, and on the green sign at the start of town – *Pop 2,396 / Elev 7,410* – which someone has scrawled out and changed to *7,420*; someone else has blasted with a shotgun; and others have covered with snowboarding stickers. Like so many towns up here in the Rockies, it was named after the sudden appearance of a mining camp that named itself after whatever wildflower blanketed the mountains that the miners were pulverizing into money. Columbine is also the Colorado state flower, so it was typical of the big ambitions the miners had for their insta-town. But right after the shootings at Columbine High School outside Denver two years ago, everybody started calling it "Dudeville."

Danny once told me the name is part of a running joke, like the name of the band over in Crested Butte ("Don't Call Me Dude"), and part of the secret handshake of living here. Nobody in Dudeville ever calls each other "dude," except as an obvious put-down, for fear of sounding like a tourist trying to sound cool. When one asks how to get to Columbine, you can say "Just hang a left at the bottom of the pass" or you can say "No idea, sorry." Sometimes I think the name really started out, or at least stuck, as a way of not having to think about the other Columbine. But I wouldn't know because I wasn't here then, and no one talks about it now.

Either way, please don't call me "Dude" either. Aside from ingratiating tourists, only Jill calls me that, and only when she's pissed at me. It's her way of trying to remind me to act more like my age and her boyfriend, and less like some guy her age blowing her off.

But I'm not thinking about Jill right now.

(Though I probably should turn on my cell phone and see if she's called again, and maybe left a message this time, just in case something is wrong. She is back from Argentina a month early, and back here in Dudeville – not off at her mother's or with the Betties – which is a little odd, given that it's mud season.)

But that's her problem. She may be back for a few weeks, but she's already gone, forever this time, finally off to grad school in a few more weeks.

And while she leaves Dudeville, once again and for good this time, Dudeville is where I now live: summer, winter, mud season and fall, girl or no girl. From right here in Dudeville, I can launch into the mountains with my morning coffee still warm. Here, no one bothers me except the pushier tourists who think they're in Vail or Aspen. Here in Dudeville, I am living the dream I dreamed all those years Back East, in a Colorado ski town too far off the Interstate and up the canyon for most tourists, in the still beating heart of the great big to-hell-with-all-of-you that is the great big American West, with Aaron and Danny and the Betties. Our mountains, our town, Elevation 7,420. Dude.

As I pull up in front of Ullar's, they come into view one more time, right down Main Street: the cirque hovering over the far end of town, Avalanche, Powell, Opal, Sunrise, and The Lady, rising up at the center. From this angle, she looks like a woman with her hair pulled back to reveal a long slender neck, propped up on her arms at a summer picnic in the park. The long ridges of her arms and legs, elbows and knees, rise to gather around the alpine lake in her lap, invisible from down here, but awash I know in midday sunshine and bathing in the Presence. And from down here – but also from up there – The Lady is as indifferent to my gaze as any other woman at a summer picnic in the park.

Just like Jill, in the end. She may not sound indifferent right now, but she will leave, finally and forever. And Dudeville will be called "Columbine" once again, when the stain of Colorado's worst memory fades like any other nightmare that makes the news. And life will go on.

Here in the midday glare of the almost-summer sun, Dudeville still looks like a place called Columbine, or Trillium, or Larkspur. It could be any other 19th century mining town turned ghost town, then turned ski bum town in the 60s when the T-bars and first chairlift went up the easy ridges below Prosperity and the hippies moved in. Even as Prosperity swapped out the T-bars and added newer and faster chairlifts, a hotel at the base and a couple hundred condos, Dudeville stayed mostly Columbine. It was too far from the Interstate for full-on denuding by the big ski companies, and its terrain is too crazy and steep – too up and down and *terra interrupta* – to put in big long cruisers for Mom and Dad and the kids.

Which is why the rest of Dudeville/Columbine wasn't bulldozed, then re-constructed into just another "quaint former mining town" advertised in the travel magazines. (Because nothing says "mining town" like sushi bars and Gucci stores under the twinkle of permanent Christmas lights, with big fake versions of little old Victorian houses.) The American Recreation Corporation (NYSE: SATAN) may have bought up Prosperity, spiffed up the hotel, and added another hundred condos. But there's still the looming terrain problem: the steep ridges cutting back and forth along the bottom of the cirque they could probably make with a chairlift; but few could make them coming down on skis or snowboards. And yes, there are rumors about them actually trying. But there are always rumors. If they did, at least I'd make out on the house I bought a couple miles up the hill from town, when I cashed out and chased the dream up here: I'd just sell out and move further into the mountains.

Until then, Dudeville – where I sleep at altitude and train out my back door, and there is always someone to go climbing with – is my home. And wherever it might be dumping is no more than half a day's drive: Taos, Telluride, Steamboat, Snowmass, the Butte. All of Utah and Jackson Hole and Sun Valley are another day or day and a half away. And, until lately, I had the perfect non-girlfriend – hot, ripped, young, smart, cool, the works – who, when she was not halfway around the world on skis for work, could pound out all of it to the top and beat me to the bottom, every time. Until she had to screw it up and get serious on me.

But I'm not thinking about any of that.

I sit in my truck in front of Ullar's, empty but for Maggie behind the bar. Before I go in, I turn on my cell phone.

No voicemails. But the signal is always hit or miss up here, as it is in most of Colorado outside the cities. Someday, they say, it will be everywhere, even everywhere up here. But not today. And it's not like I was expecting anyone to call.

As I'm starting to turn the phone off, it rings, and it's Jill.

She doesn't leave a voicemail.

Sure, I've been an asshole to her, but why does she have to make me feel like one? That's not how this started, right here in Ullar's, two years ago. But she was 25 years old then, still more girl than woman, or so it seemed; and 25-year-old girls look, act, drink and get it on like they are going to live forever. A couple short years later, when she turns into a woman, it's straight to The Hot Zone, always made worse by one of her friends having a baby. And Jill has two of those now: her older sister and college roommate, both new Moms, a picture of Jill holding each baby clipped to the visor of her truck. And suddenly she's staring down the big 3-0. Which was, I'll admit, also a crisis of sorts for me around then, already half a dozen years into a serviceable but dull marriage; like everything from my first 30 years, it was more grim survival strategy than part of any choice or plan.

Well before turning 30, Jill's competitive skiing career was over, even if her guiding career is just starting. For racing, she said they said she was too tall and skinny, her center of gravity too high off the snow; for extreme skiing, she said they said she was "too tentative on the steeps," which I now know means not suicidally aggressive. And now, like so many professional skiers around Colorado, she has turned into a ski scrounge – guiding here, repping for a gear company there – eventually ending up in the exact same place with everybody who is far less cool: *Oh shit, I'm broke, what should I do? Go to grad school? Law school?? Business school???*

This may be my own endless summer as endless winter, but it's Jill's own personal mud season, and it's almost over.

I get out of my truck into a drenching of noontime sun. The whole town is quiet but for the birds, and smells like spring in the mountains: damp, green, and fecund, like mud and flowers and a good clean sweat. And it really is that simple. Jill is dropping in, and I have dropped out, for now anyway; and it was great fun passing her on the way by.

She was off to Argentina last month for their winter, and I was supposed to follow her down there, like I was supposed to follow her last year to the Himalayas. So of course I blew her off again, and on her birthday no less, thanks to Freak Girl this time, a final double-blow.

And now she's back. And I do have to deal with her, once and for all.

But I think I'll have a few beers first.

Pissing Contests

Ullar's is deserted, except for Maggie, sitting up on the beer cooler behind the bar, reading an old *Mountain Gazette* (*"When in Doubt Go Higher"*), and her little old black Lab, Buddy, over by the fireplace. The air is sparkled with dust and the guitar notes of a meandering Grateful Dead show at half-volume, friendly white-noise for a quiet afternoon in an empty bar.

They both glance over at me when I walk in.

Maggie looks like she's just crawled out of bed and pulled an old ski hat on to corral her chestnut hair. Her face is ruddy with sun, except for the wide white stripe of ski goggles, the classic reverse-raccoon of everyone in Dudeville.

"Hey there, Jack."

"Hey Maggie," I crawl onto the last stool, my legs suddenly hot mush from the day's climb up and ride down. "How's tricks?"

She snorts and nods toward the big picture window. "No tricks today," she says, looking out at the empty street and mountains beyond, her gray-blue eyes bleary with days on end of sun, wind, weed, and hangover. "Mud season's in full swing."

"Yeah it is."

She goes to pour me a Fat Tire. "Good turns?"

"Oh yeah."

"Whereabouts?"

"Sunrise."

"Nice." She puts the beer in front of me, a pint of foaming joy. "Bluebird day all day. Manky up top?"

"Still corn, 'til the bottom, then mush. Post-holed the last stretch."

"Yeah, well," she snorts. "Mud season." She starts toward the back. "Guessing you're hungry?"

"If you guys are cooking."

"I need to wake Miguel up anyway. Burger or chili or both?"

"Both'd be good."

I gulp at the cold beer and look around the timbered cave of Ullar's – named for the Norse god of snow – at the old skis, snowshoes and ice axes lining the walls, the long heavy tabletops, the great blackened fireplace with Buddy asleep on its slab hearth, his snout splayed out on his paws. Up on the silent TV at the other end of the bar, a river of color runs down a tree-lined street, a roadbike race, with Lance in the lead of course. He looks like a predator, blank-eyed and grim-faced, controlling the entire race from the middle of the pack, kicking ass as usual.

The Grateful Dead finally meander their way into tune and into an old train song, and I look out the window at the empty street, flooded with midday sun.

Maggie comes back a minute later, and hops up on the cooler with the *Mountain Gazette*. She is the big sister of Dudeville's local Betties, which is to say a big sister to Betties everywhere, as so many pass through town between gigs to live cheap and out of the limelight in the off-season, crash with each other, train in the backcountry.

I don't know where their male versions end up. But the Betties seem to gravitate here (like Jill did), this tribe of women who piece together livelihoods through some combination of competitive skiing or snowboarding, guiding, teaching, and killing it out on some mountain in magazine ads for gear made by their sponsors. For the best money and worst scorn from the rest – according to Jill, anyway – the Betties who are the poster-prettiest, with their hats and goggles off and hair down, make the best money, not in skiing or riding shoots, but posing in ads for ski clothes, ski resorts, and ski town real estate.

Spend your vaca money here, disposable incomers and bucket list boys from Back East, their big white teeth and honeyed hair and facefuls of sun all seem to say, *and you'll get a hot Betty like me, for the slopes – and the apres...*

Not that I didn't fall for it too: the babes in Gore-Tex; the powder porn; the year-round spring break, where the snow is always fresh (but it's never snowing), and everyone is young, and blisteringly beautiful, and shreds it out on the mountain. But at least now I know, thanks to Jill, they're just scrounging for a living like everybody else. The Betties ended up in Dudeville for the same reason we all did: it's still cheap, a Colorado ski town not yet loved to death-by-development, with access to tough, steep technical snow, rock and ice in every direction. And nobody whistles or *Hey Baby*'s! them from the chairlifts when they're dropping chutes or hucking cliffs.

I sit at the bar with my beer, and feel the mountain run down my legs and ooze out the bottoms of my feet. A mountain bike slips by the window, and I look back at the TV – Lance still crushing it of course – then over at Maggie as she reads.

Danny was with her for a time, in between picking off random tourists or whoever's sister or college roommate was in town to mend her just-broken heart. Not sure how long they lasted, not that it matters: as they say in Dudeville, you don't lose your girlfriend, you lose your turn.

I know the particulars here, because in the wide-open spaces of the backcountry there are wide-open spaces of time to share details, usually while camped at the trailhead or on the down hike after a summit. And so we share them all, at least the important, or interesting, or odd ones. In Maggie's case, Danny says she has big red nipples and makes great coffee in a French press, standing over the bed and stirring it with a chopstick in a way that she thinks is sexier than it is (which makes it sexy in its own way, he says, and I guess I could imagine). And he says she comes fast, hard, and loud, and is then off to make more coffee and comes even faster the next time.

Maggie finishes the *Gazette* with a snort, jumps off the cooler, and goes into the back. I spin around on my stool and survey the empty bar again, Buddy looking up at me expectantly, like I might take him for a walk. The Grateful Dead is stumbling its way from the old folk song into a blues boogie.

Not that many weeks ago this place was lousy with tourists, and it would have been even worse if you could get Coors in here. (Maggie and her other bartenders can barely spit out a not-sorry *Sorry* when some sunburned guy in a red or orange one-piece ski suit stumbles up to the bar and asks for it with a big loud Texas accent.) Because Ullar's is where the Locals hang out, the beer is all made right around the corner or no further away than Fort Collins, the food all high-caloric gut-bombs for pushing through the glycogen window. Melting gear lines the walls; dogs gather around the fireplace; and all the talk is snow, trips, weather, avalanches, accidents, gear, snow again, and arguments over the best way to train or gear up for the next trip.

I look out across the long, heavy tables – a carved petroglyph of initials and names, lacquered with a thousand coats of beer and BBQ sauce – and remember the famous pissing contest from the spring of 1999. The season was winding down, the Betties drifting back from their circuits, and I had just moved to town.

Kelly and Hillary were holding court over at the big table in the back, with four or five other Betties and a bunch of guys crowded around. They were talking smack about who fought harder that season for her wins, or got a rawer deal from whichever gear company, or wrecked her knees more, or some such throwdown. Kelly – with her strawberry blond perma-braids, wrestler's shoulders, ice blue eyes, and freckled face all splashed and splotched with the sun – had raced in high school and switched to freestyle while sort of attending the University of Colorado. When backcountry skiing went from anonymous wolfpack adventure to televised extreme sport, she left the industrial bumps for the wilds just past the resort's ropes; turned into one of extreme skiing's first stars, sponsored by North Face, Subaru and Advil; and launched a short-lived line of women's ski clothing, Bettieswag.

The pitchers went down and volume went up, as Kelly squared off, again, with Hillary, her rival since their high school racing days who had skied her way to a silver medal in the World Cup and a bronze in the Olympics. Hillary was taller, thinner, and blonder, and her face and teeth seemed to grow only more radiant with all that sun; and so she was sponsored by Citibank, Aetna, and Maybelline. Kelly was the better, braver and more creative skier, and could beat Hillary down jagged plunges of mountain most people wouldn't venture near let alone think of skiing. But Hillary – with the prettier face and longer legs and Olympic hardware – eventually struck sponsorship gold: fashion modeling. She started out dressed in ski clothes which, shoot-by-shoot, started coming off, until she was essentially naked in *Sports Illustrated* one winter, nothing but a pair of racing skis held crosswise, at just the right angle across her big boobs and shaved cootch.

I missed the first part of the argument – I was out back smoking a bowl with Danny and one of the Betties, then back at the table with Aaron still rattled about and processing that day's avalanche rescue – but then the whole of Ullar's went quiet, when Hillary yelled: "Oh to hell with you! I piss all the time standing up outside the starting hut."

"So what?" Kelly yelled back. "You think you're the only girl who can take a piss standing up in ski boots?"

"Bet *you* can't."

Kelly rolled her eyes. "Oh puh-leeze, honey. Of course I fucking can."

"Hundred bucks says you can't..."

...and so on, until there were bets all the way around the big table and the three adjacent tables.

"Come on then," Kelly stood and barked at her, starting off toward the bathroom to prove her mettle.

"Oh, the baaath-room," Hillary half-slurred, "Thought you were so hardcore. I piss standing up – outside the starting hut – in front a hundred guys. You think I give a shit who sees?"

"Fine then," Kelly said, "I don't care who sees."

And Hillary may or may not have been kidding, but there was money on the table and alpha-female in the air, so Kelly just went ahead and launched, not unlike she does off the lip of a mountain. She clomped up onto the table, her half-buckled ski boots nearly knocking over a pitcher of beer and crushing a plate of nacho leavings. Then she leaned over, and put an empty beer pitcher in the center of the table. Then she pulled down her worn-out ski pants.

The entire bar went dead-silent, every pair of eyes on her.

"It's actually easier in ski boots," she announced all around, thrusting her hips even more forward than the angle of her boots.

She pulled the front of her bright blue sport panties aside, and out popped a big bush of strawberry blond hair, and then – *weeeee!* – a perfect half-parabola of piss, right into the empty pitcher, only the last flickers missing the rim and trickling down onto the table.

The bar erupted into cheers.

"That's gross!" Hillary yelled, her voice cutting off the cheering.

"What's gross?" Kelly laughed, pulling up her pants. "Gross that I win the bet?"

"We all eat off this table!"

"So what," Kelly said as she clomped off the table. "Pee is sterile, honey. You know that from First Responder. Why else would they tell you to drink it when you're stranded and dehydrated. Not that you get stranded a lot when there's a *Sports Illustrated* photo crew around."

"It's still gross," Hillary said, throwing a hundred bucks at her.

More cheers and laughter, money changed hands on the bets, and the bar went back to the usual drunken ski, snow, gear and mountain chatter.

I went over to the bar to pay my tab, and there was Jill, the first time I ever saw her. She was propped up in her own ski boots, hunched over a beer, still shaking her head over Kelly's little demonstration.

She was as tall as me, but all legs and long tapering waist, her dirty blond braids poking out at odd angles from under a white ski hat she'd pulled all the way down to her eyebrows. It was obvious that her height made her self-conscious. She was wiry from the waist but rounded over the bar like a question mark.

As I walked over, maybe a little more riled up than usual by the flash of Kelly's bush, I thought: *Wow. If I were ten years younger, I'd have just the answer.*

"Hell of a thing," I said to her.

"Those two," she shook her head, looking over at me with big seawater green eyes, her tanned, unlined face glowing like dark, warm honey. "They're like that about everything."

"You know them?"

"Who doesn't? Hill and Kelly are the rock stars out there. I've raced with Hill and worked on trips with Kelly. They're even more bad-ass when they're NOT working it for some camera."

I couldn't think of anything to say, other than *Of course they are and you too I'm sure, and you're so fricking hot, and so young, why are you even talking to me?* I was 38 years old, even if I didn't look or act like it, and there was nowhere for me to go from right there and then but straight to Dirty Old Man Hell.

And yet, and yet: here she was, talking Pure Uncut Betty Bar Smack, then looking sideways at me from under her white ski hat, like I actually had something interesting to say. Or was she waiting for me to hit on her or say something stupid, just so she could roll those big green eyes and laugh at me?

I let all that percolate through my addled brain for a good minute, or maybe a good minute or two too long, which is probably why the only thing I could think to say back to her – from a vast and snappy vocabulary gleaned from 38 years of the verbal bullshit fest that is the east coast – was: "Cool."

"Yeah, sure dude," she muttered and turned back to her beer. "Actually, they're not cool at all. They're both wound to the teeth, and it's kinda a drag hanging out with them. But they can crush it on the mountain, and the trips are sick, so it's a pretty good job."

"That's your job?"

"For now. What's yours?"

Oh boy, I thought. "Uh," I looked into my beer for an easy answer. "It's uh – a little complicated."

"I figured."

"How'd you figure that?"

"Well," she took a long swallow of beer and looked down at my ski pants and half-buckled boots. "Your stuff is too new for a ski bum, but not all new like a tourist. And you don't have the bullshit it's-all-good stoner vibe of a Trustafarian, so you still have like the business thing going on somewhere."

"Huh," I replied.

"So I'm guessing you're some kind of corporate drop-out guy."

"Uh – yeah."

"And you're trying to figure out what to do next."

"Damn, you're good. X-ray vision."

"It's the ski guide thing," she said. "You figure people out pretty fast."

"Because they're out of their comfort zone and overcompensating in some way?"

She looked over at me with a stunned look that gave way to a half-smile. "Exactly. Like I said, it's a sweet job. For now. But it's changing."

My tab came, right then of course, but I was welded to the spot, thinking I should order another beer, not because I wanted one, but because I wanted to keep talking to her. And I could tell that she could tell I wanted to, but that was probably just to see how fast I'd run a line and make an ass out of myself. Had to happen to her ten times a day.

"Oh well," I finally said and paid my tab. "Enough pissing contests for one night."

She looked almost disappointed that I was leaving, which had me already kicking myself for it before I had taken a step toward the door. But pride always got the better of me; and I'd rather die alone, wondering, than die failing and alone anyway.

I remember standing right over there at this very bar next to her, running it all out in my mind like a new software product that worked and looked great, but no one wanted to pay for. There was nowhere for me to go with a woman that young, hot and cool, other than hurried disclosures about my actual age, right before the clothes came off. And then the sex would be mercy sex, or pity sex. And not that many days later would come the hard Heisman or maybe the soft Heisman, after maybe some more pity sex. I knew I could take all manner of body blows on the mountain; could live through a maelstrom of missed revenues, busted budgets and crashing technology markets; but this thoughtless venture would puncture my little Dudeville bubble before it was halfway inflated.

"See you around, Corporate Drop-Out Guy," she said as I turned to go.

"See you around, X-Ray Vision Girl," I said, stiffened my spine, and walked straight into the sunset.

And then my luck changed, mostly because Dudeville is a small town – *Pop 2,396 / Elev 7,410* (or 7,420, I mean).

Our paths crossed two weeks later, in a CPR class Aaron was teaching at the mountain rescue headquarters at the end of town. Jill had to take the class every year as part of her guiding job, and I was training to be a Wilderness First Responder, something Aaron had been talking to me about since the day we met back in Vermont.

I was psyched to be taking the class, and then psyched to the point of my head almost exploding when I walked into the clinic a few minutes early and there she was. More legs and a longer tapered waist than I remembered, in a pair of beaten Carhartts that looked custom-tailored for her; an old fleece jersey open down the front; the same white ski hat pulled down to her eyebrows. But I caught myself, stopping just through the doorway – after I rolled in and she looked over and saw me and smiled – even more acutely mindful, without any beer on board, of Dirty Old Man Hell.

Under the bright domelights of the clinic, Jill looked even younger and taller and hotter than she had here in Ullar's, and I'm sure I looked every miserable bit of 38. But she came right over, punched me on the arm, and said, "Hey Corporate Drop-out Guy!"

"That's hilarious," I said.

"Well, you left the other day without even telling me your name."

"Yeah, sorry about that. I'm Jack. And you are –"

"Oh you're kidding," she sighed, "that's terrible."

"Why's that?"

"Hey Jill," said Aaron as he walked over.

"That's why," she said, her green eyes rolling sideways like the first time we'd talked.

"You two," Aaron said, his always serious voice trailing off, his big brown eyes widening even more than usual. Then his always busy, slightly worried face – with that perfectly trimmed brown beard tracking all of it – broke out into the mischievous grin he usually reserves for camp pranks and Really Stupid Tourist stories. "I guess around here, when you two go up the hill to fetch a pail of water, it'll be snow – so don't forget your camp stove to melt it."

Jill rolled her eyes at him. "Really, dude?"

"Sorry, dude," he said. "Couldn't help myself. Ok then," he turned and said to the rest of the room, instantly serious again, gesturing us onto benches with the others there for the training. "This is where –" and he looks down at the two of us and points at me – "where we deal with what happens when he falls down and breaks his crown."

Jill hung her head and shoulder-butted me, and a glow spread through my body, like I was a teenager (I think; I was never actually a teenager) and it felt good.

"Sorry, man," Aaron said to me. Then his voice went deadly serious and he looked around at the others. "This is where we learn how *not* to die in backcountry."

I am jolted back by Maggie's voice.

"Here you go," she says, as she puts a big glistening burger and steaming bowl of chili in front of me. "Sorry for the wait. Miguel did the wake and bake, then drank a pot of coffee, then got inspired to paint the whole back of the place."

"What color?"

"He couldn't decide," she sighs, "so he used a little of everything down in the basement. Whole back wall looks like a Jimi Hendrix album cover. And so does he."

"Sounds scary."

"Well," she says. "It'll be perfect for everybody getting high back there."

I chuckle and she pours me another beer and a glass of water.

"One-for-one," she reminds me of the cardinal rule of drinking at altitude, as she jumps back onto the beer cooler with a new copy of *High Country News.*

I look around the still-empty bar. Lance is still crushing it on the TV and the Dead are tuning again, each little guitar wiggle floating around on the air like more dust.

I start in on the food and go back to that CPR class with Jill, where she's bent over that CPR resuscitation dummy.

I'm not sure how much I learned that night, pre-occupied as I was with trying to avoid her eyes; with trying not to look down the break in her fleece; with trying not to stare at the stone penduluming over the honey-brown skin rising behind her taut undershirt, a bear fetish carved from jade that matched her eyes.

After the class, we were standing in front of the clinic still talking about the guiding business and her upcoming trip to New Zealand – Jill's endless winter – when Aaron came out, in a big backpack jangling with gear like an adventure sports Christmas tree, the resuscitation dummy under his arm.

"You guys wanna go grab a beer?"

Jill and I both looked at the dummy.

"Think of it like a double date," he said.

We headed into the first bar down Main Street, the Fat Chance Saloon, and sat in stools along the window, the resuscitation dummy slumped in the last one up against the wall.

I went over to the bar and came back with three beers.

"Good idea," Aaron said, pointing at the dummy, "we need to cut her off."

And then more clinic talk, animated even for him, enough to distract me, mostly, from Jill's piercing, looming presence.

With his whole body, Aaron told a series of terrifying misadventures in the wilderness, his hands and arms standing in for peaks, gendarmes, seracs, cols, cornices, couloirs, icefall, and some very unlucky climber or skier. He would jump from his stool when the collision occurred, all of it playing out in agonizing slow motion in his mind's eye. And then he'd sit back down, and go suddenly quiet, solemn, far away.

We were rapt by the stories, but when Aaron finally stopped and drifted off to some story maybe too terrible to tell us, he avoided our eyes.

Jill stared down at her long, tanned, strong but still fine fingers.

And I looked around the half-crowded bar: at the embers in the fireplace, a chocolate lab asleep a few feet away, two mud-splattered guys at our end of the bar watching the bike race on the TV, a string of colored jerseys like prayer flags winding up some mountain, Lance, in the lead of course, his eyes on fire, jumping off the front and sprinting away.

I was glad for Aaron's weird silence, because I wasn't sure what to say to Jill but I didn't want her to get bored and take off. All I wanted was to sit there, not looking right at her, but watching her turn to silhouette in that picture window as the sun set behind the bar and turned the weathered storefronts across the empty street bright gold, then burnt orange, then dark magenta.

Three guys crashed through the door full of gruff laughter and lots of "fuck yeah, dude!", their biking clothes covered with mud.

They spotted Aaron and waved, and he went over to them for the usual trip de-brief.

I turned toward Jill, who was staring at me hard. Then she just blurted it out: "so who the hell are you, really?"

"I told you. I'm corporate drop-out guy."

"Corporate drop-out guys are still corporate dudes, working on their resumes or whatever, even when they're not. And they're all pretty lame up here."

"Because they sell too hard?"

"Or not at all," she said, "which is even more stuck up –"

" – because that's the hardest sell of all," I filled in for her." I guessed I'm screwed then."

"Naw," she smiled. "You sell. A little."

Despite her tall, rooted athlete's presence, and her subtle but sharp tongue, she really was still just a big kid. And I was *not* hitting on her. But I was taking immense pleasure just sitting there in the bar, as the street went dark behind us and the lights came up just a little. The air in the bar grew warm and damp, and filled with quiet laughter and the groovy pulse of a slowly coalescing Widespread Panic jam, all long aching guitar lines and plaintive growl.

"So you had a job, and just blew it off. But you're still working. From up here."

"Sort of," I said. "With email, you can work wherever you have a good phone line."

"You mean like consulting?"

"Sort of. I stay plugged in a little, and people actually ask for my opinion on business stuff every now and then. Not really sure what I'm going to do next, but I don't really have to worry about it. For a while anyway."

"My dad does something like that. He used to be an investment banker. Now he just moves money around and tells people what to do."

"Good for him," I said.

"Not really. He's kind of an asshole. And his wife hates me."

I was desperate to change the subject away from all that and back to all this –"Lance is kicking ass again...check out how wasted that guy is...I heard it might snow tonight" – but Jill wouldn't stop with the interrogation about my old life Back East.

I handled it all like a work meeting, like slides running up on the screen, part of me paying attention, but the rest wondering. Because it really was happening, even though it really could not possibly have been: her long lean body was turning slowly toward me, her arms propped up on the windowsill bar, that three-dimensional question mark again, this time turning and opening to me.

Somewhere in the middle of all that, Aaron came and got his gear and the dummy, giving me a strange look and saying goodbye and leaving, and that's when I noticed that she was really staring at me.

"What?"

She looked down at her hands and started to ask a few times before blurting out, "So what do you think about business school for me?"

"Business school?" I almost spat out my beer. "Are you kidding? But – " I gestured toward the darkening street, the mountains a few blocks away, and the thousands of mountains beyond, where she worked and I played and who wouldn't want to spend the rest of our lives if they could? "– you have all this. Why blow that off? At least not until you have to?"

"Because I might have to," she said, pulling her ski hat off for the first time since I'd met her, running her fingers through her sun-streaked hair and letting it fall wherever. "This whole thing," she nodded out the window, "it looks like fun, but it's all business. And they want to build it around people who can do more than just ski."

"Yeah, but – you're –" and I really didn't know what to say, so I said nothing.

"I'm a *domestique*," she muttered and took a swallow of beer, pointing with her head at the bike race on TV, referring to the majority of a team's members who do all the hard work and get none of the glory. "I never placed high enough to get sponsored or any of that. I'm just a backcountry grunt. And everybody tells me I should go to MBA school, if I want to step up and help them run stuff."

She searched my face for any of the bizarre reactions she must always get when she blurts that out in a local's bar in Dudeville, which is about as far as you can get from the joyless, soulless grind of MBA school.

"Business school isn't so bad," I shrugged, trying not to shudder with the memory of dragging myself through it, twenty hours a week for four years, while working sixty hours a week at my day-job. "Just think of it like getting dental work every day, stretched out over a few years. Without any Novocaine. But hey – then it's done."

"Did you get one?"

"At night, part-time, while working. No Novocaine."

"And it didn't kill you," she said.

"No, but it was a major suckfest. I was working insane hours, and going to school. I traveled every week and studied on airplanes till midnight every night. I didn't take a full week off for five years. *Five years without a vacation*," I said it again, for emphasis, because the thought shocked me more and more, the longer I lived out here in Dudeville.

"Looks like you're making up for it now."

"Trying to."

We drank in silence for a minute.

"Then there's this other thing," she said.

"What other thing?"

"When we travel to all these cool places, I meet ex-pats who are working for these non-profits. Helping people, doing stuff for the planet, cleaning shit up. And I think – maybe I can do that? The enviro groups need people who know how to manage things, right?"

"Of course. They're in business like anybody else."

And that's how she would rationalize herself into and through MBA school, I realized there and then. She can tell herself she is going to work for an NGO when she's done; she'll get one of those "green MBAs" I'd just read about in *Forbes*; and with her ski background, maybe she will actually do it, like go to work for someone like the Nature Conservancy. I'd been thinking the same thing since running away from my own career, which may have been by choice for now, but can't be by choice forever.

"In fact," I said, "I was thinking about working – "

"For someone like – "

"The Nature Conservancy," we said at the same time, and then laughed.

So she was reading my thoughts. Scary.

We sat and drank in what was suddenly an easy, comfortable silence. She was not just hot, young, cool and a total Betty; she also turning out to be smart. Maybe we'll call her "Unicorn Girl," I thought, knowing Danny would want to hear every detail about what happened next.

"My mother's a psychotherapist," she finally broke the silence, "but she's all political too. And she's always saying 'If you want to fix yourself, go fix the world.'"

"Why? Are you broken?"

She looked up at me and rolled her eyes sideways. "Dude. *Everybody's* broken. Because the whole world is. A great big vicious cycle. That's why I think my mother kinda has it nailed."

Then she stared right into me: big black pupils in seawashed green eyes, ringed with little orange flares, like a controlled fire. Her warm but piercing gaze looked especially odd radiating off her big kid face, liked she'd been at the pool all summer, except her pool had been the backside of the Tetons the previous winter.

They say in Dudeville "you don't lose your girlfriend, you lose your turn." Ski towns like Dudeville – and there are narrow slices, if not whole chunks, of Dudeville in every mountain, canyon, river, and surf town across the American West – were 80 percent men. But it cuts both ways, because for women like Jill, Kelly, Hillary, Maggie, and all the other Betties around here, "the odds are good, but the goods are odd," as they also say in Dudeville.

And so, finally, it was my turn, the odds going for once in my favor. For her too, she said, though who knows: women think men want to hear that, so they always say it.

Indeed, it had been a long time for anything like that -- unless you count Amy the Rebound Girl coming out for that truly long weekend. Or the one time I tried to bust a move on that Third Wheelie, or what Danny calls a woman, just recently dumped, who is hanging out with a friend and her boyfriend to get over Dumper Boy. (Of course the Third Wheelie spent the night *not* sleeping with me, but crying every time she let herself get mildly aroused in my hot tub, finally throwing up and passing out in my guest room.)

So maybe it really was just my turn: Jill was only 25, as I eventually found out, the last year that still rounds down to *hell-yeah-I'm-still-young*, not up to *oh-shit-I'm-getting-old*.

But that was about to change, like it does for all of them. Like it did for my wife, a few short years after we finally dug ourselves out and got on our feet, and she was pushing 30 and suddenly had to have a kid. Like it did for Amy the Rebound Girl, after her own protracted divorce and belated ovarian awakening. Like it did for a bunch of the younger women who worked with me, who started hitting the after-work bar circuit with special ferocity and, the minute they met someone on it, disappeared forever.

I knew then and there that Jill would go the same route. But I also knew that she still had a good cache of time. In a few years, she would use the save-the-world rationale to capitulate to business school; meet a guy her own age or thereabouts; get married and get pregnant; and flee these mountain towns for some nice suburb outside Denver or Salt Lake City or Seattle, trading out her mud-splattered truck for a nice new minivan. The rest was just color choices and baby names. She was heading straight into the Hot Zone, whether she knew it or not, would one day have kids like her friends were all having kids, and that would be the end of her sweet jobs, hot body, and snow-globetrotting.

But she did still have that cache of time, so we spent the rest of that night at the Fat Chance in a blur of talk and drink and jokes, watching people come and go in blasts of ever damper, colder air, as big flakes of snow started to fall past the window. And because I would never even think to believe that she would sleep with someone my age – even though she still didn't know how old I was at that point – busting a move was pure, forbidden fantasy. Which is to say I had absolutely no plan to bust a move, which Danny refused to believe for months, until he decided it was my unconscious Zen-master plan. Which may be how and why the whole thing did actually work out in kind of a Zen way.

Jill and I closed down the place, and I walked her back to her truck, across from mine down by mountain rescue.

"So," she said, turning to me in the middle of the empty street, the town so quiet you could hear the dry rustle of snowflakes falling on everything. "I don't leave town for like a month. Let's go climb or something before I go."

"Yeah," I said, standing there like an idiot. "Let's uh – hang out again."

Then she dropped her pack, reached over, grabbed the back of my head, and moved in to kiss me. And faster than I could tune in to the fact that this was actually happening, I felt her warm wet tongue searching for mine. She pulled back and searched my face, big wet snowflakes catching all over her hat, clinging to the hair poking out from under it in every direction, clinging to her long eyelashes.

"What?" she asked. "Is the age thing weird for you?"

"You mean that I'm so old?"

"No, dude!" she chuckled. "That I'm so young."

Before I could burst out laughing, she was kissing me again, our faces slick with sudden heat and snowmelt, and I was kissing her back.

We made out in the street for a few minutes, and then in her truck, where we took it up a notch and a half. But self-consciousness and circumspection kicked in, and neither of us wanted to be the one to say *Let's go somewhere and do this!* – or the one to say that going somewhere and doing this was bad idea – so we made a plan to meet up in a few days and climb a mountain.

"Sorry, man."

I drift back, Maggie's voice.

"Didn't mean to leave you alone at the big party," she says.

I look up from the snowflakes falling all around Jill's face, and I am back in Ullar's. It's still empty but for me and Maggie back behind the bar, some ski porn on the TV now. The Grateful Dead are still dancing in the air, loopy, twisty, twirling.

"I was in the back counting bottles," she says, "then talking to my old bestie on the phone. And I left you in here with that big empty glass. My bad."

She goes to pour me another, and one for herself.

"Sure you don't want to clear out?" I ask.

"Nah, still got paperwork in the back, and nowhere to go anyway." She nods at the TV. "Good with the turns?"

"Always."

"And the tunes?"

"I'm having a grateful day."

She snorts. "I don't even hear it anymore. But it's better than the skater crap Miguel and the boys play all the time." Then a sly grin, and here comes one of her bartender jokes. "You know why you should never play a Grateful Dead song at a wedding?"

"Why's that?"

"Because the song might last longer than the marriage."

We laugh and she starts back toward the kitchen. "Just grab yourself another one if you don't see me for awhile."

I sit back and watch the ski porn and try to remember where I was. Heading to Breck?

Three days after that first night out in the snowy street, Jill and I met all the way over in Breckenridge, where she was visiting a ski instructor friend who was pregnant and getting married in a few weeks – yes, flashing red light: *Hot Zone Ahead!* – and I was driving sort-of-through on my way back to Dudeville from the Denver airport the night before.

We didn't really have a plan, just a couple truckfuls of gear and her coal-black little husky, Kettle – rescued in the 11th hour from euthanasia up in Alaska because he was too small and wiry for the Iditarod – in the back of hers. It was a late start for any kind of climb up and ski down, but the sky was a flawless blue with no wind and looked to be holding.

In Breck, I threw my snowboard and gear into the back of Jill's truck, a mud-caked, road-worn, beat-to-shit old warhorse, with a

Gravity: It's the Law bumper sticker. We drove up to the first big trailheads outside of town, off the back of Hoosier Pass, the jumping off point for several Fourteeners, none of which I'd been up yet. She had been up all of them except Mount Bross, so we dropped over the pass and drove up a winding dirt road across willow flats and frozen creeks, and found our way to the trailhead.

She started pulling gear, and Kettle disappeared up a trail that wasn't our trail.

"Don't worry," she said, reading my thoughts. "He'll find us."

"What are you going for?" I asked as she sorted through several pairs of skis in the back of her truck.

"I want to work on my tele-turns," she said, then stopped to look up the mountain, gleaming in the sun. "But it's pretty glazed up there. So probably not a good idea." She went back to her gear. "I'm thinking just alpines today."

Which meant she would be hiking up 2,500 vertical feet in big heavy alpine ski boots, with skis lashed onto her pack, along with snowshoes for when we start breaking through the crust – which would be soon at this hour – and ice ax and shovel. She'd be carrying twice the weight of my snowboard, snowshoes, ax and shovel, I was relieved to note, as I had no idea how badly she'd beat my ass up and down the mountain.

But she didn't beat my ass at all, unless she was dragging her own on purpose to go easy on my fragile, kinda almost middle-aged male ego. We actually kept pace, thanks to her working it with all that extra weight in much heavier boots, up through the trees, up to the ridge, and all the way to the summit.

Kettle, by contrast, didn't wait for either of us. He ran back and forth to the ridge and the summit, multiple times, before we caught up. Because, I remember thinking, of course Unicorn Girl would have Superdog, with a great backstory about how she saved him from death by clubbing or a shot to the back of the head way up north where it's barely half past Jack London.

We didn't bust through the crust, mostly by sticking to the rocky edge of the ridge, and then the windblown side of the face, until the last few hundred feet. Then, after a hard couple of hours of the always telescoping mind-game above treeline – head down, almost there, almost there, almost there really – I heard the jangle of dogtags and looked up to see Kettle, topped out. He was a squiggle of black ink across an electric blue sky, his tail wagging furiously at us. And then...

Summit!

And there we were, under a bottomless blue Colorado sky, standing on our own snow-and-rock island at the top of the world, lapped from all sides by mountains like standing waves breaking in from every direction. To the north, we could look down over the top of Breckenridge's matrix of ski trails; to the south and east, down into the great expanse of South Park (the real one, not the cartoon); and to the west, always to the west, a gray-granite, snow-hazy dream of range upon range of mountains without end.

We downed some calories and water, and futzed with gear, Kettle off again somewhere on the other side of the mountain.

As Jill kicked the snow off her boots and lined up her skis, I pulled out my camera to take a picture of the view like I always do. And then I could not help myself: I turned and pointed the camera at her.

"Hold on," I said.

"Aw, dude," she said. "Really?"

"Come on," I said. "Indulge me. I'm still just a tourist up here, compared to you."

"No you're not."

I don't remember what she or I said next, because I was obsessed with cramming as many mountains as I could into the frame around her.

"I feel stupid," she protested, trying to straighten the honeyed braids poking out of her hat at odd angles. "Am I supposed to smile? Or look hardcore? Or sexy?"

"You're supposed to look like you don't give a shit about any of those things."

"Well, that's good. Because I don't."

"Well there you go," I said, deeply embarrassed but not enough to stop myself. I was a lame-ass tourist dude snapping pictures as fast as the film would go, of a hot young Betty who was foolish or bored or lonely enough to go up and down a mountain with him on her day off. "Perfect. Done."

I stowed my camera and geared up for the ride down, one foot in my board, the other on the snow.

Then we just stood there, like I always do, soaking in the mountains and the sun, and all the geology, and weather, and time that had led, inexorably, to that amazing here and now.

And without even trying, and as distracted as I was, I could feel the Presence, not just there as usual, but beaming down on me, laughing, having as much fun with all of this as I was.

Jill slid her long legs back and forth on her skis, itching to drop down the snowfield at our feet.

"When we're out on some tour," she finally broke the immense silence all around us, "it's all about the Betties, and the shoots, and the pix. Takes fricking hours, messing with the gear, waiting for the light to be just so. But the girls always come out looking all spontaneous," she said, mostly to herself. "Always so fricking rad. Kinda weird, because it all looks so fake and cheesy and lame when it's getting put together."

I stood on my snowboard, one foot down for balance, and not in any hurry. I was happy to spend the rest of my life right there on top of the world, watching her stand there on her skis with one leg cocked back for balance, drenched in sunlight, angled for the drop like a surfer waiting for a wave.

"It's all bullshit, you know," she said, "all just marketing."

"I know."

"*This* is what's real," she said, sweeping her ski pole out over the rolling sea of white-capped mountaintops. "Not us. Not going huge." She let out a long, deep, peaceful sigh. "Just them."

I looked out at "them," at the great swirls of white frosting on the whole cake of the planet, the Presence sitting at the head of the table, ready to cut into it, as drunk on the glory of the day as I was. "I know."

Then she smiled at me, pulled her goggles down over her eyes, and launched.

The sun had turned the late season snowfield from hard silvery glaze to soft creamy corn – we'd been breaking through those last few hundred feet, but only boot deep – so it would be a slow, easy ride down. It was avalanche terrain, even though we had noted the risks were low on the climb up, which meant that we couldn't hit it at the same time. One drops in and the other watches, until the first one stops and watches, a rule we both knew and didn't need to say out loud.

I stood perched on my snowboard and watched her drop straight down the fall line, her long lithe body pulled with the first turn into an unspooling of graceful, slow motion curves so even and precise they seemed suspended in time and space. My head filled with chamber music as I watched her weave back and forth across the axis of gravity, a human cello playing one perfect semi-circular note after another.

I finally had to sit back on the rock behind my snowboard because my head, or my heart – or was it both? – exploded with joy. As I knew at the top of so many of these mountains, I could have died right there and then, and my whole life would have turned out just fine. And then, I realized, of all goddamn things, that I was actually crying.

I was still sitting on that rock, perched over the snowfield and trying to gather myself for the ride down, when under my arm there was a sudden wet poke, a long skinny coal-black nose flecked with white, Kettle, nuzzling me.

I stroked his head and we watched Jill as her turns tightened up around the axis, and she came around the last one, and pointed it straight down the bottom of the snowfield. Then she shot out onto the flats, gathering speed up onto the long rocky ridge that connected our peak with the next one over. Her figure, suddenly impossibly tiny against all that mountain, came to a stop on the ridge.

She waved *All Clear* with her pole, and Kettle bolted from under my arm, straight down the mountain.

I watched him shrink to a speck of black energy on all that snow, then shoot up the ridge to Jill and run around her twice before stopping next to her.

Then it was my turn, and I felt the first hammering of adrenaline on the back of my head before I could even stand up.

I strapped my other foot on the board, and more adrenaline surged through the rest of my body. Popping to my feet, I rocked back and forth to find the sweet spot where my center of gravity merges with the earth's...waiting, breathing, drinking it all in...

...and then I slipped soundlessly off the edge.

A full flush of adrenaline surged through me as I dropped in and found the rhythm of the fall-line, the chamber music jumping the needle – to grunge? no! jazz? no! punk? NO! – there was no music at all. Just the high steady thrum of the wind in my ears from the drop, louder, faster, and steadier, like the Presence whistling at me.

On those first few turns off the top, I probed with the edges of my board for the slip and give of the softening snow; shimmied my shoulders to check the swing of the packweight; then slowly picked up speed, cutting back and forth across the jagged fall line. The back of my brain processed all the numbers, running them up against the ten thousand turns I'd made on a snowboard by then, and sent all the data on arc degrees, attack angles, and throw-weights back down into my core, hips, thighs, knees, legs and feet. With all that going back and forth between my body and brain, and the mountains looming up around me, and the Presence singing in my ears, suddenly there was no Jill to impress, no me to embarrass, no age, or fear, or agitating world, just gravity and fall-line, mountain and sky, motion and emotion, the cool cleansing flush of all that good adrenaline as I pointed it straight down that wide open mountain.

I crouched into the last turn and cut it hard to gather speed, and shot up onto the ridge toward Jill and Kettle.

"Strong work," she said.

"Strong work yourself."

She turned toward the bottom and made a little clicking sound, and Kettle shot down the rest of the open face toward treeline.

I rode after Jill down into the treeline, then down into the boggy bottom, the whole run taking maybe fifteen minutes, for a better than average return for a four-hour hike up.

We slogged and bushwhacked the last mile through treeline corn mush and willow-bottom slush, then geared off at her truck in a warm, late afternoon breeze.

As I was pulling off my boots, she pulled out a bowl – because I wasn't high enough at that point? ha! – and we smoked it and packed up.

"Ket-tle," she called out, in two quiet, high-pitched notes.

Thirty seconds later, I heard dogtags jangling through the trees and there was Kettle, popping out of the woods and running straight into the back of her truck.

We drove down into Breckenridge, jacked from the climb up and ride down, high from the weed, and laughing about one dumb thing or another. At the bottom of the pass, the mountains gave way to cabins, then houses and condos scattered through the woods, and then finally an explosion of condos and resort sprawl and we were back in Breck.

I was hungry from the back of my burning eyes to the bottoms of my aching feet, my parched tongue twitching for a cold beer.

"This place has great burgers," she said before I could say anything, pointing at a brewpub. "Usually a bunch of tourists. But it's mud season, so maybe not so bad. You down?"

The Breckenridge Brewery was all glass, gleaming stainless steel, and huge copper beer kettles. It was also packed with people waiting for tables, even though it was mud season. We overheard that there was a small film festival and a big dentist convention in town; half the place was young pale hipsters in frumpy old wool, and old pale fat guys in bright new fleece. The last of the large oil-and-water crowd was still gathered by the door waiting for tables.

"Let's just eat at the bar," Jill said, towering over most of them and starting to push her way through.

The guy holding back the crowd – carrot-topped, red-faced, and barrel-chested, like a former football player from Ohio or Michigan – pointed at Jill and asked for her ID. She reached into her ski pants pocket for a lump of plastic and cash wrapped with one of those thick rubber bands used to hold skis together, and showed him the ID on top. Then he turned to me.

"What?" I asked.

"Let me check your ID real quick, dude."

I realized I still had my sunglasses and ski hat on, and took them off. But he just stared at me, so I fished out my wallet and handed him my driver's license.

He studied it a moment, looked over at me, and handed it back.

"You're like – 38, dude," he said.

"Afraid so."

He looked over at Jill, then back at me, and then put up his fist – to fist-bump me. "Good for you, dude."

I caught up with Jill as she jumped up onto a barstool.

"No shit," she said.

"What?"

"You're really 38?"

"You heard that, huh? Hope that doesn't –"

"Hell no, dude," she said, sliding over and making room for me at the bar. "I don't give a shit. Most of the guys running the stuff on tours are older, and they all go huge too."

It was nice of her to say, even if both parts of it were bullshit salve for my ego. But the age thing has been, for the past several years, like a crappy work question – there's no good answer – so I did the same thing I always do with crappy work questions: changed the subject.

She noted this with relief, I could tell, and we went back to trading stories about mountains and people we knew. Tyler was always good for that, his latest impossible feat running up and over and back around some range in one day that takes most of us three; or pulling himself up something by ice axes in the middle of the night; or crushing the Grand Traverse, or Leadville 100, or Hardrock, or Badwater. And Kelly was even better for great yarns, and not just because she could piss standing up in ski boots on a table in here, as I would find out later on that big group hut trip.

I look up from that crowded bar – the shine on everything, the emerald glow in Jill's eyes, the little cocoon we made in the crowd just beyond our *Back off, we're locals* radius – and over at the long, empty tables in this one.

"Another one, man?"

I turn and Maggie is holding up my glass.

"Yeah, one more," I tell her. "Then I have to roll."

"Yeah, me too."

She goes to pour me another one, and one for herself, and we both look up at the TV, a surf competition now, an impossibly long and perfect wave and beach full of impossibly bronzed and beautiful people.

Maggie has switched out the Grateful Dead for the manic jangle of a hippie bluegrass band. The raucous, racing hoedown fills the empty bar, as out of place with the surfing as the surfing is with the heavy timbers, stone fireplace, and old skis and ice axes on the walls.

"There's Jeremy," Maggie says, when the TV cuts to a bronzed commentator with a big afro and barrel chest straining against a Hawaiian shirt. "I know that guy. Used to come in here all the time. Bald as a cue ball."

"Gotta do what you gotta do," I chuckle. "For work and all."

"I guess," she says. "Frickin' Jeremy. Always so full of himself."

The phone rings on the wall.

"I guess it really is mud season if they're surfing Banzai already," she says, going over to answer it. She grabs a clipboard from behind the bar, and heads into the kitchen with both.

I try to lose myself in the surfing on TV, which looks a lot like snowboarding, if on a permanently collapsing mountain. But after a couple waves, the whole thing starts to agitate me, which might just be the hippiegrass spinning around in the air. Or maybe because all I really want to think about now is Jill. Back then anyway. On that perfect first date.

Back at the bar in Breckenridge, sinking deeper into our *Back off, we're locals* cocoon, we tossed back beers and burgers. There was an endless loop of alt-rock "hits" oozing out of a dozen invisible speakers – Eve 6, Maroon 9, Blink 182, Matchbox Whatever, and a dozen other noisy sugarpop-punk bands that sound like Matchbox Whatever – but were an appropriately absurd soundtrack for the intense, then bizarre, then silly stories we traded about mountains, people, the world.

After we finished eating, it was no small effort just to stay propped up on that barstool, sinking into the physical space opened up by an exhausting day on the mountain; then the weed and beers; and then the huge burger and numbing soundtrack. It may have been just another day in Jill's life, going that huge; but it was my first year in Dudeville, and a big backcountry snowboard summit was still special.

Actually, no, it wasn't just special. (Any big snowboard summit still is, of course.) It was everything I had ever dreamed about, all those late nights drooling my way slowly through the latest issue of *Outside* while stuck in some crowded airport or sterile business hotel. So what if I was on a first date that would never amount to anything, especially now that she knew how old I was, I remember thinking: I finally just surrendered to slumping on the bar, deliriously happy, both full and empty (another of Dan's *koans*?), and at peace.

Half a beer later, and she was slumping too, curled back into that question mark, her arm across the bar and head cradled inside her elbow. She looked tired herself, and peaceful, but still curious, her green eyes soft in the fading light, searching my face. I knew she was thinking the same things – my age, her age, birth control, ex's, STDs, should we hook it up, and if so where? – and I knew it best to talk our way back into the mountains.

But we were out of Tyler and Kelly stories, for now anyway, and before I could say something snotty about the music, she just blurted it out: "You're really 38?"

"Yes."

"Were you ever married?"

"Yes."

"For how long?"

"Nine years."

She sat part way up, her eyes suddenly alarmed. "Do you have any kids?"

"No," I answered, and watched her sink back onto the bar and breathe a literal sigh of relief. "That help?"

"Help what?"

"You know," I muttered into my beer, wanting to say *Help you not freak out about the age thing, because nothing makes someone older than being a parent?* But I could muster only: "Help with me being so – you know –"

An odd look came over her face, her eyes crossing over sideways, but I kept digging.

"You know," I said, "with you getting all tangled up – with some old guy and his bitchy ex and his kids and – "

"Dude," she rolled her head around in the crook of her elbow. "What's the big deal? We're just hanging out."

"That's right," I said. "Just hanging out."

She sat up and took a long swallow of beer. "I just hope *you're* not freaking out about the age thing."

"Why would I?"

"Because I'm only 25," she said. "And I feel kinda goofy." Then, suddenly, she reached over for my hand, like she'd been planning the move awhile and finally forced herself to make it. "And I think you're hot," she said, running her fingers through mine.

"Doesn't matter to me," I managed to say, with a shrug.

And it was a shrug more contrived than anything I could ever muster during my toughest business negotiations. Because over in the parallel universe of my wildest imagination, my head – yes, both of them – was exploding.

I felt like jumping up on the bar, dancing to Matchbox Whatever, and shouting out to the hipsters and dentists swirling politely around us, *Can you believe how freaking lucky I am? Look at this girl! And she's a total Betty! And she wants to sleep with ME!!!* But I had to say something, and I was drawing blanks on everything else, so I said: "Your age doesn't matter to me at all."

"Really?"

"Really." (Because yes, really, but not in any way I'd care to admit and she'd care to know.) "Though I have to admit – for 25, you really do seem to have your shit together."

"Thanks," she said, with another visible sigh of relief. "And for 38, you're still going pretty huge."

"Just making up for lost time."

Her eyes went sideways again, and I kept digging, and almost blew it.

"You may have to grow old," I said, "but you don't have to grow up."

She almost spat out her beer. "Really, dude?" she said and rolled her eyes again. "I don't know if this will make you feel better – but sometimes you kinda do sound like some guy my age."

"Thanks. I guess."

She pulled off her ski hat, and combed out her hair with her fingers, looking around with a suddenly devious smile.

"What?"

"So maybe," she lowered her voice, but it was more purr than whisper, "you're not too grown up to go poach a hot tub?"

A few minutes later, we walked out into the suddenly quiet, empty streets of Breckenridge, all *faux* Victorian storefronts and gingerbread-house restaurants and shiny new timber-framed condo buildings. The sun was dropping through an orange, then pink, then purple ribbon of cloud into the mountain range cradling the west side of town, turning the opposite range a glowing ruby red.

We wandered off Main Street into a maze of mostly dark condos, looking for a hot tub to poach, a ski resort game I've since played many times with Danny, but hadn't heard of until that day. (When you poach a hot tub, you have to wait until it's dark, not just for the stealth approach and escape factors, but for the reconnaissance factor: after dark, you can spot the wafting of just the right amount of steam up past the roofs. Most tubs are covered most of the time and let off little or no steam; a big funnel cloud means an open tub full of people; a faint, twisting shaft of steam, like smoke from a fire, means an empty tub somebody left open, which is what you're looking for.)

I followed Jill around more corners and past a few big clouds, toward a hazy column of steam, and there it was: the perfect hot tub. It was sitting in the shadow of a mostly dark condo complex, on the other side of a waist-high iron fence, bubbling away like a stewpot beneath a cover someone had hastily put sort of back in place.

Jill looked around quickly, then in one quick leap jumped clean over the fence, and I followed. And then, just as fast and smoothly as she skied, she was out of her ski pants and sweater, down to her sports bra and panties, and plopping into the furious, bubbling hot water.

A minute later, I was down to my underwear and slipping into the deliciously hot water.

We soaked in the tub in silence, our heads back against the edge of the tub, watching the last of the color drain from the sky and the alpenglow on the opposite range fade to black. The tub bubbled away, and I felt every muscle let go, along with the burn encasing my mid-calves and shins from the rub-rub of the hike up the mountain in my snowboard boots. And just as I was settling in, and no longer thinking about security guards and cameras and cops, Jill glanced around quickly in every direction, then sat forward and pulled off her sports bra and then her panties, and dropped both with a wet *CLOP!* next to the tub.

"That's better," she said. "If you're gonna get busted, might as well get busted in style."

"There you go," I said, hoping if not assuming that my body hadn't run off on its own tangent, and yet terrified that it might have or would at any moment, a fact which would be quite unambiguous the moment the tub's jets turned off.

I pulled off my own undies, greatly relieved they were a clean pair, and dropped them with a wet *CLOP!* next to Jill's.

We soaked in silence for a few minutes, looking up at the stars because I dared not look anywhere else. And just as I was settling in again, she asked me if I'd ever been to Breck before, which was the last thing I wanted to think about right there and then.

"Yes," I said.

She waited for me to elaborate, but I didn't want to, and I think she could tell, because she just said, "cool."

I had in fact been there, several years earlier for a work thing, all of which I'd almost forgotten about until Jill asked.

It had been our first company-wide meeting since a big messy acquisition. Everyone from our offices on both coasts had gathered for three days in what may have been the same conference room used by the dentists that week, maybe two hundred feet from that very hot tub. It was supposed to have been as much play as work, a little bit of corporate boondoggle in the middle of a corporate "busy season" that never ended. But Tom, Becky, Leah and I had all spent it grinding our way through the business crisis *du jour,* and the last minute details of the protracted, on-again, off-again negotiations over the next complicated acquisition, which would fall through three months later anyway.

On that first trip, I'd rented skis and planned to get up on the mountain with some of my staff. But the Breckenridge boondoggle mutated into sixteen hours a day of running numbers, arguing about org charts and money, and eventually carrying it all into the hotel bar every night, where we kept arguing until we all went to bed pissed (in the British sense of the word) and pissed (in the American sense). As usual, Tom and Becky had been fighting about something they wouldn't share with Leah or me. We'd thought it might have been a deal that affected us and so they never disclosed any of it, but you never can know what's exactly going on with other people, so why waste your energy trying?

A door slams, and I'm back in the empty bar.

I look up from my half-finished beer over to the door, and there is Tyler, sticking his tanned, sculpted, always busy face into Ullar's. His wiry body is still halfway out the door, propped up on a mountain bike.

"Hey Jack," he calls into the bar from the bike. "You seen Deputy Dog?"

"About an hour ago," I say, "right down the middle of Main, like always."

"That's my boy. He heading north or south?"

"North."

"Cool, man, thanks!"

The door slams behind him, and he shoots past the window on his bike.

Where was I? Breckenridge? With Jill, sure, but also with Tom and Becky, sniping at each other in the hotel bar every night.

Leah and I had killed far too many hours on the subject of Tom and Becky at the bar by our office Back East, but none of us could ever figure it out.

Tom and Becky had known each other since childhood in the Midwest somewhere, and had reconnected at MBA school. They started the company with a little bit of Other People's Money, and a great software patch to encrypt big, standardized PC files. (Yes, 1991 was a very long time ago.) We eventually turned this software patch into the music industry's last-ditch effort to stop the theft of its IP on PCs. And its popularity with both software and record companies was how I actually did end up in the music business, sort of – if about as far from a guitar or microphone as you can get and still technically be "in" the music business.

On that last afternoon in Breckenridge, when everyone else was heading home to their families, Becky said she'd hang out for the weekend and go skiing with me, something we'd talked about for months. But she had also been fighting, as usual, with her creepy stay-at-home husband Sidney every night via phone, who decided to fly all the way out there that week, unbeknownst to her, and fight with her in person. (Hers was yet another ugly, screwed up marriage I got to witness or hear about every week, another to remind me how bitterly glad I was that mine, right about then, had finally died of natural causes, if not been buried.)

Three years later, there I was with Jill, back in Breck for the third time. I was sitting in all that percolating water, trying not to look at that impossibly athletic *and* sensuous body, thinking: *How can I possibly explain all that messy, boring corporate stuff, all that dull, numbing work and worry, and all that starter-marriage heartbreak, to this – this **kid!** – in the hot tub with me?*

At least the sour memory of the earlier Breck trip was a good distraction to keep my body from going rogue while we bubbled away in our birthday suits.

She didn't press, but I could tell that she wanted to know, if only because she didn't say anything else after that.

But how to explain any of that to her? How to tell some version of all that business and personal dreck, without making it sound middle-aged and pathetic? While trying *not* to sprain every muscle in my eye sockets – trying to look, and not look, but really how could I not look?? – at those sweet little breasts, and those hard little nipples, perfect round chocolate drops in the ambient light off the untanned middle of her chest, roiled by all that hot water, her now familiar jade bear pendant bouncing up and down in the foam, beckoning me toward nirvana???

And how to explain my only two solid images of the whole of Breckenridge until that moment: the diamond dust snow, falling for hours through the security light outside the meeting room window; and standing in the courtyard of the hotel with rental skis, maybe two hundred feet from that very same hot tub, waiting an hour and a half for Becky to emerge, finally, in her jeans and designer sweater and black leather boots, Sidney moping along behind her. Just in time for the mountain to have drowned in a wet, heavy fog.

"I think I got in maybe three runs," I finally said to Jill, looking up at the stars through the steam. "That first time I was here."

"Inbounds?"

"Inbounds?" I snorted. "Inbounds was all I knew back then."

"So you *are* making up for lost time," she said.

"That is definitely what I am doing."

"Good," she said.

An instant later, there were long, strong, pulsing fingers crawling across the top of my thigh, and then her presence all around me in the bubbling water.

I closed my eyes, and sank lower in the tub, and there were arms and legs all around me, long, lean, muscled, and insistent; and her hungry mouth was all over mine, her tongue instantly familiar; and I wasn't sure if what was running down my face was sweat, or splashes from the tub, or tears of pure joy.

If all that counts as a first date, then it was a first date that lasted for nearly a month, when she was set to leave for New Zealand. We went from doing the everything-but in the hot tub in Breck to doing the everything-plus in my bed back in Dudeville. And then, to my great delight, we spent most of the next six days back at The Treehouse – five days in my own hot tub, all over the living room floor, on the kitchen counter, passing out in my bed, waking up for another go-round and passing out again, each morning running out to and up another new mountain.

On the seventh day, Jill moved herself and all her gear from a spare bedroom at Kelly's and the back of her truck, into what she called "The Treehouse." Along with Kettle, of course.

In just a few weeks, she would be hauling people and gear around glaciers on the bottom of the planet – goddamn, what a lucky girl! – and she needed to stay in shape. And I was all too happy, up there at altitude, to do what I could for the cause. With that quick an expiration date and never a mention of any future, I was all in. Dude. She would be off to New Zealand soon enough, and tomorrow there would be another mountain much closer to home: Shavano, Sherman, Blanco, Tabaguache, the Spanish Peaks, Kit Carson, Antero, and the best of them all, Wheeler Peak, the highest in New Mexico and goddamn, what a mind-bending summit!

So by all means, Jill, I remember thinking: move your gear into The Treehouse, my house – or more precisely my garage, so it will be easy to move right back out when it is time to move on. As all that was happening, each night the last of the sunset turning to liquid fire through the budding aspens, the Treehouse suddenly dark, I felt like I was watching it in a movie or music video: it was a shadowy, clove-scented Gen X romance – quirky and sexy and tragically doomed – like a Lisa Loeb song full of young lust, benign neurosis, and delicious pain-to-come. But rather than puncture that whole dream state with excessive appraisal and self-reproach, I just opened another beer, packed another bowl, and chased Jill into the hot tub to watch the stars come out. I was choosing every day and every night – with all the Zen consciousness I could muster – not to give a shit about how ridiculous the whole thing looked.

Especially after Becky called a few days later to complain about the latest with Tom, asked what was new, and laughed at me when I told her.

"Well," she laughed. "At least she's legal. Best to hold right there at 25 – and not go full-blown creepy old divorced guy."

Which should have pissed me off, but did give me pause, prodding me to insist that Jill was actually completely together for her age and my ending up with someone even younger never could or would happen. Because 25, I'd realized only the night before that call with Becky, was bad enough.

Over our entire dinner down at the tourist restaurant in town, Jill and I had gotten the death-ray stare from the original issue wife sitting at the next table with her MIA husband, who just stared at his plate the whole time. No doubt Jill's and my presence had sent him wandering back into his version of the collective daydream, the oft-discussed and occasionally attempted fantasy about The Eternal Promise of the Younger Woman, which goes something like: *If I can keep up with her – or more importantly, if they see me keeping up with her – I'm not really as old as I look. I'm vital, and virile, and not dying for a very long time.*

But aside from that odd outing, and notwithstanding Becky's ribbing, I was *not* that guy and I didn't give a shit how it looked. I had been in a grind of a marriage for nine years: all work and scarcely any sex, as my wife and I put in grueling seven-day weeks – full-time work and full-time college – to lift ourselves and each other up and out of *de facto* orphanhood; then through more economic struggle, thanks to my brief but foolish music detour; and finally on to good jobs, business school, and eventual capitalist rescue and reward. I may have looked, to the angry old wife at the next table over, like a lecherous old fool, but it wasn't like I was cheating on anyone. It was for only a few weeks and then Jill would be gone.

So why shouldn't I play house with a hot young Betty who'd skied her way through private school and Dartmouth, and lived in an eternal present? Even if all Jill wanted to talk about was my old job, career path, what I was doing on email every now and then and why people paid me for it. Or how small businesses got funded and non-profits worked. Or LEEDS certification as a business model, though she was the one telling me about that last one, which she'd read in the latest issue of *Fortune* sitting on top of my mail.

So yes, even toward the tail-end of that perfect, month-long first "date," Jill's work questions irritated me a bit, especially because they could be so jarring. We would be driving to or from one great mountain or another, past what felt like our own private mountainscape, with Kettle and our skis or snowboards or rock climbing gear in the back; and she would stray from whatever book one of us was reading aloud – on western history, or nature, or the environment – while the other was driving. Her questions about business were intrusions, mental farts in the cab of the truck, and the discussion that followed always felt like a terrible, tragic exercise, like I was helping her plan for life after some partial apocalypse.

Even more irritating, right from those very first road trips, were her increasingly worried-sounding probes about my parents. What was it like growing up with a drunk for a father? When and how exactly did my mother die? Where was my sister now? Why hadn't I seen or spoken to them in ten years?

I have never had good answers for any of that, for myself or anyone else, so I end the conversation one more time and look up to see Maggie standing across from me, smiling and shaking her head.

"What?"

"You sure do know how to keep yourself busy on a slow day," she says.

"Sorry. Just spacing out."

"Yeah, well," she sighs. "Good day for it."

"Mud season."

"Mud season," she sighs again. "So are you good? I think I'm out."

She reaches up with the remote and turns off the TV, then goes to shut off the beer neon in the window.

I pay her what I owe and half again – for the company when I wanted it and solitude when I didn't, she has a real gift for that – and head out the door.

Main Street is deserted, the sun almost to The Lady now, casting her face in shadow, the angle of the light turning the dust in the still air a bright, harsh gold. My truck is the only one in the entire block, waiting out front, mud-splattered all along the bottom and all the way to the top of the cap in the back, a trusty horse of the new west.

I climb in and wonder what to do with the rest of the day, evening, night. There is plenty of food up at The Treehouse, and maybe a message from Jill, or not, not that it matters.

So I just drive.

I head out the south end of town, past the road up the side canyon to The Treehouse, and climb up the pass, looking south. I pull over and sit in my truck and just watch the landscape change slowly from gold to red, the start of the high desert reaching down into New Mexico.

New Mexico.

I try not to think about the trip down there. Jill was dark and dreary from seeing her old hippie aunt and her aunt's girlfriend – or maybe she was just that way from some kind of hangover from the mushrooms we all took. But something was bugging her that day – until that great trailhead camp, and amazing climb, and summit, and drop on our skis. Because that's what the best mountains do: re-calibrate everything to its proper scale. The mountains and desert are what is real. All the rest of this human business is ephemeral, messy, bittersweet bullshit.

Because it was right after the New Mexico trip that Jill started to get clingy. More of her stuff started finding its way from down in my garage to up in my bedroom, and I was counting the days until she left for New Zealand and we could both get on with our lives.

That was two summers ago, and I'm still wishing we could both just get on with our lives.

I heard from Danny that she's back in town from Argentina, where she is supposed to be working on some ski film all summer. But what would be the point? She will be leaving at the end of this summer for grad school in California. Environmental science and not business school, as it turns out. Smarter choice for her and cooler path for anyone, so I guess my grousing did help her, maybe a little anyway.

Below the pass, the road turns west toward the sinking sun, so I start the truck and turn around and drive back toward Dudeville and The Treehouse.

I pull up just as the sun is slipping below the ridge across the canyon, bathing everything in a soft, golden light.

The house is still warm from the day, but deadly quiet in a way I never used to notice. The message light on my answering machine is blinking 3.

"Hey Jack..." says Aaron, confirming our trailhead time for the climb tomorrow.

"Hey man..." says Danny, confirming the same thing.

And then "Hey there..."

It's Jill, but she doesn't say anything else. The recording is so quiet, it sounds like I can hear her breathing, even though I know I cannot.

"It's me," she finally continues. "I'm back in town. And um – it would be good to hang out. Heading up to Cheyenne for a couple days, but back Friday." Long pause. "So give me a call, dude. I hope you're good." An even longer pause. "You good? Ok. 'Bye."

I sit out on the deck with a cold beer and the phone in my lap, and watch the trees and canyon beyond fall into shadow, then darken and disappear.

I can't decide if I should call her back. Two years now, round and round, ever since those first literally wonderful, and uncomplicated, trips. Two years of now-we're-hooking-up, now-we're-not. Of we're-not-together, but she's not fooling around on me. And then she's with this guy Brandon, and then she isn't. It will never change, and it needs to end.

Jill turned out to be a little tough to read at first, but now she is impossible. And she is definitely in the hot zone, if a little early at 27. But she's acting exactly like women who are about to turn that age when they say they are in no hurry to settle down and have kids – and most of them probably actually believe that when they say it – but they don't mean it one little bit.

I may be 40 years old now and acting like an idiot, still chewing on the bitter cud of a belated divorce after a long and useful but ultimately failed marriage. I may have dropped out from a career that peaked a little too fast and a little too early. But Jill's real life, i.e., her "adult" career, hasn't even started yet. And she is just starting to feel like she is reaching that suddenly brisk age when many, many women – no matter what they think, do or say – want to build a nest and lay eggs.

Jill has outgrown me, and I need to stop missing her.

LSD

I try not to look up too often: it can be heartcrushing to see how far up this frozen river of snow we still have to climb to reach the summit. At this altitude, for this many hours, my brain goes woozy with endorphins, gnawing at itself for more oxygen and taunting the rest of my body to get to the top.

I look up anyway.

We are still nowhere near the top.

Ugh.

Danny is a dozen paces ahead, head down, slogging away, his snowboard, snowshoes and avy shovel lashed to his pack, the duct tape patches on his baggy black pants reflecting sun.

A dozen paces ahead of him is Aaron, his pack heavy with skis, shovel, and coils of rope, his head down, slogging away.

Today's mountain and route were Aaron's call – they usually are – and he was not kidding when we said "Let's do some LSD," for Long Slow Distance. So we are headed up Apache Peak, four hard trail-miles into the Indian Peaks Wilderness, after a five-mile slog up the still-closed access road outside Nederland. Normally an overnighter, we are ten hours in today, we just hit treeline, and the real climb hasn't started yet. And the weather is shit.

At this altitude, for this long, there is no time to think about anything except where and how I am: trying to stay inside the aerobic box, trying to crunch my way to the top.

Breathe in, breathe out, I say, over and over, trying to drown out the wind screaming in my ears, trying to pull myself back to here and now from wherever I've drifted. Back to this wild mountain and wind; back to this exhausted body, raging with weariness inside its bundle of nylon and fleece; back to a pack heavy with gear, pulling me off the shoulder of this exhausting mountain.

Aaron finally pulls up under a great pile of boulders, well short of the summit.

Water, calories, and a moment's rest. We are all too winded to talk, and so we don't, another benefit of a good climbing team: you don't have to talk at all, unless you want to. And when you do, it either matters, in a life-or-death way, or it's interesting or funny or both.

Good climbing teams, like good friendships I suppose, can't be planned. They just happen. I met Danny through Aaron, whom I'd met Back East through Amy the Rebound Girl. He and Danny were both in their late 20s and had been climbing out here a couple years, so they were in great shape and had a routine: Aaron handles the gear and Danny handles the food. I always get to the summit or turn-point or drop-zone well behind them both, to find Aaron futzing with gear or digging a snow pit to check for avalanche danger, and Danny sitting and looking out over the firmament, meditating.

Aaron is the intense and natural leader, always focused on the task at hand. His dark hair and beard always look like they were trimmed the day before, his mind's eye busy with what is in front of him or the story he's telling, usually right at the edge of outrage about it. Danny, in perfect contrast, is the wild child and comic relief, always a week's worth of whiskers on his face, with laughing blue eyes and a huge head of blond hair usually streaked with pink or purple and sticking out from his hat in whatever direction he woke up that morning. Aaron is the smart, resourceful guy who steps up and fixes whatever it is you are dealing with, even if you don't want or need the help, explaining the whole time why the way he is fixing it is the right way; Danny is a glorious mess of an overgrown boy, the gregarious alpha-rebel-dreamer that all of us overgrown boys want to hang with and the alpha-women want to break, and he is happy to let them try. Aaron seems beyond the reach of any woman, though the ones he has pulled off the mountain in the patroller's sled – or their single friends skiing with them, as I've seen a few times – have certainly tried.

I have no idea what either of these guys really think about me. But I'm around, I show up when I say I will, and I can keep up with them at altitude (barely); I'm learning mountain rescue and wilderness first responder skills from them, and had a chance to prove it solo last year with those kids; and I can always amuse them with another installment of my Theater of the Corporate Absurd, another story from my old life back in the world, usually involving some huge business ego doing something hugely stupid. ("FTW!" – for Fuck the World! – Danny always ends up saying when I'm done.) And three is the exact right number for a safe but fast mountaineering team.

We've been climbing up and riding down these mountains for two years now, and we know all of each other's moods and moves. If we are talking on the hike in, Aaron leads the way: details on the route up, weather and snow conditions, avalanche danger, when to switch out gear, and details on the route down; and he is always checking in on how we are doing, even though he can read it in our faces and hear it in our breathing. When we are talking on the hike out – once we are off the peak and safely back in the trees, and Danny gets a big bowl of weed going – it'll be non-stop, all the way back to the trailhead: Aaron about Tyler's latest impossible feat of endurance, or some tourist's unlucky misadventure out in the woods, or the latest bulldozing of some fragile landscape near and dear to us – or far and dear, if only we could see how beautiful and what a crime; Danny about sex, meditation, women, the Tao, the relative merits and tradeoffs of big boobs versus little boobs, some mind-blowing new mindfulness practice, Zen Buddhism, some mind-blowing new sexual position, Kerouac and what Danny calls his *kinda lame alcohol-withdrawal version of the Dharma*, and lately, Danny's emerging theory about female orgasms. (He insists they are not only *not* binary, as generally accepted – by women themselves, he has noted – but are actually a complex continuum that have "maybe 25 percent to do with female pelvic anatomy.") He has been working to support this theory for years with copious evidence and details – or "deets," as he calls them – always copious deets, always when the hard work is behind us, and we are still drunk with the views from the summit and adrenaline from the ride down, the weed has kicked in, and life is good.

Except for today.

This endless today.

And this unreachable summit.

Today, with the route this long, the going this tough, the wind this loud, we are not talking. Today, the hike down and out cannot come soon enough. We *will* summit. But for all this wind, there is a hard gray ceiling clamped down at about 17,000 feet, a cold, gray, indifferent sky. Today, we are making the climb in these conditions for the usual reasons: because we can, despite these conditions; because it's brutally hard, and Aaron has always wanted to; and because it has some technical challenges near the top – good practice for the top of The Lady back in Dudeville.

But today, the process isn't pretty. It's just long, and hard. Besides, all of Colorado is socked in today; so we're up north in the Indian Peaks because Aaron needs to do something down in Boulder tonight, where Danny and I will drive him when we're done.

So here we are.

Yay.

It's on these kind of climbs when I actually do want to follow the long-slog chatter in my head: going back through some odd, funny, troubling, or even upsetting files in my database of memories, dangerous as that is on any climb. I want to float up and out of my body and off the mountain, to mechanize the hard, grueling, repetitive, boring, chomp-chomp-chomp up the snowpunch footsteps of Danny and Aaron, ten and twenty paces above me. But such digressions back into the past can be dangerous distractions. And on crappy days like this, the ones that turn up can be grim, and turn even grimmer as the body and spirit wear down, stories darkening with regret, anger, maybe even sadness, my age showing like it rarely does since dropping out and moving west.

Best just to focus on staying in the aerobic box. On the breath. On not thinking about anything.

Because today, if I went there, it would be all the way to the 1980s, thanks to some clattering industrial disco thing turned all the way up on the radio when I started my truck his morning, which has since burrowed in and swollen up my ear like an infection. Ah, yes, the 1980s: the grueling, numbing fights we had over cash, the ATM under 20 bucks again, which bills to pay and not pay: the back rent, the maxed out credit cards, or the medical ones gone to collection, as we play cat-and-mouse with the landlord, the hit man from VISA, and the bank check-clearing system. And so much for college for either of us for one more year, all while Reagan yammered on in the background about Morning in America.

No! Back in the box!

I am hungry and thirsty and keep climbing. Best just to focus on these steps, on breathing in and out. And not thinking about any of that.

But yes we did climb out of that hole, circa 1989, about the time that popular music was rediscovering the guitar. There were lots of screaming that went with it around then; but what I remember best was the venomous rage in the barely medicated psychosis of my mother's voice on our answering machine. Dozens of messages, one after the other, a soliloquy of viciousness inspired by our eventual escape, thanks to belated degrees and new jobs, to dry economic ground and full, final disentanglement from all four of our sick, broken parents. My mother mistook a greeting card from my wife to my sister – forwarded to my parents' house because my sister was homeless at the time – congratulating her on her new baby, as some kind of promise to show up after five years of estrangement for the baby shower. It was a promise my wife had of course never made; but my mother left another string of increasingly violent messages, culminating with a promise to come over one night while we were sleeping and set the nice little house we were renting on fire, "So you two yuppie shits both die and rot in Barbie doll hell where you belong!"

No! Breathe in, breathe out.

I am thirsty and tired, but I keep climbing. Best to tighten it up, now twenty paces behind Danny's hunched figure, inky black against the snow.

Best not to think about that house fire, especially because it never actually happened.

Even if there was a different kind of house fire, circa 1993, in the little dreamhouse we'd finally scraped enough together to buy. I'd been working till 9 every night and drinking till midnight with whoever was still in the office – almost always young and single, and often female and lonely – because I couldn't face my wife anymore, only to find the place empty and my wife still out with her favorite client ("No I am not cheating!" she screamed at me till dawn, "but God knows I want to and should be!") because she just knew I had to be out cheating all those nights myself.

But I knew if I started cheating with any of those interesting and ambitious young women out drinking with me every night, I'd never stop, it would be a professional disaster, and my slowly leaking lifeboat of a marriage would sink forever. Especially because things were about to get really ugly with the company.

In the winter of 1996, a bunch of deals fell through, all at the same time, just as our share price was soaring six months after the IPO. Then came the three 24-hour days in the office doing damage control when we announced the miss and our share price crashed. And then the iron chill of the courtroom a month later, empty but for Tom, Becky, Leah, me, and our nervous, geeky lawyer at the table in front of us; at the other table, two reptiles with cufflinks and perfect suits for the absentee shareholders suing us over the fallout of the crash; and a stern, stone-faced, 100-year-old judge, sitting up on the bench and staring at us kids like we'd just been caught playing hooky and it was all a matter of procedure before he gave us a good ass-whipping.

Ugh.

Breathe in, breathe out.

I am exhausted. Danny is now 25 paces ahead of me, and Aaron a black dot up on the blank snowfield.

I put my head down and keep climbing.

I wish I were by myself and could just give up and turn back. Today, I really might. But these guys are counting on me, so I have no choice – because I'm the guy who shows up, shitstorm or no. (Except maybe for Jill or Amy the Rebound Girl, but they knew the terms.) But even Jill used to say, when I'd ask her why she was bothering with me, "because you're the guy who shows up, shitstorm or no, doesn't complain, doesn't make it about him, just gets it done."

I guess. Though I haven't exactly shown up for her the last couple times it really mattered.

But that is who I am the rest of the time. And it's who I was on August 16, 1997, a day entered into my calendar three years prior, then deleted, then re-entered, then deleted again, then re-entered for good. It was the day of Leah's daughter's *Bat Mitzvah*, two months too late. Quiet, dutiful, workaholic CPA turned workaholic CFO Leah, dead from breast cancer at age 37, nine months after diagnosis and the slash, burn, and poison of treatment – right through the middle of that terrifying but ultimately pointless shareholder litigation.

We all went to the B*at Mitzvah* anyway: Tom and his wife; Becky and her husband; and me and nobody, because my wife and I had finally pulled the trigger and I'd just moved out of our little dreamhouse and into the Marriott down by the office. The *Bat Mitzvah* was a river of tears, three hours of what sounded like a collective death wail in Hebrew, one long, aching, yearning melody in something older and sadder than any minor key I'd ever heard before but was still oddly familiar. I remember the brave, skinny little girl choking it all back over the ancient flesh-toned Torah scroll, surrounded by the shattered grandparents, the weeping aunts and uncles and cousins, and what was left of the proud father overwhelmed by the broken husband. And all I could do was feel sorry for myself for my own dumb little professional and personal dramas, and despise myself for feeling sorry for myself, and remind myself once more that "family" is just a hyper-elaborated word for "pain," and I would have none of it.

I stop 30 paces off Danny now, exhausted, crushed suddenly from the inside by the weight of that terrible day.

Screw this mountain, with its ugly indifference, and screw this shitty low ceiling, and this nasty wind.

I will summit.

Poor Leah.

I will survive.

Poor miserable human race.

I pull out water and calories, and gulp them down, then chase both with the papery air. I *will* get to the top of this mountain. And then I'll get the hell off as fast as I can.

Where is the Presence today? Holed up, obviously, higher than 17,000 feet. Which is where I'd rather be.

I push down more water and calories, but the words keep coming back up after each swallow: *Screw this indifferent mountain and the whole miserable indifferent world.*

Or "FTW!" as Danny would say. And he is right. Better to spend your time thinking about big boobs versus little boobs, arguing with the ghost of Jack Kerouac, compiling data on the continuum of the female orgasm. Testosterone may make the nasty little world go 'round, but oxytocin keeps everybody smiling in the very mean meanwhile.

I stop and look up the snowfield at Danny, now a small black huddle of man and snowboard etched against the blankness, everything else washed out by the crappy light.

Tiny surges of energy – the calories and the water – burst into the bloodstream, little electrical shocks into my arms, legs, feet, ass.

I pick up the pace and laugh at myself for going, once again, down into the cellar to fondle my collection of fine whine, my litany of former frustrations, bitternesses, and self-pity. This mountain, like all mountains, and canyons, and the desert, does not care about my troubles, does not care about all that messy human business Back East – so why should I?

The only occupation people really have is preoccupation with nonsense, with endless grasping at what ultimately amounts to nothing anyway: the little dreamhouse you could lose with a few missed mortgage payments or one very bad decision at happy hour; the needy, whining kids who consume what life you have outside of work; the stupid lawn that sucks up what little is left after that. "All bullshit, illusion, attachment," as Danny would say.

But I digress, yet again, because it's going to be that kind of day. Great.

I pick up the pace, one measured step after the next into Danny's and Aaron's bootholes.

Breathe in, breathe out. Stay in the box. Up, up, up.

Long tough hikes in dreary weather like this are where my demons come out, the blankspot of snow in front of me flashing with snapshots from the longest, toughest climb of all. Those endless weekends, all gray skies and cold wet rain, stuck at the end of the road in that shitty little town. The blood-stained eyes and annihilating ridicule of my drunken father. The screaming, fuming, cursing rebukes of my mother, hobbled always with pain that never ended, pulling herself with a gnashing of teeth to her canes or crutches, not to defend me or my sister, but to counter-annihilate him. Then the slaps and shoves, the slaps and shoves back, and his drunken indignant howls and threats to flee.

Fine, get the hell out of here, I used to think. But all I could do was make sure my sister was somewhere safe, and then take flight myself, always to the sanctuary of the woods.

The woods began where our street dead-ended, a couple hundred feet away. It was an easy sprint off into the sudden quiet of all those old oaks, maples, sycamores and pines. Everything was green canopy and silence, with footpaths and deer trails I knew better than the streets of that town, the quiet giving way to birdsong and skitterings through fallen leaves. The woods were alive, peaceful, and safe.

It was in those woods, when I was maybe eight or nine years old and pretending to run away from home – dreaming of when I'd be big enough to run away for real and somehow survive out there – that I first came across the Presence.

I had to blaze my way through a long dark stand of pine, which opened into a wide circle of old oaks, their leaves down for the winter, their arms waving up toward a blue patchwork sky. It was a small, perfect, untouched meadow, a place no trail had cut through, a place no one would be able to find me, yell at me, or hit me. I could not see or hear the Presence – and back then I certainly had no name for it – but I knew it was there. And I knew it was aware of me, watching over me, wanting me to know in what sounded like my own voice but wasn't: *No, you cannot run away to these woods and survive, not just yet. But you will be alright. You will be. Just hang on.*

What I have since come to know as the Presence wanted me to know that it was not me who was crazy, or bad, or broken, no matter what they screamed at me every day; that my father was just a crazy, mean drunk who had made my frail, hobbled, helpless mother crazy and mean too; and one day I would grow up and be able to run away forever, if only I could just hang on a few more years.

Just hang on.

I look up the snowfield and see that I'm finally catching up with Danny by a few paces. The water and calories are working, liquid electricity pouring into my weary legs.

Stay in the aerobic box, one step at a time, and just keep climbing.

One day, I found out where the path through those woods led. I kept going until it punched through and came out on top of a hill, along the county highway running west. It wasn't until a few years later – after I'd saved enough money from shoveling snow and mowing lawns and delivering newspapers to buy my first bicycle – that I discovered the path from the other end, riding out that same highway. And only a dozen more miles west from there, another discovery: a little local ski area, the worn nub of an ancient mountain with a T-bar and rope tow that doubled as a driving range in summer. But a few months later, when the snow fell and the lights came on, that scruffy little ski area turned into someplace magic, at least to a 14-

year-old who hadn't ever been anywhere beyond a few counties and a couple trips into the city for hurried visits to my aging grandparents. I got my first job there, shoveling snow, cutting and stacking firewood, digging cars out of ditches, and dreaming of saving up for one thing: a little used pickup truck, so I could get the hell out of that town forever.

Danny's voice jolts me back.

"Hey, bro."

His voice sounds as weary as I feel. He has just made the ridge, dropped his pack and snowboard, and sits down on an exposed rock with a tired grunt.

Aaron, a few steps further up on the ridge, has already pulled on his climbing harness and is sorting ropes in the howling wind.

I drop my skis and pack and collapse onto the rock next to Danny.

We've clawed our way to the bottom of the top of Apache Peak, a flat white pyramid against a flat gray sky. Everything else around us is black and white and without form, drowned out with screaming wind.

We rope ourselves together for the final summit pitch, the last few hundred feet of vertical class IV – something we could climb on all fours without ropes and only crampons and ice axes for help, if we had to. But disaster looms on either side of the ascent, yawning a few feet off either side of this ridge into thousand-foot drops, straight down onto the boulders and ice below. The wind is a factor too, so loud we have to scream over it when we have to communicate anything. But mostly we work in silence, tying knots, roping into our harnesses, tethering ourselves into a three-man machine: six legs, six arms, three ice axes, three sets of spikes.

This is a team, I think, laughing to myself about all the old business clichés they wouldn't get.

We check each other's ropes with hard yanks, nod at each other and exchange fist-bumps, and without a single word, start up the peak. We line ourselves out at steady ten-foot intervals. No need to set protection; just keep good intervals, and maintain good clean contact with the crampons and axes.

And up we go: step, ax; step, ax; step, ax, step.

Back in the world, corporate guys would throw "team" and "teamwork" around all the time, almost always when they were in charge of it and wanted to make everybody on it work harder. I did that all the time myself, but knew how forced it sounded when I was forcing it out.

This, up here, by contrast – on this deadly mountain – is a *Team*. Because up here, we need each other – not to launch a product or land a deal or make more money – but to survive. To live through the audacity of what we are attempting. To be willing to risk our own lives to save one or the other of the two, if shit were to happen. Because up here, shit does happen. "Summiting is optional," as they say in Dudeville and in climbing schools and camps around the world. "Returning to the trailhead is mandatory."

Just don't try explaining any of that to most of the guys back in the world, making random small talk before the meeting starts. I made the mistake of doing that those first few months when I was half out here but still half back there, trying to cash out of the company and figure out which way to let the big muddy river of midlife take me.

"You moved to Colorado? Good for you! We took the kids to Keystone for spring break last year. Beautiful! And you're climbing mountains? Like with ropes and those things on your boots? Cool! I heard about those Fourteeners. Doing one of them is on my bucket list!"

Sure it is. Dude.

All that big mountain fever, adventure travel, bucket list bullshit started in the mid-1990s, about two weeks after it started for me it seems, somewhere when Krakauer's book came out about all those horrible deaths up on Everest and the first Wall Street lawyer strapped a snowboard or mountain bike onto his BMW. Suddenly, heading outside and going big wasn't just my own private way to deal with the work madness; everyone else lost in that madness was heading outside and trying to go big too, thanks to my cherished *Outside Magazine* suddenly on every airport newsstand. Hotel gyms started filling up with slouchy guys reading *Outside* on treadmills. The roads started filling up with these hulking new SUVs ("Sport Futility Vehicles," Aaron calls them) for their daily commutes, grocery runs and kid-schleps around the suburbs. And technical fleece and designer backpacks started showing up in offices.

Right around then, all outdoor sports were suddenly *extreme.* Frat reunions, guys from the bank, doc-jocks on drug company junkets, platinum sales performers on boondoggles – it's as if all these groups out here on their ski vacations, gunning the cruisers along the edges of the resort, suddenly noticed what was just past the frosty orange rope bounding the edge of the corduroy: there were wild mountains full of snow, snow like in the magazines and movies, snow like oceans that swallow everything; and yet it was all right there, beckoning you, calling to baptize you, drown you with joy, set you free.

Or kill you. Especially when you get summit fever, if only to get the whole miserable thing over with. Like on a shitty day like today.

Which is why we practice, over and over at altitude. Because in any conditions, the summit is usually a long tease. You can see it, or you think you can, right there, every time you look up from your next foothold or handhold.

But it's never right there, not just yet. It's the light bouncing off the rocks or icecap ringing the summit, kissed by the sun from the other side of the mountain, beckoning, seducing, taunting. If it's just a straight hike or easy Class IV scramble, and you have a dog or two along– Jill's Kettle, Kelly's Sampson, Maggie's Buddy, Scott's Tashi, or Tyler's Deputy Dog – they always get there first, pacing back and forth, tails wagging, tags clinking and flashing in the sunlight, tongues out in bubble gum pink against the blue sky.

And yet, and yet – it's still not the summit, not for another hour.

I put my head down and work the crampons, my ice ax and the rope; and just as I am reconciling myself to this usual fact of life up here, the rope goes slack and Danny's last boot hold stops in its track, a few feet from my face.

I look up and...

Summit.

Oh.

No long seduction, no lengthy last grind to the pinnacle. Just a sudden, frozen knob of rock, snow and ice.

Up here, the wind is screaming twice as loud as it has been all day, the ceiling as flat and endless and gray as the Great Plains running east into dusty brown void. The roof of the world is without its usual raucous dimensions today; the colors, shapes, textures and light usually reflected off the mountains in the other three directions are washed out gray and flat, with thousands of black dots of rock poking through waves of frozen milk.

We do the high-fives, far more wearily than usual, drop our loaded packs, and stand back to back to back, looking out in silence at the wind-blasted blankness.

On a summit, normally drenched in screaming sun, Danny usually wanders off to one edge, looking for just the right rock, testing this one and that before finally sitting, quietly and reverently, to meditate. Aaron usually pulls everything out of his pack, maps and compass and snow probe and shovel and little weather gauges, studying the terrain and marking notes on the map, taking readings, digging at the snow. And I usually pull out my little binoculars and camera and go off by myself, less to study the mountains and try for a good picture than to commune with the Presence.

But today we are beaten from the twelve-hour haul and shivering with the cold, so Aaron pulls out his survival poncho and without shouting a word over the wind, we sit on the flattest boulder poking through the snow, and huddle inside the poncho against the warmth of each other's backs.

We down water and energy bars, and slowly the shivering stops as we start to warm each other up.

Apache Peak, elevation only 13,441. No, it's not one of the coveted Fourteeners, another reason besides the weather we are alone on it today – but it has been a huge hit of LSD from the lower trailhead. The cloud-layer way off to the south and west is electrified with a long narrow filament of yellow light; and as I watch, the filament seems to burn a little brighter and hotter by the minute, and the tops of mountain peaks just start to poke out of the gray-white goop.

We eat, drink, and warm each other for another few minutes, not saying a word, just resting, and the filament brightens, the light climbing upward to break up the ceiling; and as if someone had just thrown a switch, the wind downshifts, in an instant, from the all-day, numbing one-note roar, to an odd cacophony of whistles.

Danny pulls himself up and wanders off to the edge, then Aaron, over to his pack.

I stand and pull open my own pack and find my camera. Not that there is any kind of picture to take up here today; but it is my usual excuse to wander off by myself for a minute, see if maybe I can feel the Presence. I don't expect that today either, after reaching out and feeling nothing at treeline, and nothing again on the last ridge, but why not.

I walk out onto the biggest slab of exposed rock at the other end of the summit, as far from Danny and Aaron as I can get, and look west at the long golden line of new light. I follow the line left and look down the spine of the Continental Divide, then right and back at the ceiling, then finally west again, toward the light.

I breathe out, waiting, breathe in, wait some more.

Here I am, I say to myself, and breathe out again.

And there it is, the Presence, but just barely. I sense it beneath the fluttertones of the wind, impatient and bothered, like it does not want to be here, doesn't want me to be here, wants only for all of us to hurry off.

I take a few more deep breaths, in and out, in and out.

And as I am turning to head back toward Aaron and the gear, the words well up in my head, in that small still voice that sounds like my voice but isn't: *Did you really just say 'Screw this mountain?' Really???*

Yes, but it was a hard climb today, I reply.

Yes, it was a hard climb today. And all the rest of it is a hard climb, the whole hard history of the world, one long hard climb out of the dust, back to the dust, all just stories.

I take another deep breath, in and out, and want to argue, but before I can think of what to say, more words: *All just stories, and yet, look where you are right now. RIGHT now. Amazing! So chill out. Dude!*

"You guys still want to do the rappel?" I am jarred by Aaron's voice, yelling over the whistling of the wind.

I make my way back toward him, Danny from the other direction.

Aaron is re-coiling purple and red rope, over near the cliff edge that drops straight off the western edge of the summit.

"Do the rappels down there?" he yells over the wind. "Ski out and around the bottom of the ridge to the trail, like we planned?"

"Kinda sucks up here today," Danny yells.

"Kinda does," I yell.

"Yeah, I know," Aaron yells. "But it'd be good to practice while we're up at altitude." He glances over at his pack, with its mobius-shaped spool of blue and green climbing rope lashed to it. "And since I carried up that extra rope . . ."

"Would be good to practice," Danny yells.

"Yeah," I yell, because what else can I say? A big rappel would also serve up a big adrenaline cleanse, which would help me make some kind of peace with the mountain after the shitty things I'd been thinking on the way up – an especially good idea before the long and tricky ski off its flank and down the last ten miles to the trailhead. "Let's do it."

"Ah, screw it," Aaron yells. "If you guys aren't into it, that ups the chance that something goes wrong."

"No way, man!" Danny yells. "We're cool. Let's rally!"

"Yeah, we're cool," I echo him. "Let's do it."

Aaron looks back and forth from Danny to me and back to Danny and huddles us in so we can hear each other over the wind. "You guys sure?"

"Fuck yeah, dude," Danny says.

"Ok, just one pitch then. We still have to ski off this bad boy before dark."

Aaron goes down onto his knees over the pile of gear, and Danny and I watch him set up the long, double-roped rappel from the ridge down onto the back side of Apache.

I clench and unclench my fists as Aaron knots the ropes, try to lengthen my breath, push back on the adrenaline welling up in my core. I've rappelled only four times before today – two of those times in climbing gyms Back East, the putt-putt golf of rock climbing, laboratory-controlled experiments for the real thing out here today – so I am nervous, excited, engrossed, and terrified.

Best to look away and just breathe. The sky is slowly lighting up from the crack widening along the horizon, as if the unseen sun were coming up, even though it is actually on its way down.

Aaron stands and we all rope in to our climbing harnesses. Knots are tied, re-tied, checked and re-checked, not *like* but *because* your life actually does depend on it.

We make quick work of the rappel, on two 60-foot lengths of rope tied together in a big circle anchored around the boulder nearest the cliffdrop. This is the same rappel sequence we will be using off the frontside of The Lady, how we will drop with our snowboards down onto the forbidden snowfield below her chin. And so we replicate every element, including the boulder anchor, the added weight of our skis, and the ascenders in case something goes wrong. With one major difference: if something goes wrong here, one of us can bail at the bottom of the drop, and take the very long way back around to the ridge at the bottom of the summit – though he misses the ski down from the top, and the other two have to get all his gear down. On The Lady, there is no such escape route, so it is good to proceed today like we don't have that option: all three of us practice using the ascenders, with all that weight, to pull our way back to the summit.

All of which goes exactly according to plan: a 50-foot controlled fall, down into the void, hanging from purple-and-red and blue-and-green ropes – starter strands for a psychedelic spider web – with the wind pushing you around like a ball on a string. It may be only 50 feet, but it feels like five hundred, five thousand, infinity – because there is no feeling in the world like dropping into space, at altitude in all that wind, your stomach dropping to the rocks and snow below, the adrenaline gushing out of the top of your head, and until, until, until … pop! Your boot hits *terra firma*, which isn't *firma* at all but it is *terra*; then the other boot; and your stomach is back and the adrenaline ebbs, leaving a cool, empty rush in its wake.

Aaron is the first down, and the last to re-summit.

Danny and I hang off the boulder up top, and watch him clamp his way back up, left, right, left, bouncing with all his weight to test the ascenders, practicing, training, checking for points of failure, always worrying, always working it, always perfecting what must always be perfect. A few minutes before he gets back to the top, the sun drops below the gray ceiling, into the widening crack and splashing us and everything else on the summit with golden light.

Aaron clambers up onto the boulder, his face lit up with the sun and grinning like a little kid – or more like a little kid with a tidy black beard – and this time we high-five each other like we mean it.

We chatter and kid each other as we pack our gear quickly, excited for the ski down, though we know the light will be flat and the turns hard, fast, and treacherous.

Danny drops in first, on his snowboard: long arcing turns, no aggression in the cutbacks, only an elegant carving, maybe three dozen of them, all the way to the ridge, before waving *all clear*. Then Aaron drops in, on his skis: tighter turns straight down the fall-line, clean and efficient, with maybe some tags on the corners when they widen near the bottom, before he shoots out onto the ridge next to

Danny, both of them specks down there. Aaron turns and waves *all clear.*

I linger for one last precious moment, the roof of the world all around me finally alight. A hundred peaks and subpeaks of snow and rock and ice emerge from gray shadow to show off their jumble of shapes, standing with their hands on each other's shoulders, ridge to ridge to ridge, the Great Divide in majestic repose, their western faces all painted yellow-orange with the sun.

And just before I drop in, there it is again: the Presence, all around me and this mountain top, settling in for the rest of the day, the rest of the season, the rest of history, until the 13,441 feet of snow and rock beneath my skis tumbles down, toward the brown dust of the plains.

Trailheads

We ski off all that LSD in a disappointing hurry: it took us more than twelve hours to hike, trudge and climb up Apache Peak, and maybe 40 minutes to ski it from top to bottom. The long trail out from the ridge below the final ascent is just the right pitch – and the snow firm enough from the overcast day – for Danny to keep moving on his board, and Aaron and me to keep gliding along on our skis.

As the trail cuts through the still snow-blanketed backcountry campsite and widens into unplowed forest service road, long ago closed except for emergencies but still tracked up with cross country skis and snowshoes, I hear something odd: a faint mechanical buzz echoing up through the woods.

I catch up to Aaron and Danny, who have stopped in the middle of the trail. Aaron looks over at me with a troubled look: *Do you hear that?*

We ski another hundred feet or so down the trail, and the buzz is now a gnawing hum, deepening, louder and closer, buzzing our way.

Aaron pulls up on his skis and turns his head to listen. "What the hell is that?"

"Chainsaw?" I think aloud.

Danny rides up, stops, and sits in the snow next to us. The buzz grows, splits into two buzzes, louder, insistent, coming our way. "What the hell is that?"

"Snowmobiles," Aaron says, his face knotting with sudden worry.

"They can't come up here," I say. "This is wilderness."

"Must be a rescue," Aaron says, looking around the meadow's unbroken snowfield. "We didn't see anybody up top. Must be somebody in trouble on another trail out of here," his voice trails off. "Wonder which one."

Then, out of the shadow of the woods, the flash of lights and whine of two snowmobiles, flying up the trail.

We step off to the side, expecting they'll stop and tell us the situation. Then Aaron will tell them he's with Mountain Rescue and that Danny and I have First Responder training, and he'll ask how can we help. But as they get closer, we see that they are not rescue snowmobiles but sport machines, crotch-rocket motorcycles for the snow, their front ends tricked up like scowling faces, each topped with a huge guy in a black leather suit and cowboy hat instead of helmet.

Aaron waves and they slow down and pull up between us, their engines putting off a stink cloud of blue smoke.

"Whadda ya'll want?" the first guy says, looking us over, his eyes resting on Danny, who has pulled off his hat and is running his fingers through his great nest of blond hair, streaked with purple. He guns his engine to keep it from stalling.

"What are you doing up here?" Aaron yells over the engine. "Rescuing somebody? This is a federal wilderness area, closed to –"

"Closed, huh?" the other shouts over his engine. "Well we just opened her," and then he guns his engine and shoots up the trail.

"Hey, you can't –"

"Like the man said," the other yells.

"But this is protected land!" Aaron yells. "You can't –"

"Hell, yeah we can," he says, "and if you hippie boys don't like it, you can go fuck yourselves." He guns his engine and shoots away.

"Yeah?" Danny shouts after them, trying to scramble to his feet on his snowboard. "Well fuck you too!"

But they are already gone, a trail of noxious blue smoke and chainsaw noise through the forest.

"And fuck the stinky-ass horse you rode in on!" Danny yells up the empty trail. "Redneck piece'a shit!"

He turns to ride back down the trail, but Aaron just stands there, his mouth half open in horror. A trail of blue smoke rises from the woods, and the chainsaw buzz winds its way up the hill to the sound horizon.

Then, an odd moment of silence, the woods perfectly, unnaturally quiet, for just a few seconds . . . and then an explosion of energy out of the woods, a doe, two fawns, two more does, three more fawns, another doe, running across the trail twenty feet up from us and scrambling up the opposite hillside, into the trees.

"Redneck dicks," Aaron mutters, as he turns down the trail.

I push after him, and Danny is on his feet and behind us a moment later.

We ski down in silence, back and forth across ruts torn into the thinning snowpack, a confetti trail of dried mud and broken twigs kicked up by the snowmobiles. The trail drops around a big bend, into an open snowfield, crisscrossed with circular snowmobile ruts, the old snowpack churned with new mud. They did a bunch of donuts before starting up the trail, tearing up the long sloping meadow.

Aaron and I wait for Danny to catch up.

"Redneck dicks," he says again. "All hat and no cattle."

Danny rides up and looks out across the muddy hash of the meadow. "Nice work, assholes!" he says. "We should monkeywrench their shit down at the trailhead."

"Monkeywrenching," Aaron snorts. "Right. Might make you feel better for a while. But vandalism isn't exactly Zen, or in the Tao, or whatever, is it?"

"Oh, come on, man!" Danny yells, "Hayduke lives!"

"Actually, no he didn't," Aaron says, going with the classical interpretation of the purposefully vague ending of Edward Abbey's wild eco-romp through the desert, *The Monkeywrench Gang*. "But Glen Canyon Dam still does."

"It's a book," Aaron mutters. "A fantasy."

"Yeah, well," Danny mutters back at him. "It's a pretty damn good fantasy."

Aaron shoots straight down the middle of the snowfield and Danny yells after him. "Lucky for them I'm all about the goddamn dharma then!" he shouts. Then he turns to me, "or I'd fuck their redneck shit all up at the trailhead."

Aaron is back at that trailhead when Danny and I catch up.

His skis are already off, and he is maniacally piling and jamming downed tree branches into a gap newly chainsawed through the willow thicket next to the locked gate at the start of the trail. He hasn't bothered to open Danny's bus, or change out of his ski boots, or even stopped to pull water from his pack.

There is an enormous pickup truck in the middle of the parking area, empty but for Danny's van, with a snowmobile trailer, its ramps down.

For the next ten minutes, Aaron keeps piling up more and more branches into the gash next to the fence. Danny and I work out of the back of his open bus, unpacking gear and changing out of our boots. Aaron finishes packing tree branches into the gap, but when he comes over to us, he is still fuming and does not speak.

Danny packs a bowl, and as he and I smoke it, we watch in silence as Aaron walks over to the glove compartment, fishes out pen and paper, and writes a note I imagine he will be leaving somewhere on their truck.

"I still think we should monkeywrench their shit," Danny mutters.

"That's a great idea, *sensei*," Aaron snaps at him, as he walks over and carefully tucks the note under the windshield wiper. "So they can trash the next hippie van they see at a trailhead?"

"Hey, fuck you, man," Danny snaps back, handing me the smoldering bowl. "You have no idea what you're talking about." He lowers the tailgate and points at the bumper sticker on the back: *NON-HIPPIE BUS*. "We're good to go, man."

Aaron finally breaks into a smile and Danny smiles back. "I stand corrected, *sensei*. Monkeywrench away."

"Nah," Danny says, taking the bowl back from me. "That'd be bad karma. And I'm all about compassion these days," he exhales a cloud of pot smoke. "All about loving-kindness."

He hands me the bowl, turns and looks at the enormous truck and trailer, studying the black double-crew cab coated with a haze of road grime. Then his big blue eyes widen, a mischievous smile crawling into his face.

"What?"

He says nothing.

Aaron and I watch as he walks over, one mindful step after another toward the front of the truck.

He stares at it a moment, sights along his thumb like an artist, and bends down next to the front panel. Then he lifts his hand to the truck, and with his middle finger, writes in giant block letters – filling the front left panel, then the first door, second door, and all the way down the side of the truck's bed – *I ♥ REDNECKS.*

Boulder Canyon Blues

A few minutes later, Danny and Aaron and I are driving down out of the mountains to "Ned" (what everyone calls Nederland) in Danny's Non-Hippie Bus. We will grab beers and burgers, then head down the canyon to Boulder, to spend the night at a friend of Aaron's before we drop him off at the Denver airport and head back to Dudeville.

I am sitting in the back seat and Aaron is up front, with a short length of climbing rope and a carabiner, practicing knots, as he always does when Danny or I are driving. The snowmobile stink from the rednecks is finally gone from my nose, and I can feel the bone-deep exhaustion from a long day on the mountain welling up among the three of us as if we were one weary body.

"It was like those idiots from Texas down in Durango," Danny says as we settle into the ride. "Remember them? The guys who went out four-wheeling up on the tundra outside Durango?"

"Outside Silverton, you mean," Aaron says, sounding spent, like he was done talking about it. "They were four-wheeling *in* a Durango."

Which will be the last word on that old story, for now.

I slouch into the seat behind them and watch the passing woods, interrupted by the occasional log home or roadhouse or rental cabin, then back to the rhythm of the empty road and long stands of white aspen, the canopy greening with spring.

But I can't help but laugh to myself about that old story, legend now in places like Ullar's and all around Colorado.

It goes something like this: a couple guys up from Texas were out roadtripping one summer with their brand new 4WD SUV down in southwestern Colorado. They were way up on a forest service road, above treeline, surrounded by tundra, when they thought it would be fun to go off-road. Except that, as everybody up here knows, tundra is softer than it looks: all sand, fine gravel, tiny flowers, and even tinier cacti, much of it capped with microscopic crypto-biologic material, a fragile living shell that keeps the entire tundra in place against the wind. And this rare and exquisite ecosystem is especially soft in early summer, still wet with the last of the snowmelt. The minute these idiots pulled off onto the tundra, they started spinning out – all four wheels of course – so for momentum or traction or whatever they were thinking would get them back up on the road, these fricking geniuses decided to gun it further down the hill, away from the road. But they just kept spinning and couldn't climb back, so they decided to keep going, straight down the wide-open tundra to the road's last switchback, way off road. They drove all the way to the bottom of the ravine, before plowing into the fall-line runoff at the bottom, leaving four wobbly sine-waves, each a foot deep, across the face of the tundra – four ugly gashes that will be there for the next few centuries.

After they ditched out at the bottom, they hiked out and back to town, looking to hire a local wrecker willing and able to drive back up there and tow their SUV off the tundra. Most everybody in town refused of course, so it took them a day to find someone; and it would take a 200-foot cable and all of the next day to pull it up and out. By that time, word had gotten around every town in southwestern Colorado, and a bunch of locals went up there to watch the tow-out, jeering at the idiots and saying things a lot less loving-kind than I ♥ REDNECKS.

The story is now great bar lore passed all around the state, though the exact details have been hopelessly jumbled except to guys like Aaron who remember everything. It was in fact on the tundra outside Silverton, not Durango, though I've heard people say it both ways. Others say that it was actually a Tundra on the tundra, while still others say that it was a Tahoe or a Suburban, though no one ever said it happened anywhere near Tahoe, and certainly nowhere near any suburb.

"What's so funny about that?" I hear Aaron ask me, and look up and realize they're talking about something else, and I've been laughing to myself.

"Nothing," I say, "just laughing about that old story."

"That's a relief," Aaron says, turning back to the road. "You had me worried you might be a pyro. And that'd be the last time you carry the stove and fuel."

Danny looks at me in the rear view mirror. "We were talking about oil dripping from chairlift towers in the spring, onto dry grass, and sometimes it catches on fire."

"Are you serious? That really happens?"

"Serious as a heart attack," Aaron says.

"Dry grass. And all the weird crap people drop under the lifts," Danny says, then a wry smile.

"What?" Aaron says.

"Nothing."

"Are we down hiking?"

"Always," Danny says.

"Well that's good," Aaron says. "I thought we'd missed out today, with the snow holding up all the way out."

"Well, technically," Danny points down the road, "we sort of still are down hiking."

I can tell that this will be a good one, but I can't imagine what it will have to do with littering or fires under chairlifts.

"So . . ." Aaron eggs him on.

"So . . . " Danny laughs and shakes his head. "One time I was hooking up with this Betty on the gondola at Telluride. Maybe you know her. Lisa somebody, crazy red hair and huge boobs, tends bar at The Buck. Big mountain biker, batshit crazy."

"Oh yeah, I know her," Aaron says. "*Batshit* crazy. Big drinker, tats, bone through her nose or something?"

"That's her. Looks like a punk rocker, with a tan. And totally ripped."

"Of course," Aaron says.

"So we start getting a little crazy at some swanky bar up at the resort, where her buddy is comping us all these shots."

Aaron turns to me. "I don't think this one's going to end well."

"Well, you're right there, man," Danny continues, "which is what made me think of it. 'Cuz we sort of end up littering off the lift. And it kinda killed the whole thing for me."

"How's that?" I have to ask.

"So we stumble out of there with our boards, all drunk and making out and too buzzed to give a shit who's around. And it's the end of the day, so we can wait for our own gondola."

"Uh huh," Aaron says.

"And the minute we're on the thing," Danny says, as if pleading his own helplessness at this point, "and those big tits are out and all in my face –"

"Oh yeah?"

"Oh yeah," he sighs. "And they – are – awesome."

"And?" Aaron asks.

"And then she's all over me. And the gondola's rocking all crazy because it's just us on the one side. And I'm thinking, *wow it would really suck if this thing flew off the cable, but there are worse ways to go.*"

"And at least you'd be unconscious or dead," Aaron chuckles, "when the patrollers' finally got up there and found you guys – all spread out like that in your full nuptial glory."

"I guess," Danny says. "But I wasn't really thinking it that far through. Not at the time."

"I'll bet not."

"I was actually pretty focused, right about then, on getting the deed done, before the gondola gets to the bottom. 'Cuz THAT is gonna be embarrassing – all those lifties standing around and I'm still in my – what did you call it? – my full nuptial glory and whatnot."

"Uh – huh."

"So anyway," Danny finally continues. "She's all over me, and I am good to go, even though I'm pretty loaded. She's working the boy with both hands, and I'm trying to get her snowboard pants off. And all of a sudden she's like, 'Oh shit, dude! I totally forgot! I'm on the rag!'"

"Nice!" Aaron laughs. "Timing is everything. But I'm guessing you don't really give a shit about that at this point."

"Shit no, dude! I'm like 'So what, dude, I'm new school, I don't give a fuck about that.'"

"Committed to the core! All Zen, all the time."

"Fuck yeah, dude," Danny says. "All Zen all the time. And you know my politics. I'm a fuckin' feminist, dude. I don't give a shit about any of that."

"You *are* a feminist, dude."

Then a long silence and I can't stand it.

"So what happened?" I burst out.

"So what do you think happened?"

Aaron turns to me. "He had sex with her. Very quickly."

"Fuck yeah, I had sex with her, dude! What else am I supposed to do? She's like 'Cool, New School – if that doesn't weird you out' and then she reaches down and grabs the rag –"

Aaron groans. "And she tosses it out the window of the gondola. Great."

"Yeah," Danny says. "Kinda bummed me out, when I thought about it later."

"But not at the time. Because those gondolas are fast," Aaron chuckles. "And the bottom's coming, and she hasn't yet. Now that's some pressure. But I'm sure you managed."

"Well – yeah!"

Aaron chuckles. "Some guys play even better with the shot clock running down."

"I wouldn't exactly say 'shot clock,'" Danny sighs. "Turned out there was only one happy ending in that ganjala."

"Aw, the demon rum."

"Nah," Danny waves him off, "I wasn't *that* loaded. It was the rag thing."

I have to chime in. "But I thought you were all New School about that?"

"Oh I am," he says. "It wasn't the Being-on-the-Rag thing – it was the rag itself – down there under the gondola. That's how we got on this whole trip. The whole time she's riding me – fucking me to beat the band – all I can think about is that freakin' bloody-ass rag down there on the snow, stinkin' to high heaven. And every deer and raccoon and other critter in the woods are all gathering around it, sniffing at it, saying to each other in critterspeak, 'What the fuck is that, dude?' But still – she's ridin' high, and the bottom of the mountain is coming faster than she is, and the gondola's rocking and rolling – and I just start laughing."

"Nice," Aaron says. "But you rang the bell anyway."

"Fuck yeah, man."

"All Zen all the time. You ARE my *sensei*."

"Yeah, I rang the bell," Danny sighs. "But just barely and it was mostly her doing. Like she had to will the shit out of it, and I just had to hang on."

"Till the bloody end," I say. "So to speak."

"Because you are a feminist after all," Aaron says.

"Fuck yeah, dude."

We all laugh, then ride in silence down the mountain.

"But you know what the shitty part is?" Danny finally says.

"She never called?" Aaron asks. "No second date?"

"That's funny. No – seriously. The shitty part is: I don't litter. I hate that. And there was that goddamn tampon up there on that beautiful mountain. I really hope none of those critters ate it."

"Oh, one of them did," Aaron says. "Probably didn't keep it down long though."

Half an hour later, I'm jolted from sleep as Danny pulls off the side of the road.

Aaron's head is pitched to one side, fast asleep, his left hand down between the front seats, still half-clutching the knotted rope he'd been practicing with.

I look down through the woods at a clutch of log buildings. It looks like we are pulling into the west end of Nederland.

"Piss stop?"

"Yeah," Danny says, "and I told Julie I'd check in with her and let her know we got down ok. My cell phone should work here."

I watch him pissing off the side of the road and think I could use one myself; but he's got his cell phone in his other hand and it looks like he could use his privacy.

"How's she doing?" I ask when he climbs back in.

"She doing," he says, nodding, sort of smiling, his usual Zen look but something else around the edges of it.

We drive into Ned, a mud-caked patchwork of old wooden houses, small barns, geodesic domes, and shacks shouldering into the wind, half the town painted in odd colors, the other half the chewed grays and browns of old wood eaten raw by weather. Ned is a ramshackle mountain town for people who love mountains but hate towns, a funky way station for tourists drunk on the scenery of the Indian Peaks Wilderness, and a leaping off point for mountaineering adventures 20 minutes from hot coffee and cold draft beers. Working out of Ned, you can hike up and ski down a dozen peaks ten months out of the year, and still get to the Wolf Tongue Brewery in time to catch the early band with your buffalo burger – exactly our plan today. Except there is no band, because it's mud season.

After the burgers and beers, we climb back into Danny's bus, Aaron crawling into the back seat and going straight to sleep.

We drive out the east end of town, gathered like water around a mirror lake that drops down suddenly into the canyon toward Boulder. Right before the drop, we pass the field where they hold the music festival, Nedfest, every summer.

I was there with Danny and a bunch of his friends from college – I'd just met him through Aaron – my very first summer in Dudeville.

It was also my first exposure to jam bands, and the one I remember best was Yonder Mountain String Band, Colorado's version of a bluegrass band on acid. Their set was a blur of musical color matched to the twirling crowd, addled renditions of second-golden-era bluegrass classics and originals played with a breathless ferocity.

I was sitting near the back of the crowd on the big bright colors of an Indian blanket with my new friends, watching women dance and trying not to think about Jill – off in New Zealand by then – as Yonder Mountain thundered out another fiddle tune for the dancers in front of the stage, a swirl of tie-dye, peasant skirts, and dreadlocks, and suddenly...

CRACK!

The PA went out, and then a big gasp from the crowd, but the band kept playing.

The dancers hesitated, wobbling in place, so the mandolin player waved them in tight to the stage, and the band moved to the edge and played on acoustically, no PA, faster still.

With the music barely audible from back there, I noticed for the first time the manic cloud of dust rising from the dancers, how it mixed with the joyous chaos of all those colors, and how quickly it dissipated against the mountains rimming the festival grounds.

I wanted to snicker, "Good for all you hippies in your moccasins, with your feathers and beads and facepaint, communing with the old natives," but the snicker wouldn't come. Maybe it was all the weed, or the heat, or the music, but it struck me that, consciously or not, all those kids were dancing that furiously for the same reason the native peoples of the West always did: the stomping of bare or buckskinned feet against a sprawl of earth – all in time to the same beat that gathered everyone into a collective heartbeat – was another way of reaching out to feel the Presence. It was a group way of doing what I always do alone, up above treeline or down in a desert canyon; it was part celebration and part prayer, a burst of energy sent upward into an infinity of sky that says simply: "Look at me, sky! I am alive, right here, right now! Me and my tribe and what else is there?"

I look up from the memory and over at Danny.

"Remember that time we went to Nedfest?" I ask, as he turns the big wheel around the last of the curve and the van starts down into the canyon, already in dusk. "Right over there?"

"Oh yeah," he says, looking back at the field. "That was great, man. Was Jill with us then?"

"Nope. Off to New Zealand by then."

"Huh."

I can see him trying to piece it together.

"And I was hanging with Raucous Rachel that summer." He lets out a long sigh. "She was cool."

I can barely remember her, except that she was indeed raucous, always talking, always high-fiving everybody.

"And you jammed out on guitar with those dudes back at her house."

"That's right." I'd forgotten that part, back at Raucous Rachel's house, all of us camped out in her backyard.

There were a couple kids with acoustic guitars way too good for how well they played them, and I was drunk enough to mention that I could play, sort of, used to anyway. The better of the two kids played along, and the rest of the night around that fire I dug up every old blues song I used to play on the streets of Boston for change when I was 20 years old and lost and broke and didn't care because the world would soon be ending. Those songs came right back, with all their loneliness and longing, all covered in rust, like my voice, which made my voice if not my guitar playing, sound better, maybe fifteen years after I'd last tried to play any of them.

"You were awesome, man. And that one fuckin' guy hung in there with you like he was playing with the ghost of Stevie Ray Vaughan," Danny laughs.

"Thanks."

"And you were so whatever about it. That's when I knew you'd be cool up on a climb."

"I guess." I feel weird talking about it – I hate talking about everything with music that could have been but never was – but I can tell that he is in a talking mood. I look out at the road, steepening with each curve down the canyon. "It was great camping up here at Raucous Rachel's house, so close to the festival. Though you weren't exactly camping."

"True that," he laughs, then lets out a sigh. "Raucous Rachel. Great in the rack. Kinda selfish though. But she could have just-nipple orgasms – which is always a huge thing, when you run across it."

"Just-nipple orgasms," I chuckle, trying to imagine. "I guess that could be a real time-saver."

"I guess," he grins. "If you're in a hurry."

I turn to him. "Are we down hiking?"

"Always." He thinks about it a minute. "Problem with her nipple-only orgasm thing was – you couldn't touch them afterwards. For like an hour. Or she'd go through the roof." He lets out another long sigh. "Too bad she turned out to be a lesbian."

The walls of the canyon loom up all around us, filling the bus with shadows. Danny turns on the lights.

"You know," he says, "I actually thought maybe that was Julie's dealio – when I first met her."

"That maybe she's a switch-hitter?"

"Fuck no, dude," he chuckles. "I'd know that by now."

"You sure?"

He looks over at me, and in the fading light I can see more from his eyes than anything else that he is grinning. "Oh, I'm sure."

I brace myself for an onslaught of unsolicited information about Julie's anatomy, but he goes quiet. And as we start down the canyon, it occurs to me that not once has Danny served up any of the usual details on Julie, not in all those down hikes over the past couple months. This is especially odd, as they are not technically together anymore – just friends, he says – now that Julie has moved to Portland, where she just got the Betty-job of all Betty-jobs: working in marketing at Nike. But it does mean that, technically, Danny is back in play, just like the Danny I've known for two years now, and the world is back to its old new normal.

Which is exactly the plan for tonight: we're going to hang around Boulder, do a grand tour of the bars Danny used to cruise when he was in college down there, and see if he's still got the old touch – if only that means the old touch for hitting on somebody's girlfriend and getting thrown out. He was emboldened to hit on anybody in those days, he has told me these past two years on all these road trips and down hikes, because he played football at Colorado. Yes, Danny, with his outsized appetites for weed and meditation, his disdain for authority, and the pink and purple streaks through his hair, a Division I football player. I get the athlete part: he's strong and fast, in great aerobic shape, as tall as Jill and me, and lion-hearted in the way he charges it up and down the mountain. And he has great body knowledge when he launches his snowboard into the air. But Danny? Who looks and sounds just like Kurt Cobain, if after a major rehab and few years at the gym?? D-1 football???

"Because I used to be really fast and could read guys," he once told me. "So I played safety. But I didn't get a lot of playing time. Because every time I'd mow some guy down, I'd feel bad about it – apologize – help the guy up. That really used to piss off my coaches."

Danny said the best part about being on the team was getting free shit around campus, meeting women, and scoring the best weed. And he was popular on the team, apparently, because he was an English major and could be counted on to write papers for the team's big men – which he bartered for access to more and better weed and parties with even more women. Not that I imagine he ever had trouble with that kind of access, especially as he was no doubt as much a "fucking feminist" when he was playing football and writing papers for weed as he is now.

We drive down the canyon in the growing dark, and still no details about Julie. Maybe he has some policy, conscious or not, of putting a moratorium on whichever woman is still of record, plus some fixed cooling off period, until he launches with the raunch. Julie was, after all, just another in a long line of women in their mid-20s – Danny always hung with women who were pre-hot zone – who just happened to pass through Dudeville (even if the part of Dudeville that Julie passed through was actually located up in Steamboat Springs). But she did turn out to be smarter and funnier than the rest, every bit as smart and funny as Danny himself. She was, like Jill and most of the Betties, scrounging for outdoor jobs in between a good run at college sports and a real career and the inevitable hot zone. She was just passing through, looking to go big in the mountains, just having a good time, and meet you at the bottom. But Julie had managed to stick around longer than the rest; she didn't put up with any of Danny's occasional bursts of juvenile humor or moody withdrawals – I mean his "Zen states," as he calls them – and she has been the only one, so far at least, he hasn't turned into a porn star for Aaron's and my benefit on a down hike.

I was there when they met, at a party up in Steamboat. I'd driven Danny up there because most of his left leg was still in a cast from a snowboarding accident down the technical side of Quandary Peak that could have killed him. He was chasing some new woman he'd met at One World Festival down in Crested Butte while on a month-long spree to deal with the fallout from the accident. She, as it turned out, was on a decade-long spree to deal with not having much of a personality; at that party up in Steamboat, she was more interested in whatever guy was standing next to the keg or pouring the shots.

"Drunk Girl," as she came to be known a few hours in, shared a house with a couple other ski instructors; a skinny, surly preppie trying to get into law school who kept asking me how old I was; and a garrulous tomboy-next-door whose heart had just been broken by an extended-stay tourist who turned out to be just bi-curious after a sexless marriage and before rotating back to dudes. That night was all keg, shots, weed, and B.B. King – though it was clearly just another regular night up there – and Danny and I, as the new kids in town, were the main attraction.

Drunk Girl and her housemates and the rest of the locals were just heading into mud season, many seriously banged up, and all of them bored with each other: a couple guys on crutches; a woman in an armcast and another in a sling; a grungy guy with two black eyes from running into something on his snowboard. There was an even grungier guy in a wheelchair who hadn't bathed in awhile and kept playing – and slurring along with the chorus to – B.B. King's "The Thrill is Gone," until he went from funny, to sad, to pathetic, to part of the peeling wallpaper. Everyone's face was brick red and bloodshot from the previous months of sun, blasting snow, and the cold hard winds that howl out of the north up there.

"I'm a physical therapist," a very drunk, very heavy woman who was hitting on me said.

I couldn't help but laugh, look around the room at all the walking wounded and say, "You must very busy."

The entire party took turns checking out the new guys. Danny held court with his cast up on a couple milk crates, telling the story of his accident every time someone would come over and ask; I fetched him beers and provided color commentary on the story as necessary. (And a hell of a story it was: Danny lost an edge on his snowboard on an unseen patch of ice sticking out of the top of the couloir, and launched into what they call in Dudeville a "hairball carcass" – a full surrender to gravity and a violent end-over-end tumbling, all the way to the bottom. He hit the ice and rock at the bottom at full speed, and only his helmet and dumb luck kept his head damage to a concussion and his leg jam to a simple tib-fib fracture. But his rescue was complicated by Sampson, Kelly's enormous, big-hearted, dumb-ass blond Labrador, amped up by Danny's out-of-his-head screaming, who kept the mountain rescue guys at bay for another half hour.)

At that party in Steamboat, they came over in twos and threes, pulling out their bowl and weed, asking Danny about his leg – hour upon hour upon hour of the same damn story, "the thrill is gone away, and you're gonna be sorry!" playing endlessly in the background – until Danny and I were so skull-baked that neither of us could actually talk for whole minutes at a time, only laugh: laugh at them falling all over each other; laugh at the "thrill is gone" guy, finally passed out and slumped over in the wheelchair; laugh at Drunk Girl as she stumbled up to us and beckoned, in what she thought was a sexy way (her eyes crossing and uncrossing), Danny to go upstairs with her.

But that night, Danny went home with Julie instead – to sleep on her couch, she'd made it clear – as she helped me and my gigantic helium head figure out how to operate the latch on the cap to my own truck, and crawl into the back for the night outside Drunk Girl's house. I think.

The next day, we all hung out in town, then went up to the hot springs in the hills east of town. The two of them had already morphed in each other's presence, somehow, from heated up to chilled out, goofing around, teasing each other, punching each other in the arm like old buddies – all of which made me feel like a big square third wheel, the wingman who needed to fly away.

Which is exactly what, like a good wingman, I did. I told them I was itching for a little solitude and a big walk – which I was, after the circus the night before – so I left Danny and Julie to their spontaneous honeymoon and headed up to Mount Zirkel, Julie's recommendation for big, beautiful and empty.

The Mount Zirkel Wilderness Area is a few hundred thousand acres halfway between Steamboat and the Wyoming state line, all empty mountains and enormous trees, raw, wild, and completely unpeopled. It is too far out of the way and most of its little peaks too unremarkable for climbing, counting, or even naming; from the moment I turned off the highway, I didn't see another person or truck for the twenty clambering miles up the muddy forest service road that terminated at a snowed-in trailhead.

I set up camp out of the back of my truck in the frozen hush, made a quick meal, and studied the topo map under my headlamp for routes where there were no trails. It was too cold to stay up – and I was probably still stoned from the weed-bombing the night before –

but as I turned off my headlamp, the sky erupted into a mushroom cloud of stars, the milky way spread across the width of the valley. A thousand stars yes, and not just white stars, but blue-gray-blue, fire-yellow, lime-green, translucent-orange, the milky way broken into bands of thousands more, too small to see as stars but all bathed in star-mist, dense, in streaks, like very high cloud cover, except the vapor was not vapor but thousands of tiny stars beyond the stars, beyond everything.

And then the Presence, suddenly welling up within me and spilling out all around me.

I was perfectly alone in the universe but not alone at all. Here I am, I said, the same words that arise from within when I'm up above treeline.

I sat back on the cold metal tailgate of my truck, staring up into that miraculous void, and tried to put numbers on all of it. I dusted off my geology and history books, my Euclid's *Elements*, and physics texts, and Einstein's *General Theory* – along with the one thing I could remember from that one poetry class in college – and I diagrammed the whole shebang in my mind's eye: I am halfway up the rotating surface of a rock, near a place labeled Steamboat Springs a hundred years ago by someone from maybe five degrees around the surface of rock, because that's what the steam rising from the river looked like; the rock spun around on an axis, and the axis went around a ball of fire, and the ball of fire went around on a plane that expanded outward in every direction including the expanding direction of time, until it joined itself inside itself in a great mobius strip, all exploding outward from the same place and time that were neither. Rocketing back 15 or so billion years from not-then and not-there, I was a shadow on a jot in some pulverized wood cells between two brown squiggles on a wrinkled topo map, in a squiggle of time labeled 2001, a few days into April – which is the cruelest month, I remember from college, because someone once counted on it to keep some promise it never made. And absolutely none of it meant anything to those stars because they were already come and gone, and I was already come and gone, and yet, and yet: I was still there, my imagination reaching out beyond those stars, from finitude's meaninglessness to infinite meaninglessness and back again, which meant that maybe the Presence and I really were one.

Or maybe it was all that weed from the night before.

I crawled into my sleeping bag, where it sucked the warmth from my body in less than a minute. My body shivered back, slowly pushing the cold out of the bag, and I fell asleep thinking about topo lines, then meaninglessness, then more topo lines.

The next morning, I was up with the sun, shivering, intensely awake, the dope cloud finally gone as I quickly turned boiling water into coffee and oatmeal over my little backpacking stove. By the time I pulled my gear together, the sun was climbing into a sky so intensely and bottomlessly and radiantly blue that it ached. The sun glowered down on everything, screaming off the snowfields surrounding the trailhead, like liquid fire splashed onto trees drooping with snowpack and a frozen trail softening back to mud.

I started up the untracked trail, obvious only by breaks in the aspens and thickets of willow, through gaps in the big pines, an occasional old blaze in bark grown thick around the wound.

A mile or so up, the trail opened out into a sweeping, still snow-covered meadow. It was surrounded to the south and east by an aspen grove running up toward a ridge of small peaks, and to the north and west by a thick stand of pines. I guessed the trail as running right across the middle, through a snowfield spiked with the dried husks of last year's wildflowers, thousands of yellowed stalks, tracked by dozens of hungry deer.

Up ahead I could see what I knew from the map was an unmarked peak, a snow-capped horn, standing there like another old uncle I'd never had but had always missed. He was showing me his neck of the woods, just up ahead with his hands on his hips, waiting for me to catch up. I felt the burn on my face and knew I was smiling, so I quickened my pace, imagining what it was going to be like standing up there on that pristine upper snowfield, the view spread out over the whole valley back toward town, the steam rising from the river like a boat in another century, and then . . .

"CRAWWW!!!"

An anguished scream, like a baby – a human baby! – squawking across the open meadow, and a flash of movement.

I kept walking toward it, toward the treeline at the other end, all curiosity and no caution, and suddenly there was a blur up ahead, a wild commotion, but my eyes were frazzled from the snow all around me.

And then a second "CRAWWW!!!" like something screaming, guttural, from deep within a human throat.

My eyes made out the thrashing of a large bird across the meadow, all wings but no flight, as if it were screaming for help, not at me, not at anyone, just screaming.

Then I saw it, and froze to the spot, maybe fifty paces away, along the edge of the woods: a large gray heron, or something like it, flapping desperately into the air, all wings and weaving head, caught by its leg. Something tugged at its leg, one big pulsing muscle of a husky dog, pointed ears swept back over its head, long nose and mouth clamped down into a growling grasp on the bird's leg, the most powerful dog I've ever seen, all chest and upper body, trying to tear the huge bird to the ground. The bird was trying to take flight, trying to pull itself loose; then it seemed to turn toward me, flapping harder, and the dog turned to me too; and in that instant, as its jaw released and the bird flew away, I realized that it was not a dog at all, that it was a wolf.

I stood there, still frozen in place, thirty paces away, time melting, my brain oozing out of my ears and my head filled with the addled chorus of a dozen adventure and outdoor writers all urging me in one voice...

Do not make eye contact and do not run! Make yourself look bigger and do not run! Do not make eye contact, and DO NOT RUN!

...singing louder and faster and finally breaking into the cacophony of the dozen things I'd read about encounters with mountain lions and bears – never about wolves because when would that ever happen? – and here was one anyway, staring me down, a long, hard, muddy two miles into the wilderness, fifteen miles from the highway, ten more miles from town.

And no one had any idea where I was, except this wolf. And I'd just messed up his bagging of a warm breakfast.

I could not run, I had to fight, and the only thing I had was an ice ax strapped to the outside of my pack. So do I drop the pack, and go for the ax???

The cacophony stopped, on a beat, as fast as it had started, but time was still stopped and I did not move.

The wolf just stood there, staring at me, absolutely present and utterly blank.

I realized I was wearing sunglasses and could not make eye contact; but maybe the black lenses looked like huge eyes? So I turned my head slowly, but did not stop looking and I tried to breathe, to force as much air in as I could and pump myself up bigger.

The wolf just kept staring at me, time still stopped...

...and then it finally, slowly, turned toward the woods, squared its shoulders, then looked back at me as if to say, *Nah, I don't feel like running over and ripping out your throat. So I'm just going to go off over here. But you get the hell out of here. NOW.*

I could not move. I turned my head the other way, toward the peak, and watched him out of the corner of my eye.

He trotted into an invisible break in the pines, and was gone.

That could not have been a wolf, I stood there in my muddy tracks saying to myself over and over. *Because there weren't any wolves in Colorado, right? That had to have been a coyote – a very large, powerful, aggressive coyote. Except that coyotes do not hunt animals that large.*

I knew that the closest wolves were way up in Yellowstone; they'd only just been re-introduced up there, after years of human howling on both sides of the debate by the Love-the-Earthers and Kill-the-Earthers. (I ♥ REDNECKS, right, Danny?) But that re-introduction was several hundred miles to the northwest; and wolves were smart and strong but they weren't that smart and strong, right?

I stood there wondering, second-guessing myself, thinking I should just look at the tracks to see if they could explain anything. But when I went to move, my feet had sunken, maybe an inch or two into the mud, and the simple sensation that they were stuck shot through me with a raw screaming terror, and as I desperately yanked at my legs to free them with a sucking noise, there it was on the breeze.

"Yip-yip-yow!" just off into the woods.

I froze again.

"Yip-yip-yow!"

No different than a neighborhood dog, I tried to tell myself; could have been a coyote still.

Then further back into the woods, the answering "Yip-yip-yowls!" of three, four, maybe five more "neighborhood dogs." Dogs? Coyotes? Those are wolves! Shit!! Run!!!

The same adrenaline that had frozen me to the spot flushed down into my legs and made me want to run, but I could not run, so I threw my pack down in the mud and yanked my ice ax out of the loops – and the air went perfectly still as I stood there, holding the ax like a weapon, no more yipping, just the breeze again, and then birds.

I yanked my pack on and hurried across the meadow, electrified with adrenaline, holding the ax with both hands, the way you do for self-arresting a fall and slide down a glacier or snowfield. I knew I couldn't pace any kind of run in all that mud and melting snow, but I could not stop, so I busted into a jog and then, despite what I knew, an outright run anyway, my heart beating up into my throat, burning, everything burning, all the way back to my truck, where I collapsed onto wet grass and burst into tears of immense relief, my core letting ago, my own death howl.

Half an hour later and halfway back toward Steamboat, there was a forest service office, so I stopped and went in to tell somebody what I had seen.

At a battered old desk behind the counter, there was a tough old woman in a brown uniform, with granny glasses and thick platinum hair back in a big braid.

I told her the story but she said "No, it must have been a coyote. There is no way a wolf could have migrated all the way down to northern Colorado, not already, from the Yellowstone re-introduction." But she had me point to a map anyway and took down every detail I could remember.

But as I turned to go, feeling like a bit of a tourist chump, she said, "It's not impossible, mind you. Just not very likely."

After Danny and I got back from that Steamboat trip, I read up on the wolves in Yellowstone. Articles in outdoor magazines across the adventure spectrum were full of the same arguments and counterarguments from the love-the-earth and kill-the-earth crowds: it was all ecosystems versus economics, each side with their data and anecdotes and bitterness at the other side, another classic squaring off of environmentalists versus ranchers, of those who shoot cameras and those who shoot guns, one of the wilder outposts in America's permanent culture war. There was no right or wrong – only competing visions for the shared landscape – and these visions would never be reconciled. Love the earth, kill the earth, I ♥ REDNECKS.

The most interesting idea I came across at the time was not in any magazine, but from Aaron, who heard about it from some guy in his wilderness medicine clinic, who heard it from some other guy who works as a fishing guide up in Yellowstone.

"The guy told him the re-introduction of the wolf up there has been great for the trout," Aaron told me.

"The trout?" I tried to guess at the link.

Aaron left me hanging a minute, seeing if I could figure it out for myself, always teaching, always training, always testing.

"The wolves are thinning out the bears? So there's less pressure on the trout?"

"Good guess," he said. "Actually, the wolves are the only natural predator of the elk, which have been totally overpopulated up there until the wolves came back. Elk rub their antlers clean on aspens and other trees, which then die and fall over, and beavers use the downed trees to build dams. The dams slow the rivers, which muddy them up, and let them heat up – which reduces trout populations. Add wolves, restore the trout. It's all connected."

Like Danny is always saying: all connected. The web of life, the path of karma, the dharma wheel – or something like that. I have no idea what he means when he goes off about it, but I'm starting to learn a little of how it might work.

Maybe it's no more complicated than knocking a guy on his ass on a football field, like you're supposed to, but then apologizing and helping him up. But no wolf would do that. And of course if you did that in business, you'd be slaughtered on the next play. But maybe that's why I blew all that off, so I could end up in a place where you can play hard just like that, and not have it matter – except when you don't see the ice poking out of the top of a couloir, or you run into a real wolf. Maybe that's the real reason I'm hanging out with a guy ten years younger than me who does exactly that without thinking there's anything weird about it, who really is just Zen about everything.

"Hey, man," I turn to him, the inside of the Non-Hippie Bus now completely dark as we curve our way down the canyon. "You remember that time up in Steamboat, when I ran into what I thought was a wolf?"

"Hell yeah, man," he says. "That what you been over there daydreaming about?"

"Yeah, still trying to figure all that out." I look into the backseat, and see the shadow of Aaron slumped over, fast asleep. "You know what happened up in Yellowstone, after they reintroduced wolves?"

"Hmm," Danny says. "Little Red Riding Hood moved to Texas? And became a spokeswoman for the NRA?"

"That's funny. But no. I mean to the other animals up there – all of the animals in the food chain."

"Like the deer and elk?" He thinks about it a minute. "Definitely bad news for the deer and elk. Not so good news for the beavers, because they have to downsize –'cuz the elk knock down the trees for their lodges. So – definitely good news for the trout. Right?"

"Exactly."

"Everything's connected, man."

"That's what I've heard."

A few minutes later, the canyon widens and lights appear up in the cliffs, as we drive down into Boulder.

"Hey man!" Danny yells Aaron awake, as we pull into a long driveway threaded through big creek boulders. It's Aaron's friend's place, an old cabin along the creek, and we'll be camping here later.

I'm tempted to stay and hang out with Aaron and *not* do wingman duty for Danny. But I said I would go; so I go. We are supposed to meet an old friend of his later on, along with her roommate, who Danny says might be hot, and who knows. And I haven't been to Boulder since 1994, and I'm curious.

That one trip was in and out for work with some barely funded startup that never became a client. And I was too busy with problems back at the office to do anything except stare out the hotel window at the wild tilt of the Flatirons, skyscraper slabs of red and gray rock, falling backwards into the front range of the Rockies. Since then and since moving out to Dudeville, I've been meaning to go back, remembering it as a funky little college town, all hippies in old Volvos and climbing bums on old bikes, and one of those perennial "Ten Best mountain / outdoor / adventure / downshift / telecommute / chase Betties towns" in all the magazines. So I am long overdue to see if any of that is true, even though I made my choice on that two years ago when I moved to Dudeville to downshift, telecommute, hang with Jill then avoid Jill, and watch Danny chase Betties.

Danny and I climb back in the Non-Hippie Bus, and head down the last little bit of canyon into Boulder. It takes 20 minutes to find a place to park.

"Look at all this fuckin' traffic!" Danny says, circling the same blocks for the third time. "And parking meters? What the fuck, dude?"

Even well after dark, Boulder is all traffic and people, lights and horns, shiny new Audis and SUVs and Subarus with empty bike and kayak racks on top, the sidewalks a whirl of people in bright workout and hiking clothes, all with perfect bodies, perfect tans, perfect smiles.

Danny finally finds a place a couple blocks into what he calls his "the old frathood," a tree-lined street lined with frumpy old Victorian houses.

"Great karma, dude," he says, as we park behind a big shiny SUV with a big empty multi-sport rack on top. "Hater douche."

"What?"

He points at its bumper sticker: *Jerry's Dead, Phish Sucks, Get a Job.*

He packs a bowl and we smoke it before heading back toward the bar.

"You know, man," he says, exhaling a cloud of smoke. "I really am all about compassion these days."

"Uh – huh."

"All about loving-kindness."

"Ok."

"But some people?" he points at the SUV and offending bumper sticker as he's jumping out. "They just live for conflict."

He takes a quick look around, then unzips his fly and takes a good long piss on the bumper sticker, then across the bumper and license plate, and all over as much of the back of the SUV as he can. "Sure would hate to disappoint him."

A few minutes later, we are walking into the Walrus, a loud, crowded, cavernous bar where Danny says he used to hang out when he was down here in school, and where we are meeting his old friends, or roommates, or friends of roommates, I forget.

"Besides," Danny says as we walk into the roar of the place. "I need to get back in play. And this is the playground."

We stand in a long line of mostly college kids, while a beefy doorman leaning on a stool checks IDs, one right after another without looking up. Which means he will be checking mine. Which should be amusing.

He takes Danny's ID, looks at the picture and does the math, then looks up at Danny's face, and hands it back.

Then he takes my license, looks at the picture and does the math, frowns and looks at it more closely. He looks up at me, nods his head, and says "You're like 40, dude."

"That's right."

He hands back my license. "Hang in there, man."

Danny and I stand in the corner drinking beers and watching the kids, all of whom are dressed like everybody else in town. Tans and smiles, bright fleece and shorts, hiking boots or river sandals, they all look exactly the same, but for every third or fourth dude's big fashion statement: a cap worn backwards.

They drink and shout over the crowd at each other, and Danny makes a few feeble attempts to engage with some of the women who walk by. They eye him nervously, notice the pink and purple streaks in his hair, then look over at me standing there in wingman position, and hurry off.

I pull my ski hat down over my eyes and stare off at the bank of TVs: baseball, basketball, and hockey; and on the farthest one over, Lance, in yellow of course, surrounded by teammates in blue, in a river of a dozen other colors on a fast and flat stretch.

Danny keeps working the crowd, so I just stare at the TVs. I am suddenly exhausted from the long hard day in the mountains, feeling not forty years old but more like a hundred, wishing I'd just hung out with Aaron and his friend next to that quiet creek.

Danny's friend finally shows up with her friend – tans, smiles, bright fleece, shorts, river sandals – and they shout introductions over the crowd. They are both named "Jen," which would make it easy to remember their names, if I cared to. But Danny and Jen and Jen turn and ignore me for the crowd, to my relief.

I wander through the crowd and realize that it's going to be a long night, so I scout an empty barstool at one end of the back bar, right in front of the bike race, and order another beer.

I feel something in my pocket: it is my cell phone coming to life, back in range for the first time in a few hours. I fish it out of my pocket, just in time to miss another call from Jill. It looks like she also called an hour ago, and left a voicemail.

"Screw this place," Danny's booming voice startles me, as he plops down on the empty barstool next to me. "Total waste of time."

"No shit," I shout back.

We down our beers, unable to talk over the crowd, and watch Lance and his team charging it down a winding country road: a perfectly tuned, multi-human machine. It is beautiful.

A few minutes later, we are finally back out on the crowded street.

"Thought you wanted to get back in play," I say to Danny, just to rub it in a little.

"Yeah, well, maybe," he mutters. "But not in there with those idiots. Julie can kick any of those girls' asses."

An hour later, as we are crashing in the tents Aaron had set up behind his friend's cabin and along the sweet burble of Boulder Creek, I remember the voicemail from Jill. But we are up into the canyon and my cell phone doesn't work. Which is probably just as well.

I *will* call her back, I think, as I drift away to the gurgling water. She's a good woman, even if I need to let her go, just like Danny needs to let Julie go. And no more go-rounds with her for old times' sake, which is what happens every time we get together for the last time. One more go-round with her would be as dumb, and pointless, and embarrassing as me actually trying to pick up one of those college girls tonight.

I just need to let her be, let her float away like a pretty leaf fallen from a tree, twirling into this sweet little creek, down the canyon and gone.

Memorial Day

It's Memorial Day Weekend, the tourists have flooded back into Colorado, and I'm right here in the belly of the beast –Vail – reluctantly, in every way describable, to catch up with good old Tom and Becky. The bars are packed; the whole overdeveloped mess of Vail Valley jammed with traffic; and in case every tourist isn't revved up and agro enough with booze and altitude, there is a full moon following me back to the hotel.

Tom and Becky are working on some new venture down in Denver they've been trying to rope me into for awhile and I don't want to know about. They thought it would be a good idea to fly their spouses out for the holiday weekend and some resort / spa / golf / altitude sickness fun; and each of them has told me they want to see what all the fuss is about with my new life in the mountains. They had suggested coming all the way to Dudeville to see me in my new natural habitat; but there would be no better way to blow my entire cover with my new friends than expose them to my old colleagues, so I suggest somewhere more civilized and so of course they picked Vail, because that's where everyone like Tom and Becky go.

I always had mixed feelings about Tom. He's all affable, all the time, and self-effacing in a way you don't quite believe, the perennial team-captain and fraternity president who makes it all about you because it really is, in the end, all about him. But you'd never know that because he is keenly observant, clever, and resourceful, and he is always exquisitely defended. It was inevitable he'd end up the young superstar tech CEO, the good guy everybody likes and wants to work with because they fall for his making it all about them – which blinds them to the cold, ruthless streak few have ever seen in him besides Becky or Liz or me.

I should have hated Tom for all the breezy falsehoods and impossible promises over the eight years and eight months I worked my guts out for him. And I should have hated him most of all for caving in and selling the company in the middle of the night for a near rock bottom price when our stock was at what Liz and Becky and I hoped was a temporary rock bottom. But, as with everyone, I liked him anyway, with my own reasons for hating myself for it, just like Becky did.

As for Becky herself, prim and proper and even more defended than Tom – except when we were out drinking our 10 PM after-work dinners – I have no mixed feelings, just sentimentality for the years we spent grinding it out, pissed about whatever jam Tom had gotten us into. I also had direct, real-time sympathy for her always having to clean up Tom's messes, replaced since moving to Dudeville by complete mystification over why she continued to do so, long after she too had cashed out and could have fled like I did.

But tonight, the mystification seemed to be directed by them at me. Over the last of a long, fancy dinner in the nicest restaurant in Vail – after Becky and her always morbidly withdrawn husband Sydney had gone back to the hotel early because of "altitude and time-zone problems" – Tom's wife Mary kept at me, the same way she used to at company dinner parties.

"So Jack," she chirped at me. "Who's the lady in your life? You must have somebody special! Lots of men your age and older are having children and starting families!"

Tom, who met Amy the Rebound Girl at some conference and heard maybe two or three references to Jill over the past two years, seems to believe I'm up here knocking off every other Betty and unattached tourist in Colorado. Or maybe he just wants to believe that. Either way, he kept brushing her off.

"Leave him alone, honey! He's doing fine up here. Look at that tan! And he's got some famous skier girlfriend," he said, turning to me. "Right?"

"But he's *lonely*," Mary said before I could answer, looking over at me with her big brown worried mama-bear eyes. "I can tell."

I kept steering the conversation back to their family. The three daughters I'd known since they were babies were now teenagers and off in Europe with another family, and the fourth – "the big surprise," a decade later, as they always called him – was still a toddler and Back East with Mary's parents for the first time so they could have a weekend alone in the mountains.

But Tom didn't want to talk about their kids, even though Mary did; it's all she ever talks about, actually, her kids, or somebody else's. And I knew from years of being around them that something else was going on. Finally, Tom – whose trademark perma-gameface is one of his great corporate assets – suddenly blew up at her.

"Stop, honey! He doesn't want to hear about any of that."

He got up suddenly and stormed to the men's room.

"Children are complicated," Mary sighed to me after he was gone. "Families are complicated."

"Yes, I know," I said, looking down at the big empty table for six, cleared of everything except linen and our drinks.

"And that's why you never had any children?"

I shrugged and avoided her eyes.

"There's still time, you know."

And sure, there is still time, if I'd ever wanted kids but I never did and I never will, I think as I walk the long way through Vail Village, under the white blaze of the full moon, back to my room, wide awake and alone. There is always time to fix almost anything until you are well into your 40s. If you're a guy. And if you want to.

But, as Mary said, families are complicated. And don't I know that? Because that is one of the few things that cannot be fixed, no matter how young you are, no matter how much time you have. Even Jill, with all her privileges, gifts, and good fortune, has had to deal with those complications; they started coming up no sooner than what you could call our second date, right after she moved her stuff into The

Treehouse – into my garage, I mean – and we started playing house those first couple weeks.

We were heading down to New Mexico to climb up and ski down Wheeler Peak, the highest in the state, hovering like a sphinx over the Taos Ski Valley. We'd each taken note of it from chairlifts at Taos, long before we ever met, and wanted to climb it; and so Jill and I drove down there on Memorial Day Weekend two years ago, with Kettle and Sampson, Kelly's big blond Labrador, in the back of my truck.

An hour north of Taos, we crashed with Jill's old post-hippie aunt Alfreda (about my age) and her young post-punk wife, Georgina (about Jill's age plus five years maybe). They lived in one of those "earthships" carved into the brick-brown plateaus all around Northern New Mexico. It was cozy and dark and smelled – as you sat down on different objects draped with tie-dyed tapestries – of sage, curry, incense, weed, and vagina. We pitched a tent on the flattest part of their property, which turned out to be on top of the house itself; ate a curried-something-fantastic over brown rice; and afterwards, as we were gearing up for a sunset hike, they passed around a little jar of dried mushrooms. I'd never done any actual drugs before, just weed, and didn't really want to run the risk of weirding out or acting stupid or worst of all, outing myself for some old guy who had never done any actual drugs. But I didn't know how to just say no, standing in front of the earthship in a circle of three wide-open, welcoming, expectant human faces – and two exultant, expectant canine ones.

In that psychedelic landscape, the mushroom's effects were mostly redundant, at least until later, when Jill and I climbed into the tent and were giggling so hard we could barely have sex – until Jill stopped laughing and started crying and was suddenly even more horny and clinging. But the hike up the big mesa just down the road from the earthship that evening could not have been more intense had the whole thing been on fire, its geology morphing into an enormous confection we were eating as we were scaling it, all those rock layers suddenly milk chocolate, mocha, raspberry, black crumbles, more milk chocolate.

The wide-open plateau atop the mesa was all gullies and cactus and sagebrush and scrub pines. It felt less like terra firma than like a much bigger and actual earthship, hovering over the brown blur of wide open plateau below, as if the whole thing were vibrating just below perception, the scrub pines twitching with the wind in my peripheral vision, then stopping when I looked right at them, then twitching when I looked away. Kettle and Sampson ran around the trees, barking at them as if they were human forms moving in the wind – which is when I realized it might be the mushrooms, and went over and sat on the edge next to Jill, her eyes wide open and wet, filled with the last of the sun.

Our boots were raspberry cream red with the dust, hanging off the last milk chocolate layer, as we watched the sun melt into an orange puddle on the furthest mesa west, and the vast cobalt blue of the sky turn electric fuchsia, then hard pink, then soft pink and lavender, finally succumbing to a flurry of stars.

"My aunt," Jill finally let out a long sigh, ten miles down the road the next morning, as we drove south toward Taos. "Mushrooms, acid, flotation tanks, meditation. If it's a trip, she's on it. Like this crap," she pulled the little envelope, with the two hits of Ecstasy that Alfreda had given her, out of her shorts and tossed it behind the seat. "Who needs it?"

Jill had been quiet as we broke camp, walked the dogs, and packed the truck, before Alfreda and Georgina were up and making us breakfast. I'd thought maybe she was mad at me for laughing after our drugged out sex, especially as she was up and out of the tent without morning sex. But then it came out the minute we were heading south, in broken, jagged pieces, bits of her family story, knocked loose by seeing her aunt.

"Alfreda and my mother were hippies growing up. But my Mom married my Dad, to get away from all that, she thought. He was a banker dude, all super-normal, even though part of him was cool. My mother tried to pretend for awhile, to go along with all the climber crap – until she went to grad school for psychology and got all left-wing. Then they split up. I was only five, so I only remember them as these people from totally different planets."

Jill had grown up going back and forth between a series of her father's ever more opulent Connecticut homes – he'd remarried less than a year later to some Junior League Country Clubber, who would torment Jill for the next fifteen years about her size, clothes, hair and manners – and her hippie psychologist mother, who was living on a farm with her therapist boyfriend, four other adults, three kids, and a yard full of goats, chickens and mud.

"It's why I'm such a freak," she said. "One weekend, it's my bitch stepmother, riding my ass for being some dirty hippie tomboy and hassling me into this freaking eating disorder – "

"Really?"

"Shit yeah, dude. For like two years. I was puking all the time, trying to fit into these gross dresses and all this preppie crap. Nasty bitch. And every other weekend, it's my mother and her boyfriend and all these fat hippies running around naked. Which one was real? Neither? Both?"

"Sounds like the perfect way to grow up for someone who ends up getting a green MBA."

"That's the problem," she sighed, her sudden flash of anger dissolving into a whimper as she kicked her boots up on the dashboard and stared out the window. "I'm *sooo* predictable. And I don't want to be that. I don't want to be either." She let out a long sigh. "I don't know what I want to be."

"Well, at your age, you don't have to – " but her look told me that I best not finish that sentence.

So we drove on in silence. And I really didn't have anything smart or interesting to say, only snark like *Whoop-de-doo for your first world problems,* or maybe *Yeah, it sucks being a poor little rich girl,* or best of all *Chill out, girl! You're 25 years old and you don't have a care in the world. So shut up and drive / hike / ski / drink / screw!* or worst of all *Oh please. When I was your age, I was married and broke and working my ass off to keep the lights on. My wife and I were still trying to get through college with no money, no parents, no health insurance, two car payments, maxxed out credit cards, overdue tuition bills, and one long traffic jam between work and school and study and back to work. So get over yourself.*

"What do you think I should do?" she finally broke the silence.

"I think you should go climb that mountain," I said, pointing at the faint shadow outlines of a mountain range just starting to loom up out of the dusty haze of the plateau.

"Yeah, right," she mumbled and crossed her arms. "Whatever, dude."

The visit with the aunt had obviously knocked some shit loose.

"Come on," I said, giving her rock-hard shoulder an affectionate shake. "You've got life licked – right now anyway – so just be that."

"Be what?"

"Be the person who has life licked and will figure it out later."

She looked over at me, and her eyes went hard and rolled sideways, her *What is THAT bullshit you're feeding me* look.

"The shitty little world is right over there," I said, nodding left, toward the endless flat brown expanse stretching to the east. "Anytime you want to drop in on it and become just another corporate drone with a jazzed up MBA, there you go. In the meanwhile," I nodded at the peaks looming into focus up ahead, and gave her shoulder a friendly shake. "I'm going to the top of that mountain right there, and to hell with the rest of the world."

The hard black points of her eyes softened back into their sea-green saucers, her pursed lips breaking into a half-smile. As I started to move my hand back to the steering wheel, she kissed it.

"You're right, dude," she said, lifting her eyes to the mountains.

Within minutes, the distant range was exploding from the plateau to fill the windshield. There were spring-green aspens spilling down through all the draws, and a long sweeping ridge above treeline still capped with snow, shimmering in the sun.

"Look at that sweet mountain," she said. "We do have life licked."

The "we" part kind of freaked me out; but she was leaving for New Zealand in ten days, and she hadn't invited me to visit her down there.

Which was a good thing, because I had the time and money, and was more snow-crazy than Jill-crazy. And I'd been curious about the place with the stars upside down since she had first mentioned it, and surely would have gone. Or maybe probably would have.

I'm yanked back by an eruption of kids' laughter somewhere behind me.

I look up from Jill's face, and everything around me is suddenly dark.

The path has crossed into a stand of tall pines, and I realize that I have lost track of where I am in Vail. It all looks the same up here – *faux Euro* condos and hotels – and I think I have just been walking around in circles when I spot it up ahead, the *faux Euro* hotel where we are all staying.

Families are indeed complicated, I think as I head in and upstairs. Mary was certainly right about that.

Jill wouldn't shut up about hers and everything they were or weren't on that trip down to New Mexico. And of course I had nothing helpful or interesting to say, so I grew dark and dreary myself. When her mumbling monologue finally hit bottom and burned itself out, she turned and prodded me about my own wreck of a family.

All I could do was shrug and say "I don't talk about that nightmare with anyone."

That's what I tell everyone who pushes, my long-perfected and oft-practiced line that sounds just dramatic enough to shut them up. How else to describe the tar pit I'd crawled out of when I was sixteen – almost ten years younger than Jill at the time – after a sixteen-year nightmare which made her family drama look no worse than an oddball family sit-com?

On the stunning drive south that morning, as we sped toward the mightiest mountain range in the "land of enchantment," my mood was suddenly blacker than hers. I drove faster and faster, because I knew a big mountain would fix it, like they fix everything. From somewhere around treeline, the wind screaming the world away, the Presence everywhere, all of it would turn to dust and drift onto the brown plateau below: family, history, frustration, anger and heartbreak.

And it didn't even take the climb to find that peace, only driving up the river canyon into the shadow of that long ridge, undulating up and down and back up to the highest point in New Mexico. It was like a massive living altar, simultaneously beckoning and indifferent, inviting and enigmatic, geologically restless but humanly eternal. I couldn't imagine a more powerful place from which to remind Jill – and myself, one more time – just how small and meaningless the rest of the world really is.

Small and meaningless indeed, I think as I pad through the hotel lobby, the bar crowded with loud, sunburned guys in golf clothes.

Back in my cold, empty room, I don't feel like going to sleep. But tomorrow will be an early one: I am "guiding" Tom and Becky "up something really big," as Tom put it. "Maybe one of those Fourteeners everyone is always talking about."

I pull off my clothes and set the alarm on the clock-radio and crawl into bed.

But all I can think about is Jill, New Mexico, and the drive up into those mountains, through funky little adobe villages, red rock formations, and budding aspens all lit up with cleansing sunlight...

Then the alarm goes off.

This is the morning I am dreading most from this trip.

Are those two serious? Do they really think they can get up a big mountain?

I know Becky used to run every other day, and said she still does; and Tom says he's working out now too – though he's the kind of guy who would more likely pay a personal trainer to do the working out for him. But he says he bought a treadmill and gets on it when he can; and he does look to be in fairly good shape, compared to the old days.

So, I think as my feet hit the floor, why not at least humor them, see how far up one of the baby Fourteeners I can get them.

But then, I realize as the minutes tick by downstairs, they're too late for that.

I'm out in front of our hotel at 7 AM as planned, my truck loaded with food, water, emergency gear and daypacks for the three of us. I have it timed out for an 8 AM start time on the other side of Fremont Pass – as late as you dare push it on a big day up past treeline, especially with newbees – and no one shows up.

At 7:10, 7:20, and 7:30, I call up to their rooms.

The line is busy in Tom and Mary's, and no one answers in Becky and Sid's.

At 7:39, just as I'm about to go out to my truck and find my cell phone with their cell phone numbers in it, Becky comes down to the timbered lobby in jeans and a sweatshirt, so much for my "no cotton tomorrow, you guys, cotton is death up there. Synthetics only!" warning.

She tells me that Sid is still sick, probably from all the altitude, and she should stick around and keep an eye on him. Which wasn't really a surprise: Sid, who had latched onto Becky a few years ago at a conference, despised all of us for reasons we never understood; and he was always pre-empting things Becky wanted to do, especially with me, as if he knew that those things invariably involved her bitching about him as well as about Tom.

Standard operating procedure from the old days, I think, as I watch Becky hurry back up the deerskin-covered stairs to their room.

I go back to the lobby phone and dial Tom and Mary's room again.

Tom answers on the first ring. "Sorry. Had a little thing to deal with back home. Be right down."

He comes down half an hour later, in hiking clothes still creased from the store and brand new hiking boots – always a very bad idea on any kind of hike. But if the boots don't fit, or require any kind of breaking in, at least we will know in the first half hour: his feet will be raw hamburger, and we can head back down.

It is almost 9 AM before we are rolling, and there are already hints of cirrus clouds up high as we pull out of Vail.

"See that?" I point at the clouds. "That means weather later, and maybe lightning up top. Too dangerous to try a Fourteener."

"So I blew it with the late start?"

"Kind of."

"Sorry about that," he said. But he looked a bit relieved, like we'd just aborted a rocket launch to the moon.

"No worries," I say. "There are dozens of big peaks around here. We'll summit something."

"Cool," he says, and I think he might actually mean it. "Gotta summit something."

As Tom's CTO, I always had to have a Plan B (and a few Plan Cs), and today my Plan B is not a bad one. We head for Notch Mountain, with its sweeping views across the Mount of the Holy Cross Wilderness, down over the Bowl of Tears, out across ranges in every direction. The hike will be tough enough to feel like something major for him; easy enough to bail if the weather does move in and/or Tom's new boots chew his feet to shit; and good enough for me because, well, it's one more day up top.

"Sorry about Mary getting on your case last night," he says, as we exit the highway and start up the forest service road to the trailhead.

"No big deal," I shrug.

"She doesn't really get it," he says.

"Get what?"

"That you're living the dream."

I have to chuckle at that, because it really does sound stupid when someone says it out loud. "Is that what I'm doing?"

"Oh yes," he says, then drifts off a moment, then bursts out laughing.

"What?"

"Remember a couple years ago, when you'd just split up with your wife and you moved downtown? And Mary kept trying to get you out to the house for dinner on Saturday nights – because she thought you were lonely down there by yourself?"

"Yeah." And more like: *Hell yes, Tom. I was lonely, miserable, and horny all the time, and back then, a big Saturday night was knocking off work or school work by 4 or 5, and going out and getting drunk with Becky after her first marriage blew up. (Even though all she ever wanted to talk about was how mad she was at you about something.) I was, in fact, overwhelmed with loneliness back there and then, Tom – every one of those swinging Saturday nights, between rounds one and two with Amy the Rebound Girl – coming back from the half-empty office and eating alone at the corner bar, living for the IPO and the first day after the day I could finally cash out, blow all of you off, and run west forever.* "I remember."

"Remember the night one of the girls was sick, and we had to cancel on you?"

"Uh-huh."

"Mary got off the phone with you, and felt so sorry for you," he says, going into a high-pitched imitation of her. "'Oh poor Jack! He'll be all alone down there by himself on a Saturday night!'" He laughs with the memory. "Man, did she bust me. So much for my poker face. I knew you didn't really want to hang out with us and our screaming kids on a Saturday night. So she said to me, 'What? What's so funny?' And I said, 'don't worry, honey – Jack will be just fine.' And she said 'How do you know that?' And I couldn't help myself – she knew something was up – and I said 'Because it's a big town, honey. Jack's single and good-looking and has plenty of money in his pocket. All he has to do is walk into a bar, and he can get some Strange.'"

"Oh yeah, Tom," I mutter, "that's exactly how it was, every Saturday night. Nothing but Strange. Up here too."

The road narrows up through the trees, turns into muddy ruts, and I have to stop and shift to four-wheel drive.

For the last half mile or so to the trailhead, the drive is too loud and gnarly for any more talk, which is fine at this point.

"You got me in big trouble that night," he chuckles, still stuck on the story as we park at the trailhead and get out of the truck. "She was totally pissed at me," he says, going back into the high-pitched squeal, 'Is that what you want, Tom? Some *Strange*??? Then you go right ahead! Run down there with Jack tonight, and get all the Strange you want! I'll take care of our children. Just don't you dare come back!'"

We are no more than ten minutes up the trail, and Tom is already winded.

I have to stop and wait for him; and when he catches up, I have to ask him – without sounding snotty, superior, or judgmental – about how his feet are doing. I know from hard experience that he's a proud, stubborn and private guy, and that he would ignore any pain long before copping to it, until it's too late, we are way up the mountain, and the cumulus cloud just starting to build over the valley turns dark and menacing.

He finally stumbles up. "Whoa, man. This altitude is for real." He tries to sit casually on the boulder next to the trail, but lands with a painful grunt.

"Yeah it is."

I squat down across from him and pretend I need to do something in my pack, but I'm really scanning his face for distress, something Aaron teaches in mountain rescue classes. Tom's face is even more blank than usual – the first bad sign – but bathed in sweat.

"You should drink some water," I say, and hand him my bottle. "How are your feet holding up?"

"They're uh – fine," he says, out of breath. "Just – fine."

"You sure? New boots are a big gamble on any hike."

"You can tell – they're new – huh?

I hold out my booted foot. Its once dark brown leather has been shredded almost to the color of tanned flesh, from ten thousand scrapings against rock and root, a few hundred immersions in cold streams, and dozens of slatherings with mink oil.

"You mean – you didn't – buy those that way," he tries to get the joke out in one breath, but is sucking wind. "Like a ratty old – brand new pair – of designer jeans?"

"That's funny."

"Ok," he says, pulling himself up too quickly, still out of breath. "Let's hit it."

I start up the trail and he is soon struggling to keep up. The cloud above is building, but not darkening.

I wait until he is mostly caught up, read his face, then keep going. I know this drill well, because I've been on the receiving end of it many times: with Aaron when I first moved out here; with Jill after she's come back from a big trip; and all of us with Tyler, who can fly up any of these mountains without breaking a sweat or drawing a heavy breath.

I also know that there are several leveling strategies. The stronger hiker carries more weight, or tells stories the whole way up, or sings. (Though sometimes, even with all three going, Tyler is still jumping ahead, so – like a good mountain dog – he summits first, then comes back to join us, then summits again.) These strategies aren't just to keep the peace in a mismatched pair or group, but to keep the stronger/strongest from going a little crazy. When someone is slowing you down at altitude, it's frustrating, even a little agitating, because your lungs want to step it up and work harder, your heart can't find the right elevated rate, you actually start to get cold, and you can't find the aerobic box.

I turn and wait and Tom is struggling up the trail, about fifty feet back.

I hurry further up the trail, around the next curve, and duck out of sight to look for just the right rock. There it is, poking out of the pine needle carpet, the size of a volleyball. It feels like about 25 pounds, so I open my pack, dump everything out, put the rock in the bottom, repack it, and wait for Tom.

"Seriously, buddy," he says as he stumbles up, completely winded, his face showing some pain. "This is tough."

"Yes it is. Altitude is serious business. Keep drinking water."

He gulps at the water, then looks past me at the view, opening up toward the south and the arc of the sun: the sudden rise in the mountains past treeline, the sweep of tundra, the alpine lakes at the bottom of the last of the lower snowfields.

"It is awesome though," he says.

"It's that too. And never more awesome than when you earn it like this."

"I think I'm starting to get that," he nods, suddenly transfixed by the view.

I wait until he's completely caught his breath, then start up the trail. My pack is weighed down with the rock, the hike is suddenly work, my heart going. I am back in the aerobic box at last, and it is all sweet release: body, mind, and breath, aligned and emptying.

The trail is clean, and so I wander off like I do on so many routine training hikes, to where I was when I was fighting sleep last night: New Mexico, that amazing peak painted with sunrise, Jill and Kettle; and yes, Tom, I really am living the dream.

Jill and I camped in the back of my truck at the trailhead, at the upper end of the ski area's parking lot. No tents allowed, just RVs for some reason. We didn't have backpacking gear, so we just set up a little kitchen out the back of my truck, while Kettle and Sampson ran around making friends with all the Ma and Pa Kettles in the RVs. Our plan was to bed down early, and get up in the middle of the night, hiking by headlamp to make the ridge by sunrise. Another hour or so of pickaxing along the ridgeline, and we'd summit and ski off before the snow turned soft and dangerous.

Jill was still dark, wanting to talk about her family as we scouted the trail to the ridge and pooped out the dogs, and I couldn't get her to change the subject. She sat on the tailgate of the truck, drinking beer and railing about her father or stepmother or aunt or somebody, while I made a big meal and packed us a bowl and opened more beers.

A few minutes after we ate and smoked another bowl, everything was right in the world again – right enough anyway for her to think maybe it wasn't early enough for bed, but early enough to check out the bed.

We loaded the dogs into the cab of the truck, and climbed into the back, and she was all over me with an anguished fury.

I was lying there in the bed of the truck as she rode and ground me – cowgirl, reverse cowgirl, back to cowgirl – all while hanging onto the ribs of the truck cab and rocking the whole thing back and forth, the gas sloshing around in the tank beneath us. The dogs up front started barking, and Jill started riding me harder and moaning with what felt like her whole body – when I suddenly realized the truck would not be rocking so much back and forth on its gear if I'd put the emergency brake on, oh shit! – but Jill was riding me harder still and finally coming. And she just kept coming, her moans turning into muffled screams; and the dogs were barking louder and louder; and all I could think about was the pitch of the lot and the RVs parked everywhere downhill from us...and then all I could see was the truck jumping gear and rolling down across the lot, Kettle and Sampson sitting up in either seat like driver and passenger barking warnings at the RVs scattered around the lot, and me trying to jump out of the back of the truck, completely naked and fully erect, scrambling to get into the cab...but I couldn't move and couldn't stop her, every ounce of strength she uses to run up and ski down mountains drilling me into the truck bed until she finally let out one last long muffled scream, and then an explosion of sobs. The swaying of the truck slowed, and she collapsed into a pile on top of me. I burst out laughing and she burst out laughing, and the truck finally stopped moving.

As fast as I dared, I untangled myself and pulled my pants on, then jumped out and put the emergency brake on, then the rest of my clothes.

On that trip, I learned that whatever ills a mountain will not cure, some good raucous sex will. Because right after that, Jill was cool Jill again. No more family talk, no more future talk, just us hanging out, futzing with our gear and playing with the dogs. We smoked another bowl, and pulled out a hacky sack, kicking it around while the distant ridge changed color.

It was early enough to sober up, hydrate, and fall asleep in the back of the truck, right after another color wheel of a sunset . . .

. . . and crawl out again at 3 AM and gear up for the climb.

The trail was steep, straight up through woods smothered in darkness. The hike up with a pack loaded with skis and gear – up through what felt like the vertical tunnel of our headlamps – was eerie, like I was still asleep and dreaming.

Jill led, her skis bushwhacking the unseen tree branches into mine, the jangle of the dogs' tags disappearing into the darkness ahead. I had brought alpine skis instead of my snowboard for the long push back out, and they were riding higher out of my pack than I was used to; they kept tangling up in the branches and pulling me backwards. Jill had her telemark skis, half the weight of alpines, and flew up the trail when it finally opened up and had to wait for me a couple times – just like I'm waiting for Tom again, even with this rock in my pack today.

But our timing was perfect. We emerged from the last of the trees onto a vast shadow of alpine tundra wiped clean of trees by avalanches. All the stars were gone, but for two at opposite ends of the sky. And just as we made the ridgeline, amber light was wafting up from the far end of the void, the first streaks of dawn breaking like electric pulses on a perfect flat black line of eastern desert plain.

A few more hours of following the ridgeline, up and down across snowfields, and up and down a heartbreaker of a false summit, finally, after the dogs had made it back and forth between the two several times...

Summit!

And there we were.

We dropped our heavy packs, sat down with a couple of grunts, and looked down at the whole of Taos Valley. It was an open, outstretched hand, its peaks like little fingers, a mesh of muddy green trails running down into the open palm, except for the fat cruisers they groomed all winter, now a crisscross of coffee-colored snow.

Up there on top of Wheeler at the start of summer, the snow was tired too, a field of frozen pellets coated with the maroon-haze of snow algae, undisturbed by avalanche, wind, or ski, baking in the great petri dish of a protected snowfield at altitude.

"You were right," she said, looking out at yet another collision of gravity and geology and color that is at once perfectly random and somehow perfectly ordered. "This fixes everything."

We downed some water and calories, and then I took my usual summit pictures, finishing with one of Jill of course, propped on her poles and looking awkward and annoyed, the dogs wagging their tails and looking the exact opposite of awkward and annoyed.

We packed up quickly, as the sun was climbing enough to hit and soften the snow on our west face route down, increasing the risk of a wet slab avalanche by the minute. We checked our beacons and clipped our probes and avy shovels to the outsides of our packs, then we clicked into our skis and turned toward the great drop.

"Betties first," I gestured down the face with my pole.

Even with her sunglasses on, I could see her roll her eyes sideways, then smile. "If you insist."

She dropped in, straight down the fall-line, her turns a perfect up and down rhythm of half circles.

The moment she got to the bottom, she swept around into a big turning stop and gave the all-clear wave. The dogs looked at me and I nodded for them to go ahead. They shot straight down, two maybe three paces before landing on their bellies and going into a full slide, their paws out like cowcatchers on old trains. Sampson barked and screamed with joy, trying to eat the snow flying up into his open mouth. Kettle, at maybe half his weight, lagged far behind, scrambling to catch him.

I took one last look around at the wild landforms and colors running off in every direction, and was suddenly aware of the Presence, beaming at me from without and within. I beamed back, managed to choke out a "thank you" through the lump in my throat, and dropped in.

With the first turn, the whole world melted away – exactly like I imagine it does for an addict when the needle goes in. That do-or-die moment on the lip of a big mountain, hours into the backcountry and away from any help, is the fix for everything, and maybe only because it could be the end of everything. Six hours of climbing with all that weight on our backs, for the rush of maybe three dozen slow, slushy turns to the bottom, and it was worth every step. Because the summit is always worth it. And whatever turns you can pull from the top is just a bonus.

And maybe Tom will get a little taste of that today, back here in Colorado today, as it looks like we just might make the summit of Notch Mountain.

I get to the upper ridge and wait, a few hundred feet from the summit, where I can see clear down the trail.

Tom is trudging up, staring at the trail, one foot in front of the other. He has obviously discovered the aerobic box, and he's staying right in its center.

I look across the basin: the weather is holding. The clouds are big white cotton balls floating by, their giant shadows drifting across the tundra, shape-shifting with the terrain.

Tom finally catches up, looking winded, sunburned, and elated. His face is relaxed, open like I've never seen it after all those years together, all the airplane miles, weekends in the office, all-night document jams in one of our hotel rooms, deals blown, deals signed. He looks like a happy, tired little boy, just like the rest of us here on top, no matter how many times we come back.

He doesn't say anything and neither do I. We just turn, hike the last few hundred feet and...

Summit!

And here we are.

The top of Notch Mountain is nothing spectacular, compared to something like Wheeler Peak anyway; but it still has the grandeur, power, and peace of any good-sized mountain up here. And I can tell from the look on Tom's face that it's the most spectacular view he's ever seen under his own steam. That is a big part of the power of any of these mountains: it's not how it looks on the outside, but how it feels on the inside, after you've earned your way up.

Tom turns and smiles at me, and we high-five – the first time that has happened since the day we stood on the trading floor at Brownstone, and heard our company go public. Then he looks at me funny, lifts his arms, and we actually hug – the first time that has EVER happened.

We sit on the summit in silence and eat the lunch I've packed, watching the giant cloud shadows move across the basin and across the front of the Mount of the Holy Cross at the other end. (Holy Cross is the Fourteener with a horizontal band of snow cutting across the vertical snow-filled couloir, hence its name and the alpine lake, named the "Bowl of Tears," draining the whole thing.)

"Wow," Tom says, looking over at the mountain. "I had no idea I'd be going to church today."

"Every day is church up here," I say.

He chuckles, something else I've never heard him do in all these years. "I don't doubt that," he says.

We finish the rest of our lunch in silence, and sit back on the rocks.

"You know, Jack," he finally says. "I never told you I was sorry."

"Sorry? For what?"

"For caving on you. For caving on everybody. For selling the company when things got a little too hairy."

"Oh well," I shrug him off. "Water under the bridge."

"Yeah, but still. We had such a crazy ride with the stock, the market was screwed up, the dotcom insanity was just getting started. And I panicked. I pussed out. And we all got hosed on the valuation and our equity. Especially you guys."

I've seen people come apart on top of mountains, but this is still shocking. I never expected to hear anything like that from him – not that I needed to – but I suppose it's still good to hear. It was a crushing disappointment, after all that work, all those plans, all the money on paper, most of which went down the drain, with so little to show for all those grueling years beyond one great resume entry and million little business war stories.

"Well ok, Tom. Thanks for saying that."

"And thank YOU for bringing me up here. I know this is just another walk in the park for you. But this is the biggest thing I've ever done out in nature."

"No such thing as a walk in the park up here," I say. "This *is* a big deal."

"If you say so," he says, standing awkwardly, clearly wiped out from the hike. "Now get me the hell off this mountain, before I have a heart attack and die."

On our way down, the rock in my pack actually slows me down enough so that Tom gets a little ahead of me, running ahead like a kid. With the rock, it's some work to keep up and I don't want to push it, or I could mess up my knees, ankles, lower back. His mood is ecstatic, and mine suddenly pensive, a little sour even.

Because I can't stop thinking about Jill again, and that perfect climb and ski in New Mexico.

I wish it had ended right then and there, right before she left for New Zealand – even though we've had so many great times since. Now, after two years of more mountains, half a dozen stops and starts, some perfect climbs and some terrible wipeouts, she and I have become like what Mary says about family: it's complicated. So I guess I really do have to call her back. Being an asshole to her didn't work, avoiding her isn't working, and I really do have to deal with it once and for all.

I never wanted her getting attached to me, but she did. So I guess it turns out she was in the hot zone the whole time, and I simply didn't recognize it. Not only did I want to avoid the hot zone altogether, I'd blown up my entire marriage over it. I'd spent years watching people make really dumb decisions because of their kids: taking or keeping jobs way beneath them; moving to the wretched blandness of the suburbs; grinding away entire years of their precious life at soccer practice, Disney world, the goddamn mall.

Nearly everybody who worked with me fell into the same black hole just south or north of turning 30: the dull pre-occupation and obsessive dissection of every detail of their pregnancy; then the sleep deprived drudgery of dealing with their infants; then the exhausting, routinized robotics of living under the command-and-control of their kids, their brains finally and sufficiently shrunken to think that the dumb shit coming out of their kids' mouths was actually clever. And for all they carp and complain about all the inconveniences of that first kid, many have another one, and some another after that. Complete insanity.

I always had – and will always have – exactly zero interest in any of that. I don't know why I don't. I just know. And for all that Jill has going on, for as hot, smart, and cool as she is / was / is, and for all the great adventures we've had together, she is headed straight into that nightmare, just like the rest of them.

I knew that the moment I saw her after she got back from New Zealand. It had been five months since we'd met at Ullar's, shacked up in the Treehouse, climbed Wheeler and all those mountains, and four months since she'd run off. And suddenly, she was back. But we were hanging out, just trying to be regular friends – until we took that stupid Ecstasy.

I had run into her the first morning of the blues festival in Telluride. Five thousand people were camped out in Town Park, and of course she and a couple of her Betty friends ended up all of two tents over from Danny and me.

At first, she was tentative and weird. I avoided her eyes and acted like I didn't care, mostly because I felt guilty. (I'd not returned any of her emails from down there, which went from glowing and expansive about the landscape to curt and hurt.) But then we went for what was supposed to be a little walk to clear the air, which turned into a long hike up the canyon at the end of town.

We didn't clear the air at all, only thickened it with tension, longing, sadness, confusion; and Kettle clung to me and nosed my hand, rather than his usual back and forth up the trail ahead.

Back at their camp after the hike – for just one quick beer I told her, before running off to find Danny – Jill pulled out the same little packet her aunt had given her a few months before.

"Remember these?"

I'd never done Ecstasy, but had heard from Danny that it was a "cleansing psychological trip" and from Aaron that it was harmless and fun – "Unless," he added because he always has to add the medical detail, "you go crazy with thirst, drown yourself with water, and die from heart failure due to lack of salt."

Thinking that a cleansing psychological trip might be perfect for the awkward occasion with Jill, I chased the pill with beer and waited for it to make me feel better, or numb, or at least different.

Just about the time I was convinced the whole Ecstasy thing was bullshit – that it was all one big collective placebo effect – I noticed something about Jill's eyes I'd never seen before. They were more intensely emerald green than I'd ever seen before, more intensely *everything* than anyone's eyes I'd ever seen before. And I noticed how they matched the last of the summer green in the aspens climbing up the hillside beyond her, changing with autumn to sunflower gold. They were flickering, alive, hungry and present, like her whole body, her whole being. I noticed – for the first time really *noticed* – that all of her youth and strength were not passing through her like the seasons on some mountain, but were emanating from within; that she would always be young and strong inside; and that I was the one passing through her, aging backwards toward childhood, infancy, helplessness, and I needed her.

She smiled and blushed and took my hand and led me through the maze of tents to the stage. Then we danced, for hours I think, to one swaggering, howling, scorching blues band after another, the sunlight splashing off all those red rocks and sunflower gold aspens.

The next thing I remember after that: another walk with Kettle and the two other dogs in the back of her truck, all around Telluride, in and out of streets lined with little gingerbread houses painted maroon, lemon, turquoise, and tangerine. We stopped by the house of some friend of hers, down at the end of a muddy street, a woman with a new baby and a yard full of chickens.

I stood there holding Kettle and the other dogs by their leashes while Jill held and fussed over that tiny baby, the chickens pecking all around her feet, the mountains welling up from town suddenly ablaze with sunset. Jill's eyes were still bigger and even more emerald, wide open now, like rivers of green and gold light. And all I could feel was a massive, impending loss, and how it connected to a lifetime of losses I could never measure or even name. My heart exploded, and I felt like crying, and I saw that she was crying.

So I knocked it off.

I knew it was just the Ecstasy, and knew it would wear off, eventually anyway, so I just made myself not feel it. I guess.

I almost run into Tom, stopped in the middle of the trail. He is gulping his water so fast it's running down the sides of his face.

I pull up, drop my pack with a thud, and fish out my own water.

We don't talk, just look out at the view a minute. Then he starts down, and I hoist my heavy pack and follow.

A few hours ago, I thought I'd have to talk him up, off, or down this mountain, but now he's leading, same as it ever was. And that's fine with me, because I want to go back to Jill and Telluride, to that walk around town with Jill and the dogs at sunset.

The Ecstasy was still swirling everything into a nice warm soup, and the words just spilled out of me.

"Don't worry," I said. "You'll have a baby of your own, you know, because you're going to make some cool young guy really happy someday. You'll see! And I'll be right there to say I-told-you-so at your wedding. I'll even bust out the guitar and play a song for you guys. And if you think that sounds weird, well, it won't be, or shouldn't be. Because I won't really be your ex-boyfriend, because I was never really your boyfriend anyway, so I'll be more like your older brother."

"And *that's* not supposed to sound weird?"

We said nothing the rest of the way back to festival.

That night, we all hung out and got a little drunk, and Jill and Danny traded places, Jill sleeping with me in his tent, and him sleeping with whatever Betty was in Jill's tent, two spots away.

For the next week or so, Jill was back in The Treehouse with me; we climbed a few more peaks; and then she was gone again, off to Alaska this time.

Which was fine with me. It was my first full winter in Dudeville, and I certainly did not want to be tied down, not that I would or could run wild like Danny. Every week, I was off snowboarding somewhere new, learning to telemark ski, going on my first hut trip. I was chasing powder, not women, still running the other way, from my marriage and from Amy the Rebound Girl. And I was a guy in Dudeville, so the odds were not good, and I was fine to be just more odd goods.

That winter, my monogamy by default still intact, I was supposed to go up to Alaska to ride with Jill. But somewhere between buying the tickets and the date of departure, Amy the Rebound Girl had shown up in Dudeville ("just taking a long weekend in the mountains after a Denver business trip" she said. *Yeah, sure*, I thought.)

It was a completely pointless go-round that ended with her cussing out the mountains on my refrigerator. It was a stupid waste of time, and unexpectedly mediocre sex after Jill. But it did pre-empt Alaska – how could I go up there without telling Jill about it? – a handy little rationalization for not going that Danny concocted, even though I know he didn't really believe it mattered any more than I did.

In the days leading up to what was supposed to be my departure, Jill sent a couple emails and left a couple voicemails, each a little more exasperated about my silence.

I finally sort of replied. But I don't remember anything else because I was making myself forget all of it. Besides, there was all that amazing fresh, dumping all over Colorado.

That first winter of powder day after powder day passed soon enough, like all things pegged to the earth's seasons do. And I had stopped thinking about Jill entirely when another one of those bizarre coincidences occurred, when I was snowshoeing alone up a mountain outside Aspen.

It was a tough training hike in a dense warm fog, a long slog through what felt like a dreamscape. And just as I was coming down off the summit, I heard the rattle of familiar dog tags – and out of the fog pops Kettle, right up the trail and straight to me.

I was bent down, petting and hugging him as he licked at my face, wondering who Jill had left him with and who would be coming up the trail any minute, when I saw two figures, both tall and thin, one pushing hard up the trail and stopping to wait for the other. It was Jill, and an older woman who looked just like her.

She just stared at me.

"Hi," I said.

"Hi," she said, her expression cold and wary. "This is my mother."

"Hi there," her mother said, smiling at me and reaching to shake my hand. "I'm –"

"This is Jack," Jill cut her off.

"Oh," her mother said, her smile and hand gone.

A few hours later, when I was well off the mountain and back in range, a voicemail popped up on my cell phone: "Dude. There just aren't enough Fourteeners in this state."

When I called Jill back on my way into town, she said that she and her mother were visiting friends for a few days, and it would be good to "clear the air," she said. "Again."

A few minutes later, we were sitting at what used to be the only good dive bar in Aspen. Over a couple of beers, she told me – while pretending to watch the ski porn on the TV over the bar but really looking at me sideways – that there was a guy on the crew up in Alaska who was really cool, and who dug her; that she was tempted and they had even made out a little; but, she said, she kept thinking about me, wrapping it up with, "and – well – never mind."

"Ok," I said. "Cool."

"Cool?" she looked over at me, her face suddenly hot and angry, like I'd just slapped her face. "What does that mean?"

"I don't know. What do you want it to mean?"

Then she made one of those bizarre leaps of logic that only a woman can make, because it is completely random and yet they think it completely rational.

"So that means you've been hooking up with someone?"

"Huh?"

"Why else would it be cool then?"

"I don't think I'm following you here."

"So you HAVEN'T hooked up with anyone."

"No," I lied.

"You're lying," she said.

"Ok, so yes. I did. But it didn't mean anything."

I told her all about it, reminding her who Amy the Rebound Girl was, that I'd been with her many times before, and that she didn't matter to me – even if I had no reason to put any of it that way.

"But it didn't – you know – it wasn't any good," I said, staring into my beer for the right thing to say. "Not like – you know –"

"Whatever, dude," she took a long swallow of her own beer. "I'm just a damn fool."

Then she laid into me with the whole bio about this guy on the crew, who suddenly had a name: Brandon.

"He's a really nice, thoughtful, attentive guy."

Which didn't bother me.

"And he goes HUGE."

Which did bother me.

"And he's really nothing like you."

Which made me want to burst out laughing. But I was only half listening, until I turned and saw that her eyes were hard, like she wanted to say something really hurtful to me. I think I knew what that might be, so I said it for her: "And he's your age."

"What?" she blinked. "Yeah, I guess he's my age. So what?"

Three beers in, and she kept at me, like she was trying to make me jealous or something. So I told her what I'd told her in Telluride – "I'd be psyched to play guitar at your wedding" – and that just pissed her off even more.

And that was that, or so I thought. And to show that we could be friends – Dudeville being a small town after all – we went skiing the next day.

Aspen Mountain was still open, that winter I'd learned to telemark, and I knew Jill was great at it. And part of me – the part that makes about much sense as her at the bar that day – wanted to show it off to her.

On that first run, we flew down the mountain in long, graceful telemark turns, like two dancers in a ballet on snow, our turns mirroring each other.

On our way up for the next run, on the upper chairlift, she told me that she and Brandon had actually broken up.

"He was too young" she said right before we got to the top, then shot off down the mountain without waiting.

I skied after her as fast as I could go, our turns in perfect sync to a sudden rush of violins and cellos, another ballet as our turns paralleled each other, fitted into each other's like the long matching curves of our legs entwined in bed after sex. We skied at full speed, around clumps of blue groomer tourists, all the way to the bottom.

We were both winded and waited at the bottom for the guys behind us to go ahead on the next chair, without saying it – wanting a chair to ourselves, I guess – and we weren't twenty feet off the ground, sitting jammed up against each other in the middle of the big chair when we both lunged at the same time, a long, deep, wet familiar kiss.

Then another blazing run to the bottom.

And then, everything else back at my hotel room in Aspen, until an awkward dinner that night with her mother.

The memory of that day, with all those unexpected turns on the mountain and turns in the big hotel bed, makes everything in my body ache.

Or maybe it's just that big rock in my backpack. Which I need to ditch before I get to the bottom, or I'll have to drive away with it.

Tom is having a big day and feeling all full of himself about this hike, and I suppose he should, coming from sea level. But he doesn't need to see me unload my ballast. As an effective CEO, he knew how to use unspoken shame to get us to carry as big a load as we could, not burdening him when we didn't have to, and to use the same shame to pass that load on down the line. Even up here, I suppose, old work habits die hard, so with no one down the line from me, I'll just carry the rock myself and let him have his big day in his new hiking boots.

I look down the trail for a place to unload it and see people straggling up, in blue jeans, which means we are almost back to the trailhead. Tom is well down ahead of me now, out of sight, so I stop and pull the rock out of my pack.

But all I can think about is Aspen and Jill: our perfect doubled telemark turns; her body, as strong and present and giving as ever, and all that howling sex in what became our hotel room for the next couple days; the awkward dinner that first night with her mother. She turned out to be maybe ten years older than me, and a little eccentric but mostly cool, even if she was blushing that night more than Jill did. Her mother was a big idealistic kid actually, which made her seem in some strange way like the youngest of the three of us when we talked about politics, the world, the people around us. By the end of that first dinner, when I got to know her mother a little, another piece about Jill had fallen into place, and she saw that I saw it fall into place.

Then she was gone again.

This time, it was for spring guiding season up in the Tetons, and work on another film. But this time, she wasn't halfway around the world; she was just a wide open 12-hour drive from Dudeville, north and west into Wyoming.

I am snapped back by noise up ahead, laughter and voices and engines.

The trailhead already, and Tom is sitting up on the boulder next to my truck. His boots and socks are off, and his feet are rubbed raw and red, his socks actually bloody in a few places.

"Wow," I say, dropping my pack and pulling out my first aid kit. "Your feet took that much of a beating, huh?"

"No big deal," he says. "They'll heal."

I open the kit and pull out the Betadyne and special bandages for blown blisters. "They will. But they're going to hurt like hell for awhile."

"Yeah, well," he says, taking the Betadyne from me. "It'll still be worth it."

Tom may already be reconsidering that calculation by about now.

I just watched him stumble to his feet at the dinner table back in Vail, almost yelping with the pain. But at least he is off his feet for the night, helped back to their room by Mary and trailed by Sidney – leaving Becky and me alone and finally able to catch up, free of them and her husband, over drinks in the hotel bar.

"Good old Tom," she says, before our drinks even arrive. "The work stuff never changes. He makes this deal with these guys, promises them all this crap, and we can't deliver on any of it."

"Oh well," I say, because it is what I always used to say, when I knew she was counting on me as a good friend not to tell her what I really thought because she wouldn't act on it anyway. "The devil you know."

"So what's wrong with me?" she says more than asks. It's the rhetorical refrain from a hundred conversations we've had in bars after dinner, or a day in the office, or at the ragged end of some conference. "Why do I think he will ever change?"

"Seems to me like he's changed a little," I say. "Up on the mountain today, he was actually really humble. And not his bullshit, manipulative version of humble – but really grateful."

She chuckles. "Maybe it was the altitude."

"Maybe. Or maybe it was the hike. It was pretty tough going, if you're not used to it."

"You mean he didn't hire a couple Sherpas to carry him up there?"

We both laugh and drink in silence for a minute.

"Actually," I finally say, "when we were up there on the summit, I think all the beauty, or the scale, or something – really got to him."

She looked at me, not with her usual skeptical impatience over what I've just said about Tom or anything else, but with what I learned years ago was her poker face. "What do you mean?"

"I mean – that's what happens up there. People are moved by the scale and the beauty. Would you believe that he actually apologized to me?"

"Apologized? For what?"

"For selling the company when he did."

"Huh," she says, still with the poker face, then a long thoughtful sip of her drink. "I guess he has changed. A little. Part of him anyway." She turns to me and searches my face. "You don't know, do you?"

"Know about what?"

"About their new kid."

"What about their new kid?"

"Top secret, personal NDA shit, ok? Like the old days?"

"Top secret personal NDA shit, got it."

"Their little boy is autistic. Tom really wanted a son, and they tried for years and years and nothing. And just about the time they gave up, Mary gets pregnant. And the kid is really badly – that way. With the autism. Completely blank, completely withdrawn."

I had no idea. "Oh shit," is all I can think to say.

"Oh shit is right. Tom was in denial about it for the first couple years, then went through a pretty dark period. But now they're dealing with it."

"Huh," I say, "that sort of explains it."

"I don't think he wants you to know, or he would have said something by now. Especially today, up on the mountain. He's still – you know – proud, tough, private, all that crap."

"Yes, I know."

"But it's really broken his heart. And before that, who knew he even had one."

After we sign the check, Becky and I say goodnight in the lobby with a quick hug.

I watch her hurry up the stairs to her room, but I am wide awake and do not feel like going back to mine, so I go outside for a walk.

The moon is up over the mountains, just a sliver past full tonight, and still blinding with its bright white light.

I try to soak in the silent radiance of its old familiar company. But the streets of Vail are filled with people, couples mostly, a few with older kids running around screaming, flirting, teasing, goofing on each other.

I walk the long loop back through the buzzing village to the hotel, back to my cold, empty room, maybe just a little glad for the company of all those silly kids and complicated families.

Arizona Highways

It is still the tail-end of mud season, early June, and already fire season is upon us. We're in the third year of a drought; we didn't have any big spring snow dumps; and the temps picked up early and shot up fast. Under the relentless Colorado sun and wind, the trees are turning into standing timber and the forest floor into a tinderbox of dried needles and kindling.

One of the three wildfires burning out of control in the state is only twelve miles down the canyon from Dudeville, its blue haze drifting up the canyon and choking the air in town. It affects the dogs first: they wheeze, cough, hang their heads and suck at the air, their tails drooping and gaits all flat. Tyler's Deputy Dog and Scott's Tashi sit out in front of Ullar's, panting, and Maggie's Buddy mopes in the back, under the table furthest from the door. Then it starts to affect the rest of us.

I'm sitting at the bar with Tyler and Scott, Maggie across from us reading *High Country News* – all of us coughing and rubbing our eyes and bitching like we've suddenly got allergies – when Aaron bursts in and asks who wants to hit the road with him for a few days.

He's heading all the way down to Flagstaff, he says, far from the fires, to hang with an old friend, do some climbing on the way, and get the hell out of the smoke. Tyler and Scott both have to stay in town and work, but I don't, because, well, I don't have to do anything (except call Jill back, which I'm long past doing).

An hour later, Aaron and I are up at The Treehouse, where the blue smoke is even thicker than down in town, pulling gear; an hour after that, we're driving south and west as fast as we can. Aaron has a few days off and wants to visit a geologist friend from the Wilderness Restoration Project, and we have to head straight there to time it with this guy's time off. But we can run up and down an obscure peak or two on the way back, he says, or maybe go up and down the Grand Canyon, if the timing and weather hold.

In Aaron's old but impeccably kept truck – no stickers except the one for Mountain Rescue – we drive down out of the smoky haze, and shoot under a clear, soaring, perfect blue sky west. It will be a solid eight hours of mountain, then canyon, then desert, as the gray granite pyramids and ridges of the Rockies collapse and tumble into red rock desert.

On the drive, Aaron runs through a wild collection of CDs: jazz, blues, Brazilian, chamber, klezmer, Cuban, all music you'd never hear with this landscape, and it occurs to me after a few hours of this mismatched music that I've never known where and how he discovered all this stuff.

"My father played jazz," he tells me, scratching at that perfectly trimmed black beard. "Back in Boston. And jazz is connected to almost everything. So I grew up listening to almost everything."

"He played professionally?"

"He could have," Aaron says. "But he was a first-generation Jew. And it was all about getting on your feet back then. Med school, kids, money. So that's what you did. Jazz? No."

We drive a full five minutes in silence, the squawk and snicker of some jazzy klezmer unspooling with the pink hoodoos of the high desert, before Aaron finally says, mostly to himself, "Not a lot of jazz after that for Dad. Just work, lots of work."

"That sucks," I say, well aware of the problem. I dreamed the music dream myself for a few desperate years between high school and reality, before work, bills and my wife's illness – before life without money, insurance, family, credentials or connections – finally broke me. "He just stopped playing? After med school? Or after you guys were born?"

"Mostly." He thinks about it a minute. "He'd pull the horn out for holidays, a *Bar Mitzvah*, somebody's wedding. But not really."

"Does he play at all now?"

Aaron shrugs. "He's been playing a little bit the past few years, since he started winding down at the hospital."

He swaps out the CD for another, this one straight-ahead blues.

"So my friend down in Flagstaff," he says, clearly wanting to change the subject.

"Wesley?"

"Yes, Wesley. He's a geologist. I met him on the survey project. He's incredibly smart and practical, but he's kind of intense. And a little harsh."

"Ok."

He smiles over at me. "A little bit like you, actually."

"Thanks," I say. "I guess."

For the next hour, Aaron tells me about the months they'd spent working together: charting ten thousand or so of the millions of acres of federal land that Bill Clinton had designated as new wilderness in his last few weeks of office. Wesley led the crew scurrying to document whole swaths of southern Utah, every heap of rusting metal, mining scar and abandoned shack, so that once set aside, it could never be shitted on again. They'd been "out in the middle of absolutely nowhere for weeks," he says, "and now it would all stay out in the middle of absolutely nowhere, forever."

It sounded like a damn good way to spend your middle 20s, I thought, and wondered if Aaron missed it.

"What was the coolest thing you remember from all of that? What little detail you'd read about in *Mountain Gazette* or *Outside*?"

"The sidewinder trails," he says without having to think about it. "We would sleep out in the open in the sand dunes. And in the morning, there were sidewinder trails going right by our sleeping bags. Long slithering lines through the sand. And then – WHAM!" he bangs the steering wheel, his big brown eyes growing even bigger, focused and fixated on it. "A blast-spot in the sand where they struck their prey – a mouse, a little lizard – and then just more slither lines. Off into the brush. Gone."

"Cool," I say.

"Totally cool."

Cool indeed, I think: predator, prey, wham, gone. Like so much else in the world, but without the handshakes and bullshit. With all the niceties and ceremony and pretending cleared away, just like everything else in the desert.

We drive past the last of the hoodoos, their gold and purple cone-tops collapsing into sand, then out onto an ocean of red rock. There are waves of it, rock the color of old brick or half-dried blood rolling out in every direction, to the silhouettes of mountain ranges so far off in every direction that they hover, more dream than earth, hazy ridgelines against the vast blue bowl of sky.

I am psyched to be going back. The Arizona desert was my first encounter with the actual west, and Flagstaff was the way-station, the place I thought I would end up when I finally broke free and fled this way, before my feet locked into my first snowboard and whisked me off to Colorado. While travelling all over for work, I'd been back and forth to Flagstaff half a dozen times, made a couple friends there, watched the last of my marriage crumble away there, even tagged a serious Betty there – great sex, horrible mistake, but did I mention great sex? – all while still stuck Back East and wanting to get Out West for good.

Flagstaff was my first Dudeville: a mountain college town full of kids who, instead of growing up, somehow managed to grow sideways, into river rats, climbing dirtbags, backcountry skiers, and desert freaks, oblivious to the rest of the world and contemptuous only of the hordes of tourists who sped through town in their RVs and rental cars to "do" the Grand Canyon.

There's tourist junk all along the edges of town, but at its core, Flagstaff is a postcard you can't send home, because everything spools out in 360 degrees on all three axes, and it feels like it breathes. It's a mountain town at the edge of a great wooded rim, where the red rock desert of the Colorado Plateau drops down into the saguaro-studded eruptions of the Sonoran Desert, a short pause for what's actually civil about civilization in a collision of landmasses. With two snow-capped peaks buffeting it from the north, Flagstaff is the earth-scaled staff for the entire sprawl of the desert, and the flag itself is a great big blue sheet of sky.

It was down off that rim, in the eruption of saguaro desert a few hours south of Flagstaff, surrounded in every direction by searing purple desert mountains, where the eyes of my eyes were opened. It was where, for the first time in 33 years, I saw the raw and rugged majesty of the earth behind the thin, ragged curtain of the world. The special effects were not unlike those out on this empty highway today: the air fluttered with the most intense heat I'd ever felt in my life, turning the surface of the road to liquid silver. In the Arizona desert, everything I'd known about scale, size, temperature and distance was obliterated.

But at least I had a good excuse: until then, I had never been on vacation, not as a kid, and not with my wife as we ground our way through school and onto our feet. I was 19 years old before I'd seen an ocean, 28 before I'd been west of the Appalachians, and then only for work, back and forth across the country a hundred times in airplanes over the next five years. But it was always work, tied to an office, meeting, phones, conference calls, then back to the airport. And my discovery of the desert at age 33 was a complete accident: the meeting was cancelled because of somebody's family emergency, two hours before my plane landed.

Normally I would have just turned around, a windfall of time back in the office. But as we were landing, I looked out the plane at all that psychedelic red rock – at what looked like it had been plucked out of some old western and thrown down in pieces into the middle of a sprawling city – and I realized I could just get a rental car and drive out there. My wife would probably be happy for me, I thought, and no one back at work would know. Just check in with my assistant, clean out my voicemail every time I got near a pay phone, and take a day for myself. So I rented a car and found a sporting goods store and bought my first ever hiking boots and hat, and headed out into the desert.

The Arizona desert reduced everything to nothing, the nothing I'd always known was the architectural underpinning of the stupid little world. Those great piles of rock, scarred towers of cactus, and slashes of empty canyon all calibrated reality and obliterated the nasty smallness of people clinging to their pathetic little share of it. Which worked just fine for me.

I drove up and over mountain ranges the color of copper and chocolate, mountains raw and jagged as human skin but on a super-enlarged scale. The desert was like the very skin of the earth revealed, and the rental car was a tiny mite, crawling across its utter indifference, waiting for the slap of a hand so enormous none of us would ever see it coming. It was an entire planet apart from all the crummy little towns, city streets, and suburban sprawl Back East. Until that first trip in the desert, I'd known only work and traffic and crowds, bars, restaurants, campuses and office buildings full of ants, manufactured landscapes, human blight. I'd flown back and forth to the west coast by then, but it was just more of the same: newer, cleaner, and shinier maybe, but the same machine on the other coast in sandstone instead of brick. Until that trip, I had never been in the actual American West – and it demolished a world I'd always known was badly in need of it. The desert was all rock, and looming cactus pock-marked by lightning strikes, and harsh trees that stood in a tangle of spiky branches to defy the sun and wind tearing at them. It was raw, harsh, stubborn, and achingly alive in its own terrible way; and it triggered my awareness of all those things inside myself – all the things I'd always felt but had never seen expressed on the outside – as I beheld it all for the first time.

Halfway between Phoenix and Flagstaff, I hiked out into an enormous stand of saguaro cactus, and discovered that they look nothing like they do in books or movies or on TV. They are not human-sized; they tower over you. They don't grow straight, with neat bundles of three or four arms; they are enormous, raucous, living creatures, jabbed and blackened and still towering overhead, their arms reaching at odd angles toward the sky. They dance, swagger, supplicate, praise. There was a whole forest of them, presiding over a sea of sagebrush and prickly pear and crumbling rock, reducing me to a tiny speck of defenseless flesh.

I kept hiking, maybe ten minutes up along a steep ridge ringing a narrow canyon. When I reached the top and gazed down into the canyon, I became aware for the first time in decades of the same, precise, impossible thing I'd always been aware of while deep into the woods by myself as a kid: the sensation beyond all sensation. Because there it was, exactly the same as it ever was, in the middle of the desert.

The Presence.

The sensation loomed up from the unseen bottom of the canyon, in waves of heat and dust like a pulsing rhythm, as if it had originated in the very center of the earth. It also seemed to well up from inside my body at the same time, and felt like it might be moisture, but there was no moisture, dust but there was no wind, fire but there were no flames.

I've since come to understand that a big part of the Presence is the simple presence of time. That even the oldest trees and the grand cycle of nature are ephemera, and a four-billion-year-old earth doesn't give a shit that we're here. That all of us busy little ants have been crapping all over the planet for just a moment and will soon be gone, and all the horrific damage we did will heal over a moment later. That this random wonder of an earth is waiting, for just another breath or two, before shrugging all of us off with a great explosion.

And yet, and yet, while all of that is true – the Presence is also the exact same idea walked backwards in the opposite direction, from infinity to infinitesimility. This is something I can sense in the space between breaths, or maybe between heartbeats, when I get quiet enough out there on the very edge of that eternal consciousness: the Presence sits at the exact midpoint between the two, and it is something that speaks, in a voice that sounds like my own voice but isn't.

Because on that very first hike on my very first day in the desert, this is what it said to me: *This is all there is, backwards and forwards and beyond all time. I am, I have always been, and I will always be.*

And in my own voice, I filled in the rest: *I, by contrast, am just a pale smudge of flesh walking by, and that's just fine.*

And that was the rock bottom truth to everything, revealed in the hard rock desert.

There was a simple purity in all these garish earth tones, in all this desolation, in the absolute indifference of the desert. It was the first true thing I'd ever heard, read, seen or thought in 33 years; the one hard fact behind all the shadows of civilization with its manufactured realities, contrivances, detritus.

Back east after that first trip, the desert loomed larger still in my imagination; it took over my daydreams and became my principal reality, confirming once and for all that everything else in the world really was manufactured, a pathetic falsehood and unworthy distraction. I started reading everything I could find about the desert: from Edward Abbey's anarchic tales of desert rats, to Terry Tempest Williams' poems of the bittersweet dissolution of the self into all that pastel-painted infinity, to the surreal, color-saturated photo spreads of *Arizona Highways* magazine.

And I went into full business mode to contrive a reason and a way to get back to Arizona as soon as I could. What kind of deals could we do in Phoenix? Who did I know out here? That's when I remembered John, a guy from a couple of my engineering classes, who had landed a job at the observatory in Flagstaff.

Back in school, John had been a gruff, quiet, intense guy, with ice blue eyes and a big blond beard, dressed in flannel shirts and hiking boots in every class, as if he were already out here. He was always in a hurry to get through the labs so he could go off and do whatever he was doing outdoors; I was always in a hurry to get back to work. We both hated everything about where we lived, and so we went from lab partners in chemistry to friends of convenience and shared contempt. I figured I'd never see him again after our last final exam.

But he was right there with a "yeah cool, let's hang" – like he was almost expecting my call out of nowhere – when I tracked him down via phone at the observatory on my follow-up visit to Arizona.

"I can knock off work early tomorrow," he said, "and we can go hang-gliding out in the volcanoes. You wanna go hang-gliding?"

Hang-gliding? Out in the volcanoes??? Hell yes, I did!

I drove straight up from Phoenix as fast as I could and found a hotel.

A few hours later, I met up with John and Roger in downtown Flagstaff, in a truck coated with red dust and two long shafts of tightly bundled fabric on top, sticking off either end.

It wasn't clear what was happening as I got into the jump seat of the truck, until we were speeding out of town and John asked me if I was ok driving a stick in four-wheel drive on some tough roads.

"Sure, no problem," I said, not wanting to be that lame-ass dude from Back East. And I figured that I'd be able to figure it out, as the town fell away behind us and the desert opened up.

A dozen or so miles north of Flagstaff, the road turned to dirt and shot across a plateau that would have gone on forever, but for a horizon line spiked and stumped with a line of brown and purple cones, all with broken tops, the remnants of old volcanoes.

Twenty minutes later, we were driving straight up the side of the biggest of the cones when John points at the road and says, "Look! A tarantula! Cool!" as we pulled up onto the rim.

I stumbled out of the truck (though still aware of where my feet were landing) to behold the most surreal landscape I'd ever seen. Back toward Flagstaff were those snow-capped peaks, surrounded by great waves of aspen and pine forest; running in the other three directions, it was all red and pink desert plateau, studded with cinder cones like giant bubbles rising to burst in an earth stew. The horizons were all red dust, to the north sinking ever so slightly toward what John said was the Grand Canyon.

I stood on top, overwhelmed by it all, my knees shaking and stomach a little queasy, while John and Roger pulled their hang-gliders off the truck. I was torn between gaping at the view and watching them assemble two long, skinny piles of nylon, pole and wire into actual flying machines, in rapid, practiced, efficient silence.

The sun was just starting to sink toward the west, turning the dust that way orange, when Roger pulled on a helmet and climbed into his hang-glider, and John came over and handed me the keys to the truck.

"See that wind sock down there?"

I looked down where he was pointing and could barely make out what looked like a tiny orange pennant, hanging limply from a stick.

"Uh-huh."

"See you down there. Not sure how long we'll be up. Depends on the thermals. But we have to be down by dark. Cool to hang out up here for awhile, if you want," he said, looking at the camera in my hand. "But start down before the sun sets, or the drive will be a little freaky."

A minute later, he was strapped into his hang-glider, a taut and simple geometry of flight: white and purple neon sail, skinny aluminum poles, a dozen wires tight as guitar strings. Then he and Roger turned toward the lip of the cone, and without ceremony or even a word, both sprinted straight at it.

Pop!

Pop!

Their sails filled with air and their hang-gliders took flight, straight off the top of the cone, a burst of running energy exploding, silently, into the energy of flight. I'd watched them take maybe half a dozen sprinting steps; and then with two quick popping sounds, all was utter quiet as their feet left the rock and their sails lifted them into the air.

They flew straight out from the edge, then tipped away from each other in perfect symmetry, and started sinking, but for just a moment. But then, gaining speed as if motorized, they both started rising – up, up, up, turning, then up some more – into rising columns of air.

In a few minutes they were soaring straight overhead, as high above the top of that volcanic cinder cone as the cone was above the plateau.

I stood there watching them fly past the sun, circling like birds of prey, and my legs went weak again, my heart pounding, my eyes welling with tears. It was the most amazing thing I'd ever watched anyone do. And all I could do was wonder: how can anyone who tastes that kind of freedom and release ever be able to come back to earth, deal with all the petty nuisances of the world, ever care about anything else?

I scrambled back to the truck and grabbed my camera, and took pictures as fast as I could through my tears. The plateau was turning a burnt orange, the cones and peaks to the west darkening, the ones to the east suddenly bright orange with the sinking sun. The scenery was turning even more psychedelic and surreal, even more impossible for me to believe was really there, let alone there for me to try to internalize.

I blew through my one roll of film in a few minutes, wiped away my tears, and sat down on the rocks to catch my breath.

But before I could, the Presence was suddenly welling up all around me, that same small, still voice I'd heard down in the desert canyon on the previous trip, saying *Look how beautiful the real world is, always was, always will be.*

I gave up trying to control the tears, sank back on the rock, and had a good long cry.

When it finally passed, I looked straight up into the bottomless bowl of the sky, and studied its hard eggshell blue, softening at the edges into dusky violet. My usually bored and busy imagination was washed blank, my breath quiet. And for maybe the first time ever, that awful motor – the one deep within that never turns off, except in the first few moments right after sex – stopped. The constant, low-frequency vibration and noise was suddenly gone, the steady tension and reservoir of anger built up after 33 years of fear, work and worry suddenly flushed from my body, drained from behind my head, heart and gut, down into the porous rocks of that old volcano.

Then I remembered the tarantula.

I sat up, looked around, and pulled myself to my feet, laughing aloud.

I heard tiny voices just off the ragged edge of the wind, and looked up and saw John and Roger cross overhead, fabric and metallic specks against the sky. They were flying in parallel, two perfect arcs around from the east, back toward the west, picking up speed and growing larger as they zoomed by.

The sun was working its way west, igniting the dust cloud horizon into red-orange fire, and John and Roger turned into silhouettes against all that color.

I climbed into the truck slowly, no longer worried about how nasty the drive might be, or about anything.

I wanted only to stay there on top of that old volcano, on what suddenly felt like a sacred altar, a randomly holy place I had never imagined could exist and now never wanted to leave. All was Presence, all was eternal and real, and I was all in it.

I drove as slowly as I could down the side of the volcano, the truck scratching and sliding on the coarse gravel. The two ruts that were the road eventually wound their way to the plateau, and came within a few dozen feet of the wind sock, which turned out to be a large streaming tube of orange on a ten-foot pole.

A minute later, I stood out leaning on the truck, watching them swing wide of the landing zone, then turn and swoop in like birds, dropping soundlessly to the earth. John was first, his hang-glider pausing in the air as his feet came within inches of the ground, then puffed out and deposited him squarely on both feet. Roger came in with the same exact landing, soundless and utterly competent, from midair to terra firma in a breath.

I want THAT, I told myself. *I want ALL of that. I want to be able to throw myself off a mountain, leave the earth at will, and come back at will.*

I want to fly, under no power but gravity's and my own. And I will, I remember thinking.

The engine backs off, and John Coltrane is breaking out of the top of a solo, like he too is leaving the earth, hanging onto his sax, flying away.

I look up from the red-orange moonscape of my imaginings to the red-orange moonscape all around us, this one interrupted by a wire fence and line of weather-beaten stalls, squatting empty next to the side of the road. Must be a town up ahead.

Aaron slows the truck, and we pull in for gas and the usual "water on, water off," somewhere in the middle of absolutely nowhere. We are out in the middle of the Navajo reservation, marked to the south by the two peaks outside Flagstaff thrusting up out of the dusty plateau, hovering like an island on a vast earth-sea.

There is no cell phone coverage out here of course, so Aaron goes to the pay phone to check voicemails and see where exactly we are supposed to meet Wesley over at the Canyon.

"Glad I checked," he says when he comes back. "He's done with work already and heading back into Flag. We'll meet him down there."

"He works at the Canyon?"

"Yeah. Some survey thing."

"Cool."

"Actually, I think it sucks. Some dumb little project, he says, to keep his crew going. Not sure what exactly. He didn't say a lot about it when we talked last week."

We start down the road, the sad smudge of a town behind us in thirty seconds.

"You've been to the Canyon before, right?"

"Three times," I say, with an exuberant pride I'd normally find annoying in myself or anyone else.

"Been to the bottom?"

"Oh yeah."

"Cool."

We drive in silence for a few minutes, watching dozens of red, orange and purple hoodoos the size of five story buildings shoot past. Then Aaron pops in another CD, some dank Chicago blues this time, and I think back to the Grand Canyon.

Three times to the Canyon, yes. But the second time, with my ex-wife, doesn't really count, but that could be the fault of the first time I went.

During that first trip to Flagstaff, over beers and dinner with John and Shelley, his intense Betty wife – interrogating them both about hang-gliding, climbing, kayaking, canyoneering, and everything else about their lives in that magnificent place – I got the desert adventure bug in a bad way. I kept reading about it, I worked out even harder in whatever free time I had Back East, and I went a little gear crazy. All I could think about in every spare moment were John and Shelley's stories: about trekking the Canyon, rim-to-rim every fall, and end-to-end twice (so far); about running the Colorado River at its bottom every five years in kayaks (permits permitting); about running the trail top to bottom and back to the top every spring.

I will get to the bottom myself, I decided, even if I lived 2,250 miles away and was otherwise consumed with work, business travel, and business school. My marriage was dead, my wife consumed with her own work and business travel, and I would find a way, even if I had to contrive one.

It took several months, but I was able to do exactly that – a big important work thing in Phoenix, conveniently scheduled for a Friday. I would drive up to Flagstaff that afternoon, and the next morning on to the Canyon, where I would hike to the bottom and back to the top that same day. So what if all the guidebooks said not to attempt to do that, that I would fail, hurt myself, require rescue, maybe even die; that would actually be a fine way to die, I decided after reading through them one more time.

By then, at age 33, I was done being told that I couldn't.

I had grown up being told all about everything I would never be able to do by the two wrecks who were my parents, and well into my 20s, I still believed them. The odds would always be against me because I was their kid and would surely fail because that's just how life was for us. It was years before I realized it was just their own misery talking: all the booze, illnesses, lost jobs, anger and frustration, and decade after decade of constant, gnawing economic fear. For all those years I'd unwittingly succumbed to their darkness, without once questioning it, because what other data did I have? To that darkness, I'd surrendered my youth, my hunger for an education, my dreams about music, everything.

But then my wife and I found our feet, slowly, and started our steep climb out of that darkness. And it was filled with hard labor, and many disappointments, and despair. But it would not be forever. We would lift each other up, and find a way out. Which is why what I'd pulled off by 33, with Tom and Becky and the business in the intense years since, had me readily convinced that guidebooks – like all those shallow, facile business books – were written for the tourists. For the 40th percentile. For the masses who hadn't ever had to climb out of the same hell.

So bullshit on the guidebooks, I thought. *I am going to the bottom of the Grand Canyon, and I am hiking back out, in one day, or I will gladly die trying.*

I was a big, headstrong kid from a crappy little town Back East who'd just fallen madly in love with the desert. And hiking the Grand Canyon in exactly the way I was told I couldn't was going all the way with her; it was the great big vagina of the world, right there at the end of the road, and I was going all the way to the very bottom.

That's what I thought anyway when I confronted the same warning on the signs at the trailhead: *Do not attempt to hike to the bottom of the Grand Canyon and back in one day people! People have died!!!*

I read it with Darwinian swagger: it was just another challenge, just another self-defeating, catastrophizing sneer from my coward of a father, who had hiked nowhere, risked nothing, accomplished nothing, and ridiculed (not to their faces of course) everyone who ever did. So I checked the gear and water in my new backpack, and started down the trail just as the sun was breaking the rim to the east.

And I did make it to the bottom, which was like making it to the summit of a vast red, pink, purple, gold hallucination of a mountain range, turned inside out. And I did make it back in one day. And I did not die.

But it wasn't exactly pretty on the way back up and out. During those last few eternal hours, dragging my dehydrated and hypoglycemic body back up toward that faraway rim in the thinning air and failing light, I did come to realize just how easy it would be to die down there. The trailhead sign may have been for the masses, for the 40th percentile; but I would lose three toenails and not be able to walk upright for three days. Not that I cared. My limp was a badge of defiant courage, and I couldn't stop smiling for days beyond that.

I'd crawled back to the Canyon's rim after dark, too exhausted even to think about camping with all my new gear, but I got lucky: one of the historic hotels on the rim had a cancellation. After I got settled into a cozy, air-conditioned room, I limped back out to the rim and listened to the sweetest music I'd ever heard, to the cavernous sound of absolute emptiness, the great void welling up from the darkened Canyon. It was the exact same thing I'd sensed looming out of the side canyon down in the saguaros: a wordlessness beyond everything without and within; a simple, pure presence, the same one in those runaway woods when I was kid, the same Presence always waiting for me somewhere above treeline.

I went back to the Grand Canyon a few months later with my wife. I wanted to show her what I'd been talking about all those months; to open her eyes (maybe, hopefully) to its vast grandeur; to see if we could salvage our marriage (maybe, hopefully) by figuring out the baby thing, which was all she wanted to talk about, now that we'd clawed our way onto economic dry ground. If that was her agenda, mine was to see if we could maybe combine it with my sudden and obsessive preoccupation with fleeing all those horrible memories Back East and moving Out West.

After another contrived business reason to be in Phoenix, on a Friday of course, she joined me that night from her own business trip to LA and we drove straight to the Grand Canyon.

"Sure, Jack," she'd said, as if trying to convince herself. "I mean – everybody wants to see the Grand Canyon."

The next morning, after a painfully long breakfast, I practically ran down the trail ahead of her.

We weren't further than maybe the sixth or seventh switchback, the heat more horrific than I'd remembered, the trail even drier and dustier in the almost-summer, when I realized what a stupid and obvious mistake I'd made.

My wife picked her way carefully down the trail, wary of the little cactus, the muleshit, the acrid, noxious puddles of piss from the mules who had carried the tourists down ahead of us.

I kept waiting for her at the end of each switchback.

She slowed the pace, and when she finally caught up, she said words that to this day still sink to the bottom of my chest like a rock: "So how much farther do you really want to go?"

"Lots farther than this," I said, pretending not to hear what she was really saying. "It's really beautiful when it opens up down there."

But she just sighed and said, "ok."

We'd had the same thing happen every time we went for a hike or I'd tried to get her out on skis. She liked the idea, but was put off by the task, like she was both afraid of and contemptuous of it, if only because she was ordinarily given to fear about nothing in life. So I tried not to push, as excited as I was to be back in that place that had come to consume my imagination that year. After nearly a decade of marriage, she could tell how disappointed I was, so she responded by pushing herself a little further down the trail, then getting angry at herself for her hesitancy, then getting angry at me, and then sulking.

It was on that bitterly disappointing morning that I realized my expectations weren't out of whack, just out of whack with her. On those first few trips up a ski hill or out into the woods, I would see all these couples – just like John and Shelley, the dude into it, the wife or girlfriend all Bettied out and just as into it – flying down the trail together. And I would think: *Why can't I have that? Why only this old workhorse of a marriage, something I never really felt like I got to choose in the first place? We made it out of hell, and right over there is heaven, all the things we never got to do when we were young. Why can't we just make this ours now, after all the hell we went through to get here?*

Down into the Canyon again, the earth torn open into that chaos of color, I wanted to run and disappear, like the little kid I never was.

But my wife kept stopping, her hands backward on her hips, looking around, pale, sweaty, bewildered. "Yes," she said, her voice frail. "It's beautiful. But you really want to keep going? It's just more of the same thing – all the way down, right?"

"That's alright," I said, turning back up the trail, still a little kid but a suddenly pouty one. "It's just more of the same."

An hour later, we were hiking back up the rim, past dozens of pairs of hikers, chatting and laughing their way down. I waited for her every few switchbacks, trying to ignore the voice in my head. It wasn't that of the Presence, just my own sad, disappointed voice, and all it said was: *Your marriage is dead. Why are you pretending?*

We split up four months later.

The first place I went – thanks to some good luck with work – was back to Flagstaff and the Grand Canyon. I wanted to be certain that my imagination, memory and need hadn't conspired to turn it into something more wild and hallucinatory and transformative than it really was, just some escapist fantasy from the dull, stressful grind of my life Back East. I was compelled to verify that the desert and the canyon and all that rock was Reality, and that my marriage and my wife – and all her talk about buying a bigger house with a great big yard and filling it with kids – was Illusion, a false, conformist construct and complete waste of my precious little time on earth. I had to prove that I really could move west someday; that I could run up and down the Canyon but this time without losing toenails or falling apart near the top; that I could learn to climb rocks, ski off the top of those peaks outside Flagstaff, jump off a volcano and fly. I had to believe that people like me could live like John and Shelley instead of like all the breeders Back East – that I too could grow old without ever having to grow up.

That good luck with work was a corporate retreat down in Phoenix with our biggest clients. I finessed the entire schedule of side meetings so that when everyone was done with the actual work part and hanging around the pool and golf course with their families, I could run north with my new tent and camp down *in* the Canyon this time.

This time, without having to worry about turning right around and climbing up without dying – with hours just to sit by the banks of the Colorado and look up – the bottom of the Grand Canyon crushed me, obliterated my sense of scale, reduced me to a puddle of sobs. It felt like the very top and bottom of the world at the same time, both the scariest and safest place on the planet, more real than anything could ever be while at the same time completely impossible. It was the pure, raw jumble of dreams, unedited by waking consciousness, because I had never been more awake in my life.

I sat next to that mighty emerald river – the same liquid green as Jill's eyes, now that I think about it – and watched the whole wild rush of it turn from green to gold to black as the sun dropped behind the rim. The towering red canyon walls turned rose, then magenta, purple and black, and a river of stars emerged to flow between those great walls, matching the great curve of the canyon and river at my feet.

It did not cool off with nightfall. The red rock walls radiated heat all night, in waves, like an oven left open with the gas going on and off. I slept outside my tent, on top of my sleeping bag.

I woke up in the middle of the night to a half moon bathing everything in milky light. I hiked over to the river, and looked up at those great walls in the moonlight, a gathering of robed giants standing in rough ranks, unmoving and imperturbable, the black glass of the river gurgling along their feet. The Presence was everywhere, practically screaming at me to be heard over the churn of the river, howling up and down that billion-year-old watercourse as if in a dream. It felt, within and without, like the dream of time itself, but this dream was Real. Everything that was supposed to be Real, back up on the rim, back in the stupid little world, was not Real; it was all a sham, the worst dream of all, a nightmare.

Unfortunately, my permit to camp down in the dream that was Real was good for only one night.

The next morning, I packed and hiked back up to the reality that was the bad dream and the stupid little world. It was a grueling climb out with all that weight on my back, every step three times the effort of the hike down, but it was the best exhaustion of my life. That afternoon, I drove east along the Canyon, as fast as I could from the crowds on the rim. I found a nearly deserted campground, and pitched my tent a hundred feet from the empty rim.

The temperature dropped with the sun, suddenly and fiercely, and I stayed up as long as I could stand the cold. But I eventually succumbed and crawled into my tent, which turned out to be too big for one shivering person in the freezing cold.

The temperature kept dropping, and I pulled on every layer I had, shivering in my tent until my sleeping bag warmed up.

The wild swings in temperature, from canyon bottom to canyon rim – just a few miles away as the crow flies – shocked me at first and then delighted me: they gave real human measure to the earth, and made me laugh to myself in my flimsy, freezing nylon nest. That morning, I had started up the trail under a screaming sun, hot, sweaty, and at the edge of dehydration and heat stroke; that night, I was curled up in fetal position in my tent under an ocean of stars, freezing, at the edge of dehydration and hypothermia.

Toward the end of the night, finally warm, I crawled out in all my layers to take a piss with my headlamp, the waning moon already come and gone.

I walked out to the rim without having to turn on my headlamp, the trail perfectly visible in the starlight. I looked up at the stars, ten thousand of them washing out any constellations: they winked in different colors, some tiny flecks, some hard rivets; some popped and faded in and out of my vision, others seemingly close enough to reach out and touch. I looked down and saw the silver ribbon of the river flashing below, a billion years of the earth exposed and brushed with starlight. Then I looked back up and saw 15 billion more years of the universe exposed.

And yet, "Here I am," I said to myself.

Here you are, the Presence answered, like harmony notes in my head.

"I am alive."

You ARE alive.

Then I started to shiver again, suddenly intensely conscious of my tenuousness, of one simple fact: I may be alive, but at the same time I am nothing more than a cluster of living cells clinging to this tiny margin between the scorching heat of day and killing frost of night. I have been slipped at random into this margin in something arbitrarily marked 1998, on an earth shaped four billion years ago in a cosmos formed 15 billion years ago. And yet, I breathe, my lungs work, my heart works, everything else works; but without the cover of technology, it all works only between 35 and 120 degrees Fahrenheit, which barely registers on the Kelvin scale, which is nothing.

And yet and yet, *Nothing? Really? You and ten billion other people who were honed over 100,000 years by evolution, all just wiggling around within this tiny little margin of time, temperature, space and geology? Random? Really?*

"So maybe not random. But religion is all bullshit, just a bunch of nasty stories to keep people terrified and towing the line. So where does that leave me?"

That just leaves you wondering. Can wondering not be a religion too? Standing here in your impossible little margin, running all your numbers about the utter preposterous randomness of your existence, acknowledging that you are here do that? Perhaps that is your religion and if so, every place you are standing to behold your impossible little margin is a holy place. And in each one of those places, when you say "Here I Am," are you not also acknowledging a listener?

And there may have been more to it, but the cold overtook me so I picked my way back down the shadowy trail and crawled into my tent.

I burrowed down deep into my sleeping bag, and knew there and then that no matter how lonely I might ever get, I was never actually alone inside this tiny margin of time and space and geology. I had been to the bottom and the top of the crust of the earth; and tomorrow I would wake up, everything would still work, and randomness could not possibly have produced any of it.

I'm rattled by the roar of the truck as it backs off.

I look up, and Aaron is slowing down for a red light at a crossroads in the middle of sun-blasted desert. It is the exact middle of the day, the whole of the rock all around us blanched with harsh light, everything seeming to vibrate with the heat.

Aaron switches from the last blues CD to the radio. Nothing on FM so he goes to AM, and it is all static and native drumming and a DJ speaking in the muted sing-song of what must be Navajo.

We turn left toward Flagstaff, the plateau climbing out of pink and white hoodoos washed with sunlight, toward the peaks sharpening on the horizon. To their east, I make out the first faint hints of volcanic cinder cones.

Two hours later, we pull into Flagstaff, and go straight to the Flag Brewery to meet Wesley.

He is sitting at the end of the bar, with a bird's nest of a beard and mop of curls and thick glasses that magnify his eyes, reading a beaten up copy of *Scientific American*. His face is burnt ruddy brown with sun and wind, his barrel chest too big for his old *New Riders of the Purple*

Sage t-shirt. He wears beaten Carhartts and even more beaten Tevas, his knobby feet stained the same brick red and brown as the desert.

While he and Aaron catch up, my eyes wander around the place, and I realize that I've been here before. It was the last time I'd met up with John and Shelley and they'd broken the news to me about Lying Bitch April, so I hadn't noticed that it was the kind of bar I could only dream about Back East – and the kind I'd come to haunt every day when I finally made it west.

The Flag Brewery is Ullar's South, another frumpy locals' refuge just off the main drag of a high desert Dudeville. Ullar's old skis on the wall have been swapped out for a giant topo map of Arizona, and there are different local beers on tap. But the rest was exactly the same: sun-drenched, windburnt guys and Betties hunched over the bar, planning their next adventure; dogs coming and going with dirty tennis balls in their mouths and old bandanas around their necks; the air filled with dust and the wandering guitars of a Grateful Dead jam; a mountain bike race up on one TV and surfing up on the other.

"You've been down?"

I look back and realize Wesley is talking to me.

"Down the Canyon?" I ask. "A couple times."

"So you know how powerful it is. What it's really about."

"Yes."

"Good," he says, "because I don't want to sound like a dick."

He continues telling Aaron about his current project, a National Parks Users Survey, where they stake out the Grand Canyon and follow tourists to see exactly what they actually do in the parks.

"We're geared up for anything," he says. "The scientific method all the way, man. We're randomly assigned to follow people. Study what they do, record their use-patterns, down to every detail."

Aaron is rapt. "And?"

Wesley snorts into his beer. "Most people just drive on by, as you know. Hit a few turnouts, take a few pictures. Some ride the mules down, some hike a little. And every now and then, someone will go huge, all the way down. But I've never drawn one of course, thanks to sample size."

"You're kidding," Aaron says. "That's what the agency's funding? Instead of more wilderness preservation?"

"That's right," he says. "Some yuppie shit about R-O-I on new wilderness versus new parks. Or the 'business case'" – he does the air-quotes, with another snort – "for the parks. Tourism as an 'export good' and all this other corporate crap."

"Export good?" Aaron asks.

I know exactly what that means, but don't say anything.

"Yes," Wesley says, "because almost 75% of multi-day park visitors are foreigners."

"No shit," Aaron and I say in unison.

"Europeans and Asians visit America," he says and takes a long swallow of beer. "Americans visit Disneyland."

Aaron takes a long swallow of his own beer, then says, "I don't think I really want to know, but what are the findings so far?"

"No," Wesley laughs bitterly. "You really don't want to know."

We both stare at him, waiting for it, and I can tell that there is part of him – maybe the gall bladder? – that can't wait to tell us.

"Well – the results are preliminary. But the average is 832 paces per visitor, and 3.2 turnouts per vehicle. For 7.4 minutes each."

"Ha!" Aaron almost spits out his beer.

"And the two most popular items visitors buy?" Wesley lets it dangle in the air a moment. "The first is an ice cream cone. The second?"

He looks at me like I would have any idea.

"Cigarettes?" I ask.

"Condoms?" Aaron asks.

He lets it dangle another moment.

"Hookers?" I ask.

"That's funny," he says. "Nope." He takes a long swallow of beer. "A t-shirt that says 'I Hiked the Grand Canyon.'"

Aaron hangs his head with a groan. "Seriously."

"Seriously."

"Wow."

The three of us drink in silence a minute and then they go back to talking about people they know.

All I can think is that my wife may well have bought one of those fricking t-shirts, for the maybe 1,000 steps she took down into the Canyon with me on that awful visit. The ice cream cones? No surprise there. Danny always likes to joke – whenever we're pulling into a crowded trailhead – about the invisible line just up the trail where the tourists will turn around, and the trail will be all ours. ("The ice cream cone line," he calls it, which crosses the trail at approximately the distance from the minivan or rental car that it takes to eat one.)

"So what else is new," Wesley says, breaking a suddenly moody silence when our burgers arrive. "You guys still going for that first snowboard descent – the one you were all about the last time I was in Columbine?"

"That's the plan," Aaron says. "The Lady. The snowpack is already a little thin because of the drought, but it looks like she'll hold for around Labor Day."

"You on that one?" he says to me.

"Oh yeah."

"Labor Day should be good," he says. "Zero slide risk."

"That's right," Aaron says.

Suddenly, an odd silence looms up between them, part of some discussion they're having but not having. I have no idea what it might be, but it's obviously not my business. We eat in silence, watching the bike race on TV.

Wesley looks up and says "Hey" to two sunburnt women who come in with backpacks and a dog. Then he turns to us with a mischievous grin and lowers his voice. "You guys in play? I know they are."

Aaron looks down and says nothing.

"I am," I say. "I guess."

He turns to Aaron. "And you? Still no, huh?"

"Ah, you know," Aaron says.

Wesley studies him a minute. "I know you hate talking about it," he finally says. "But I was thinking about all that when – uh – when the news broke about Alex Lowe."

I still don't know what they're talking about, but I know that it has to be related to some awful mountaineering accident. Two years ago, one of the greatest mountaineers ever, Alex Lowe, was killed on what would have been yet another first ascent of an impossible mountain, Shishapangma in the Himalayas. What was weird about it though: he wasn't killed on the climb itself, but by an avalanche that swept down on him during a routine hike outside base camp with fellow climbing great Conrad Anker and another guy. Anker ran one way and survived, and Lowe and the other guy ran the other way and didn't – even though Anker seems to have dropped off the face of the earth since then as well.

"That was a totally different thing," Aaron says, bristling in a way I've never seen before, and jumps off his barstool. "It was a slide down onto a scouting hike and wasn't triggered by an earthquake, so maybe they should've sited better. And at least one of them survived."

Wesley and I watch him push his way through the suddenly crowded bar, toward the men's room in the back.

"Seven years later," Wesley turns back to me, shaking his head. "Shit, man – I loved Angie too. Not like he did of course. But seven years? You think he would've moved on by now."

I have no idea what he's talking about.

"You don't know what I'm talking about, do you?"

"No."

He shakes his head and stares at the bar. "Aaron," he sighs. "And you're his road trip and climbing buddy?" He looks at me, shakes his head again. "When did you guys meet?"

"Three winters ago, back in Vermont."

"Huh. That's Aaron. I guess."

"What?"

"Well, man – it's not like it's a secret or anything. It's just a little weird that he doesn't even talk about it with a guy like you."

"Talk about what?"

"His high school and college sweetheart, from back in Boston. They were together from like – eleventh grade. Until she bought it up in Alaska. On a trip they were on, the summer after we all graduated from UVM."

I am stunned. "No shit."

"No shit." He takes a long swallow of beer, grimaces, puts it down, and maps the movement of the terrain with his hands over the bar as he describes it. "It was an avalanche, triggered by an earthquake. Nothing they could have seen coming. Way down in the middle of a snowfield, where they'd set up camp. Aaron and two guys were back at camp sorting gear, and Angie and another gal and guy were just doing a little scouting hike. Out on what Aaron says was a totally consolidated and stable glacier. No danger, no need for roping in, all good. And then there's this little earthquake, barely perceptible Aaron says. A typical Alaska tremor. But it takes a chunk off the cornice on the cirque way up the valley, and triggers this huge avalanche. The whole thing sweeps the glacier. Missed their camp by maybe 500 feet."

"Wow," I say, because what else can I say. "That sucks."

"What sucks even more – they recovered the other two bodies from the avy debris, but they never found Angie's body. The quake opened up several big crevasses at the bottom end of the glacier, well short of the moraine. They found the other gal and the guy. But they never found her. She's still out there. Buried God knows how deep down some crevasse. And – you know –"

And yes I do know: no one ever will find her body, because it has been torn to pieces by the grinding of the crevasse, under the slow, steady movement of the glacier. Gravity, pressure, time.

"Fuckin' A, man," I say, guzzling the last quarter of my beer. "That sucks."

"Fuckin' A, man," he says, guzzling the last of his just as Aaron walks up.

He stands between us, looking from Wesley to me, then back to Wesley.

"What?"

"Nothing," Wesley says, staring at the bar.

"You guys were just talking about Angie, weren't you?"

And what can I say? What can anyone say?

"I'm sorry, man," I say, finally.

"Yeah, well," Aaron says, climbing onto his barstool. "I'm sorry too."

"Hey," Wesley calls over to the bartender. "Could we get some more beers?"

We down the last round quickly, in awkward silence, and head out.

We follow Wesley in his truck – bumpersticker *You! Out of the Gene Pool!* – to his house. The next day, Wesley has to be all the way back up to the Canyon, and Aaron and I are hiking up Humphreys Peak – the highest point in Arizona and the tip of the old volcano that stands watch over Flagstaff (!!!) – so we want to crash early.

There is even more awkward silence in the truck as Aaron and I drive out of the suddenly empty streets of Flagstaff and the cab goes dark.

He has to know I'm curious about the nastiest mountaineering accident – I assume, imagine, hope? – he's ever been directly involved with. Maybe this is why he never told me about it – because it was the ugliest and most personal? – despite the dozens of accidents we have discussed and deconstructed, down to detailed decision trees of what-ifs and an ever-growing punch list of remember-this'es and not-next-times. Maybe this is why, now that I think about it, when the news about Alex Lowe swept through Dudeville, Aaron never once discussed it. Maybe tomorrow on the hike, which I hear is an easy one – when we are back in our comfort zone of big trees, altitude and exercise – because it has to be gnawing at him, after Wesley brought it out from a place where Aaron obviously never goes. How can it not? It is certainly gnawing at me, the whole wretched unknown horror of it.

We spend the rest of the evening in Wesley's garage, where he shows us a workbench crowded with new climbing hardware he is modifying for soft rock walls. He and Aaron debate the merits of various metals, shapes, teeth, holds, knots, and whatnots, and I am fascinated by all of it.

Just as we are wrapping up, Aaron's cell phone buzzes in his pocket.

"That's weird," he says, looking at the little blue screen. "It's a voicemail from my parents' number. It's almost midnight back there."

"We have cell service out here," Wesley says. "They must have just left it."

He goes in the house to check the voicemail.

Wesley and I keep futzing with the gear, absently, silently, because we're really both listening to Aaron on the phone, or at least to his hushed, worried tone.

A few minutes later, he comes back into the room, his face drained of color and eyes fixed elsewhere with worry.

"My mother's in the hospital. I have to fly to Boston. Tomorrow."

The next morning, under a perfect blue sky, I drop Aaron off in his truck at the little airport outside Flagstaff. He will fly from here to Phoenix, then on to Boston, and I will drive his truck and our gear back to Dudeville.

The airport, tucked in a pine forest spice-ripening with the day's heat, is tiny, and I can wait right outside the chain-link fence surrounding the airfield until it's time for Aaron to board.

He forces a wave as he hurries across the tarmac.

I wave back and watch him climb carefully into the little airplane, his head down and shoulders hunched. It seems like something is seriously wrong, worse than he wants to let on – his mother has had pneumonia and it's not getting better and they're admitting her for stronger antibiotics and tests – but he didn't say exactly what it might be.

And I didn't exactly ask, I think, as I stand next to the fence and watch half a dozen people board the plane behind Aaron.

As the plane taxis, turns, and takes off, I have no idea if Aaron is sitting where he can see me. But I wave the whole time anyway, my arm aching as the plane lifts off the runway and climbs into a desert sky so bottomlessly blue it makes my eyes hurt.

I drive back into Flagstaff, Humphreys Peak watching patiently and peacefully over the still quiet little town. The weather is perfect, and there is still plenty of time to hike it; but it's probably not the best idea to tackle a big new mountain alone, at least not if I can find someone to hike it with me. Tomorrow is Saturday and maybe John and Shelley will be free; either way, I can just camp somewhere or get a room, maybe go down to Sedona for the freak show or just hang around Flag, find a good book, drink coffee, get loaded, ogle the Betties.

I turn on my cell phone and call John's work number.

His voicemail greeting says he is on vacation, so I don't leave a message and call their home number.

Their answering machine picks up right away. It's Shelley's voice, her tone weary, off, none of the usual glee.

"Greetings, friends. This is Shelley. I'm not here right now, so leave a message. And if you're looking for John, his new home number is . . ."

John and Shelley have split up? When?? Why???

I am stunned. They were *the* rip-it-up couple – completely alive in nature, alive together, just like – well, just like Aaron and Angie, I suppose, had been, for all those years, all those years ago.

I leave a message for Shelley, starting off with an awkward "Sorry" and letting her know I'm in town and my cell number. Then, without thinking about it, I finish the message with the real-time decision to say screw it and hike up Humphreys Peak.

"Heading up there by myself," I say, "from what looks like the main trailhead at the ski area." Because it's always good to let someone know where you are going, from which trailhead and when, even if you barely know them.

And what other decision could I make? I'm as eager as I was on that very first trip to Flagstaff to see it all from up there: the red rock ocean of the Colorado Plateau; the crack in the earth off to the north, where it all drops into the Canyon; and most of all, the volcanic cinder cones northeast of town, from afar and a little above, where I crewed for John and Roger on that first visit more than three years ago, and finally got to hang-glide with John and Shelley when I came back a few months after that.

I drive Aaron's truck back through Flag, out the other end of town, and halfway up the mountain to the ghost town of the local ski area in summer. The parking lot is empty but for another truck, a car, and a jeep at the sign for the trailhead.

I gear up, study the map, then start across the empty ski slope on a well-marked trail that leads into a forest thick with ponderosa pine and stands of aspen. It's an easy trail, shaded and empty, but for sun dapples and birdsong.

And as hard as I try, all the way up, I cannot stop thinking about John and Shelley – when and why and what happened? – and every time I try, they keep landing back on Aaron and this Angie. Who was she? Why didn't he ever mention her on all those hikes and climbs and chairlift rides, at all those trailhead camps, during all those miles on the road? Especially after the news about Alex Lowe, which he and Danny and Tyler and I all talked about for weeks? Despite what he said at the bar yesterday, it does sound like the same kind of accident – but he doesn't once mention it? Is this why Aaron never has a girlfriend, never hits on anyone, never shows any interest in all the women who hit on him in Ullar's, or out on the slopes when he's in his red ski patrol parka?

The more I think about it, the more upset I get and the faster I pump my way up the gentle trail, until I am winded, way out of the aerobic box, frustrated, a little angry, out of breath, shit!

I stop, grab some water, try to catch my breath.

To the north, the desert spills out of breaks in the aspen forest. It looks like a floodplain of dark red in the morning light, like the earth has been bleeding slowly and forever – like we are all bleeding, slowly, all the time, and not really saying anything about it.

I catch my breath and start back up the trail, and go right back to John and Shelley. You guys split up? Why?? What happened???

When I went back to hike the Grand Canyon that first time, I met up with them for dinner the next night. I got there early and found a table so they would not see me limping and wincing with two toenails coming off, the big one still bleeding and oozing into my sneaker. (What a proud wreck I was!)

With his first sip of beer, John said he felt bad that I didn't get to hang-glide with him, only watch and drive and ask a hundred questions about it – so would I want to fly tandem with him the next day?

"Fuck yeah!" I said, but just as quickly had to admit, "but I can barely walk."

"Ha!" he laughed. "You don't need to be able to walk to fly."

The next day, John and Shelley and I drove up that same volcanic cinder cone, in the same truck, with the big tandem hang-glider on top. He showed me how to put it together, just like we were in an engineering lab back in school – except the lab was on top of the world in a screaming wind, and getting the experiment wrong could kill us both.

I could barely pay attention, could barely put pin through hole or cable to pin for all the adrenaline surging through me, the views all around me, the cold howl of the wind.

A few minutes later, with Shelley holding the hang-glider steady in the wind, I climbed into the second harness next to John. His eyes ran once more over every strap, cable and joint. Then I felt him lift the enormous wing into the fist of the wind; felt the whole thing find its loft point and all the cables pull taut as guitar strings; felt everything in my body go taut. And then, as if from faraway, from inside a dream I can't decide if I want to stop or not, I heard him yell "RUN!" and we sprinted in unison straight at the edge of the cone, the wind exploding up into the sail, my legs still running and kicking at the air as my entire weight and John's weight and the weight of everything left the ground...

...and we were up, up, up, the curved lip of black and red cinders pulling away from my kicking boots...

...and there it all was beneath me, pulling away as if in binoculars turned backwards: the full circle of the cone, breached in one place by an old lava flow; Shelley waving and shrinking; the truck a muddy little toy; the entirety of a little volcano in a stand of little volcanoes, all of it coming into view, the great pink earth turning to dust, the Grand Canyon a gully off to the north.

"Pretty cool, huh?" John screamed over the wind.

I tried to scream back *Yes!!!* but my voice was clamped shut with adrenaline, awe, terror, joy, and release, with the sudden and absolute release of what felt like the correction and perfection of everything good or bad that had ever happened to me. I couldn't stop the rush of emotion, the flood of tears plastering my cheeks, and I was afraid to let go of the bar and wipe them off, but they blew off with the wind as fast they came.

I glanced over at John, self-conscious about the tears running down and flying off my face.

He laughed and screamed over the howl, "Don't worry! That happens to everybody the first time!"

A minute into the flight, as John steered the hang-glider out over the open plateau and found a thermal, the air went suddenly quiet. We flew higher and everything below turned to pinkish brown dust.

I gulped at the weirdly calm air to catch my breath and looked out at the horizon, past the last of the cinder cones, past the high points of the same broken volcano peak I am hiking on right now.

From all the way up there, we could see out past the great gash of the Grand Canyon in the long bending blur of the desert, and I wanted to say what I've heard so many people say, looking out the window of an airplane or standing next to the ocean: "Oh look – you can see the curve of the earth!"

Except that I know you can't actually see the curve of the earth from anywhere near there or any of those other places: it would require at least four or five arc degrees for the eye to pick up the actual curve of a sphere with a circumference of nearly 25,000 miles, which means you'd have to be looking at a horizon of 300 or more miles, which you can do from the Space Shuttle but not from any airplane, or beach, or hang-glider, no matter how fricking cool it looks and feels at the time. I know the sensation of seeing "the curve of the earth" is just a perception bound to error by human anatomy, by the rotation of a round skull sitting in the curving plane of a cervical vertebral space.

But to hell with all that, I decided in that moment. It looked and felt so fricking cool up there, liberated from the earth, from gravity, from everything, that I just said screw it, and let it be true, and surrendered to the curve of the earth and sheer wonder of it all.

Which I do all the time now, especially as I am pulling up to treeline like this one – here already? – and communing with the ancient pines, these gnarled, hobbled druids welcoming me up the trail as it disappears into snowfields and the snowfields melt down into rock.

I know these aren't druids, or priests, or goblins, or any other quasi-anthropomorphic thing; they're just trees and happen to look like they could be any of those beings.

But I always say "Hello" anyway and indulge in believing that they are saying *Hello* back.

Up here on Humphreys Peak, on the crumbling remains of this volcano, the rock is looser than the boulder fields atop the Rockies. It is sharp, crumbly, shot through with holes, a great heap of pumice, and I pick my way carefully across the shifting, tumbling rocks, looking for cairns, any signs of a trail. But there is nothing, only more shifting rocks on little dunes of pumice, rattling under each careful step.

Luckily, and very much unlike most of the Rockies, the line to the top is a straight shot, right there, no false summits, no drop-and-go-rounds, and in half an hour or so, there it is...

...Summit!

And here I am.

And so is some old guy with a big white beard in an orange cap.

He sits cross-legged over at the far end of the summit cap, facing out across the jagged lip and blown out center of the old volcano. A border collie sits next to him, tongue out, looking back at me. The guy is both motionless and intense at the same time, like Danny when he meditates up top.

So I keep to myself on this side, drop my pack, pull out some water and calories. Then I sit gingerly onto the biggest chunk of pumice on the summit, cooling and drying in a perfect mix of mild breeze and blazing sun.

Down the long, pumiced top and out past the forested slope, the whole of Flagstaff spreads out before me. It's the little town I'd dreamed of (ok, maybe romanticized just a bit) when I still lived Back East but had discovered the west. From up here, the funky mud-brown and brick-red grid of Flagstaff looks like a model railroad town, swallowed up by landscapes – alpine forest, red rock desert, ponderosa canyon – in every direction.

I could definitely live in this town, I remember thinking, every time I came here. But maybe that's only because I finally got my mojo working here, after all those years of a dead marriage. (Even if all that mojo turned out to be bullshit too, with Lying Bitch April.) But for a night or two anyway, she wasn't Lying Bitch April; she was still just April, hot, intense, and ready-to-rock-the-house April; and my mojo certainly was working, finally, again.

I met her at a bar right down there in that grid, around the corner from where we hung with Wesley last night.

I was half-loaded but fully there: a newly minted single guy, Out West for another long weekend of adventure. All April had to do, from two barstools over, was smile at me. She was tall and cut (just like Jill, hmm) and an obvious athlete (just like Jill, but not as young, and I was three years younger myself), with blond hair pulled into a tight ponytail, like she'd just finished a shoot for an ad in *Outside Magazine*.

Another smile.

I looked down at her left hand, and could see not exactly a tan-line but some odd markings where there had been a wedding band

"Yes," she finally said, holding up her hand to make it clear to me she wasn't hiding anything. "I was married. I can't believe the ring still shows. I guess after all those years out in the sun, it's like a callous."

"Or a scar," I said, holding up my own left hand, even though my wedding band had left no mark, thanks to all those years indoors, tending bar and then tending a business. "If it's been long enough. Maybe a little bit of both."

"Sounds like you've been married too."

"Nine and a half years," I said. "Just ended."

"Mine too," she frowned, pulling her hair out of the pony tail and fluffing it around her shoulders. "After a long time coming."

I almost burst out laughing at the gesture, and yet was utterly powerless against it. Thirty seconds later, I was moving two stools over, and the woman who introduced herself as April – yes, I'd figure out the Lying Bitch part soon enough – was ordering shots of tequila.

"To keep the calories down," she said.

Because she made her living, she said, as a middle-distance runner and high jumper, which I had no idea you could do. She said she'd been in the Olympics once and nearly a second time; was sponsored by gear companies and a bank, etc., etc.; and had to account for every calorie, every meal, every mile.

I wasn't sure if it was all bullshit or not, any more than the story about the ring coming off a couple months – or a couple hours – before I met her in that bar was bullshit. At that moment, with a couple shots of tequila igniting me from chest to loins, I certainly didn't care. She was hot and horny and all there; and the last time I'd had sex had been seven months and twelve days earlier, as part of the sad and desperate farewell with my ex-wife the weekend before I moved out.

An hour later, April and I were stumbling toward my motel room. And before I could unlock the door, clothes were coming off, tongues were coming out, and there were hands everywhere. She was all big blond hair, and long, sinewy legs, and ripped torso – barely any hips or ass – and no breasts really, just slight rises over her breastplate and hard little nipples. We fell onto that shitty little motel bed and went at it fast, hard, and loud, like two people who had gone without sex for months.

Then we went at it slow and deep and even louder, like two people who had gone without romantic love forever.

And then, bathed in sweat, we finally passed out.

Every few hours, one of us would stir, and stir the other, and in an instant, there were tongues again, and hands, wild hungry licking and sucking and a sudden painful whimpering and...

SLAP! out of nowhere. She said her little nipples were too sensitive to be touched at all, and what was wrong with me???

Before I could gather myself and apologize, she climbed on top of me and grabbed the suddenly loose, squeaky headboard, then more raw desperate sex until I was empty and a little queasy. She kept going, yanking on the headboard in time with her thrusting, pulling harder and harder and screaming – until the headboard snapped, and the bed collapsed.

We burst out laughing and passed out again, for most of the night, and then more sex on the mattress sitting down inside the broken frame, until dawn was lighting up the window shade.

We had a hurried, awkward breakfast in the diner next to the motel.

All I wanted to say was *Sorry about your nipples being so sensitive. My wife had big breasts and big nipples, and she loved that, and how was I supposed to know?* But I knew it was probably not the best thing to say, so I said nothing.

We went back to my room to get her things, and I was still thinking about her nipples, and suddenly there was her tongue again, and still more sex on the broken bed, slow and deep and quiet, like we'd already parted and were already off with someone else, fantasizing about each other.

Afterwards, she sprang up from the bed.

"I have an idea."

"What?"

"Why don't you come running with me down in Sedona?"

"Are you kidding? I can't keep up with –"

"I don't mean run *with* me, silly! I'm going ten fast miles today. I mean come down and hang out, while I get my run in. Didn't you say you've never seen Sedona?"

I had never seen Sedona and wanted to; had heard all about the New Age woo that went on in the canyons down there and was curious; and I could certainly keep myself busy for a couple hours while she ran around the hills down there.

She went home to grab her running gear while I got on the phone and dealt with work, and before I could call her and find out where to pick her up, she was back at my motel.

In my rental car, we headed down the wild curves dropping through Oak Creek Canyon, past soaring red rock formations and towering trees and rushing creek; and soon enough, we ran into the back-up of traffic on the main drag of that odd little town.

As we crawled through Sedona – April still rattling on about her training, or her weight, or calories, or something else that seemed far less compelling that it had been in the bar the night before – all I could do was nod and take in the whole spectacle. There was the red rock spectacle itself, sure; but as striking was the uniformity of the oddity of everyone there to take it in.

Sedona turned out to be a tourist town full of what looked like rich hippies and groovy golfers, often mixed into the same late middle-aged couple. Lots of flowing purple and pink, orange and red, khaki and gauze, denim and hemp, and lots of long platinum hair. Shops full of crystals, beads, t-shirts, cowboy-themed souvenirs, and handbags all the same colors and textures as the clothing. And of course, the ice cream cones, out for a walk and gawk, fueling the collective scurrying, head-shaking genuflections at the cathedral spires of brick-red and bone-white rock looming up over the town in every direction.

As we finally drove through and on south out of Sedona, April showed me where to go, leading out into a maze of red dirt roads that threaded through spires, mesas, and great piles of red rock.

"You sure you'll be ok just hanging around?" she asked after we parked at a crossing of two dirt roads.

I had water, hiking boots, binoculars, an Edward Abbey book, and a blazing landscape all around me, which means that I'd be just about perfect for as long as she wanted to run. "Oh, I'm sure," I said, trying not to stare as she peeled off her clothes and pulled on a tiny pair of sheer running shorts and a tank top. "I'll just hike up there," I pointed at a spire. "Keep a lookout for any hostiles."

"That's sweet," she said, pulling her big blond hair into a long tight ponytail, jumping up and down, loosening her limbs. "An hour and forty-five, maybe two hours tops." She set her watch then gave me a quick kiss, and with a "See ya!" she was off.

I watched her run off down the road in a cloud of red dust, the ponytail bouncing up and down behind her, and had a good laugh at everything and nothing. Was this really happening to me? My life was supposed to be a dull, miserable, uninteresting grind – all work and no play for all those years – and the whole time there was this big beautiful world out here in the west? And all I had to do was fly out here and find it?

After the red cloud of dust was lost to the wind, I wandered around the mesa. I walked down into a draw spiked with juniper and sage, then up the other side and out onto a long flat rock formation.

There was supposed to be magic in that psychedelic geology, or "earth energy," or "vortexes" or whatever they called it, I remember thinking, having read about it in a dozen magazines. So I sat down and listened, tried to feel something, tried to see if that whatever they called it might have anything to do with the Presence I had just rediscovered all over the saguaro desert, and up and down the Grand Canyon – the same thing I'd discovered deep into the woods as a kid pretending to run away.

But outside Sedona that day, I heard and felt only the wind. The landscape was certainly beautiful, if garishly so, like the color, tint and contrast buttons had all been turned up too high. And I could well imagine people getting carried away.

Then, just at the edge of perception, I did feel something.

It was a slight vibration, a rhythmic rumbling, and it was quickly growing stronger. But it was a literal rumbling, not something trapped between the cosmos and my imagination. It was coalescing into a steady hum, then a roar, and then around the corner popped a jeep – a pink jeep!?! – jammed with people, rolling up and over the middle of the rock formation, twenty feet away, their heads whipsawing with the crest and plunge back down the other side.

One of them was staring at me as I sat on the rock watching them: a woman in a huge sunhat, who lifted her camera and took a picture of me.

The driver was yelling over the roar of the engine about spirits or shamans or something, and a moment later they were flying around the mesa and gone.

And of course what else would I have with me, right there and then, but Edward Abbey's *Desert Solitaire*, half-read on the airplane, still in the rental car.

I went back and got it, then found a shady spot high up under another red rock ledge. And for the next hour or so, I watched and listened as Abbey – the storytelling elder of the eco-warrior tribe, inspiration to aspirational anarchists with good legs and healthy tans – paced around in a circle on the wind-sculpted slickrock in front of me, telling one cantankerous tale after another. *You see all this terrestrial magic all around you?* he seemed to be asking to me rhetorically, his gnarly, red-stained finger in my face. *It is all fragile and all doomed, if we don't stop plowing through it with, well, stinky crap like pink jeeps. And rental cars.*

Half an hour into Abbey's lyrical, sprawling bombast, the ground rumbled again, and another pink jeep came by, then another half an hour after that, then another half an hour after that. Finally, when I went back to Abbey but was too distracted wondering what he himself would actually say – or do – about the next fricking pink jeep to come by, I sensed another commotion.

I looked up to see traces of red dust down the road and heard a grunting noise. The dust and grunting got closer, and suddenly there she was, popping around the mesa: a little figure, the same pace as before, though a little ragged, chugging up the road, the ponytail wet and limp down her back.

This time, it was impossible not to stare. She undid and shook out her sweaty hair, peeled off her soaking shorts and top, and doused herself from another bottle, the water running down her tiny, hard nipples, down her rock-hard, concave stomach, down into her matted, dirty blond bush, all of it gleaming in the sunlight.

She looked over and caught me staring as she toweled herself off and smiled at me, and slowed down the towel, enjoying that I was enjoying it.

Then she came over, threw the towel around my neck and said, "Nothing gets me hot like a good workout."

And if I hadn't been completely mesmerized, or at least the part of my anatomy prone to pre-intellectual mesmerization hadn't been, I would have burst out laughing. But I was, and it sure as hell was, and so I didn't. Instead, there were tongues everywhere again, etc., etc., and there we were hanging out of the backseat, the rental car rocking to beat the band. And when she started screaming with her loudest orgasm yet, all I could think was: wouldn't it be hilarious if one of those pink jeeps came by right about now? Would old Ed Abbey approve of this as a method to scare the tourists away? Or would this only draw even worse ire from him?

Not that it matters. Ed Abbey died and was buried in a secret grave in the middle of his beloved desert, and his cause was lost a long time ago. Which was plain enough when we got back to Sedona. Those pink jeeps were everywhere, and the main drag was a tangle of traffic, families and couples, all wandering the street in a trance, gazing upward every few seconds from their ice cream cones at the cathedrals of rock.

We found a table along the crowded upstairs balcony of a Mexican *cantina*, overlooking the street and the red rock spires beyond, and downed three margaritas with a big early dinner.

We were tapped out of things to talk about, not counting another compelling analysis of her run, training regimen, diet, and caloric budget. I was also getting a little tired of watching her take her hair out of her pony tail, fluff it up, then tie it back up. So we just watched people walk by, and I tried to make jokes about them like I always do.

But she didn't seem to think I was funny – something I hadn't really noticed in the past 24 hours – and so we just sat back in the dark cool of the *cantina's* balcony, watching the last of the sunlight slip off the red rock cliffs across from town.

It was dark by the time we headed north out of town, up the canyon and back toward Flagstaff. She finally seemed to be tired of talking about herself, and I'd nearly forgotten she was even there in the darkened car with me, when I felt her hand crawling up my thigh.

"There's a beautiful turnout up here," she said.

"Seriously?"

"If you want one more for the road, I mean," she said.

I looked over at her in the glow of the dashboard light and wanted to say *You really were in the Olympics, weren't you?* But all I could say was "Wow."

I laugh to myself and suddenly there is a border collie in my face. And I am pulled back by a strange voice.

"Sorry about that."

I look up and see the old guy with the orange cap and long white beard walking over, with the help of a long knobby hiking stick. His border collie runs back and forth between us.

"No problem," I say, petting the dog, who is wound up, expectant, bursting with more than the usual dog's desperation to trade devotion for attention.

"This is Jess."

"Hey there, Jess."

At the sound of her name, she jumps around in circles and barks.

He stares at me hard, his eyes set back in dark sockets and his pupils and irises so ice blue they look nearly all one washed-out color. He is husky but solid, more hair than face, like an old rock star – David Crosby or Jerry Garcia maybe, but well out of rehab and in great hiking shape.

"You all good up here?"

"Never better," I say, gesturing with a sweep of my hand at the view all around us.

"Jess and I are happy to have the company on the way down, if you'd like."

"Thanks," I say. "But I'm good."

"If you say so. I turned around and saw you sitting over here, and it looked pretty heavy, if you don't mind me saying."

I force a laugh. "Just thinking about a girl."

"That explains it," he says. "Worse things to think about up here. Better things too." He hoists his pack. "Girls, God, the Great Spirit. Easy to mix them all up." Then he points the hiking stick at Flagstaff. "Down there in the world anyway. Like the pop songs mix them all up."

Jess runs a couple circles around him and barks, and he turns to start down the mountain.

"That's why it's good to sort out the one, from other," he says. "Up here."

Jess jumps and barks at him.

"Yes, girl – we're going." He steps off the summit onto the pumice field, Jess tearing down the slope in front of him. "See you on the other side, my friend."

I watch him pick his way down and realize he is exactly right: it's extremely easy to mix all of them up down there.

And when they stay mixed up, and follow me up here, then where is the Presence? Not up here today. Just Lying Bitch April and half an erection, despite myself, for thinking back on all that. But No Presence, and no plan. Aaron is Back East by now, dealing with whatever he's dealing with, and it's just me up here alone with my little stories.

I sit back and look out at the first cumulus clouds gathering in the west and building this way. I follow their probable path east, toward the cinder cones the other way, and realize they could mean thermals, a good day for hang-gliding. But John is gone, and who knows why. Down there is Flagstaff, my once favorite place in the universe. And I wish I could say who knows whatever became of Lying Bitch April, but I do know, hence her formal name in my formal, i.e., non-erection-based, memory.

Better to remember that it was indeed a beautiful turnout in the road up here from Sedona, stag or not. I can see from up here where it slices through the forest south of town, into the great carpet of ponderosa and spruce and lodgepole pine crawling over the Mogollon Rim and down into canyon, down into Oak Creek Canyon and the start of the great Sonoran desert.

The turnout was at the top of that canyon, a long parking area notched out of the forest, with the skeletons of stalls where Native Americans sold jewelry during the day. We leaned against the front of the parked car, and watched the stars come out through the canyon break in the forest canopy, watched them deepen and brighten as the sky filled with them, like rock salt and sugar spilling out across a black countertop. And then we had sex again, all the way into the backseat this time because it was cold, and there were no screaming orgasms, just a lot of sighing and sadness. Because by then, we were doing it not because we wanted to or because it felt good; we were doing it because we could, and because we both knew – though not for the same reasons – that this would be it.

It was pitch dark and freezing cold back in Flagstaff when we got to my motel, with the mess of a mattress squatting in the shattered bed frame.

She looked quickly around the room to see if she'd left anything, then hurried straight to her car, which was fine with me. I was ready to pass out, and I wasn't sure how we were going to leave it – this was just a great big rebounding piece of luck for me – but I asked for her phone number anyway.

She scribbled it down on the notepad by the phone, and a minute later she was gone.

The next night, I was flying out and thought, what the hell, I'll call her from the Phoenix airport. But she didn't answer what turned out to be her cell phone, and I didn't leave a message. I tried a week later and did leaves messages, twice, and never heard from her again. That's fine, I thought at the time; it was apparently a rebound for both of us. It wasn't until I was back in Flagstaff nearly a year later with my first snowboard – to ride this very mountain I just climbed, after more business conjured down in Phoenix, conveniently scheduled for a Friday – that I found out what happened to her.

I was meeting up with John and Shelley in the Flag Brewery, the same place Aaron, Wesley and I were hanging yesterday. I was still humming with all the snow and the turns and the welling energy of this very mountain – lots of the Presence with me that day – when I just sort of mentioned her to them.

"I kinda met someone the last time I was here," I said. "Same trip you guys took me up."

Shelley's eyes widened with a half-smile. "Oh really?"

"And I figure it's sort of a small town, so maybe you know her?"

"What's her name?" Shelley asked, her smile growing.

"April, uh –" I blurted out but then remembered that I'd never known her last name, had never remembered to look it up, maybe because I didn't want to find out anything more about her. "April, uh – big athlete, big runner."

Shelley's smile disappeared, her eyes hardening.

"And uh – a high jumper. I guess. She was in the Olympics, or so she says."

"April Callahan?" John asked, looking over at Shelley, who was now looking at the table and shaking her head. "Lots of big blond hair, likes to play with it all the time?"

"So. You guys do know her?"

Shelley muttered: "All hair and legs, and not a whole lot in between?"

"Yeah," John said. "We know her. And her husband."

"You mean her ex-husband?"

"No," Shelley said. "Her husband."

I am pulled back by an explosion of energy in my face.

I look up to see Jess, back up here on the summit, barking and jumping and circling. Maybe the guy in the orange cap might be in trouble and she has come back to get me?

I watch her jump and run around in circles, vocalizing "Come with us!" And I realize she isn't any more agitated or vocal than before, just exploding with energy. Like all great mountain dogs, she will summit multiple times for each one of your own. But I can take a hint, so I pull on my pack and start back down.

I pick my way down the pumice field, Jess back and forth to the treeline a couple more times. But by the time I get to treeline, she is gone.

Back in the trees, I start to think about Aaron again. I will have to call him later and find out how his mother is doing. And as the words "how is your mother doing?" form in my head, I realize just how odd they sound in my own voice. They are the exact same words I heard from so many people, so many years ago, and just about the only words I ever heard from anybody in that town, to the point where they were like a greeting: "How's your mother doing?"

My answer was always "she's doing ok, thanks," when my real answer was always "she's not dead yet, but we're all hoping, thanks."

I stop and look up at the canopy, a kaleidoscope of aspen leaves, pine boughs, blue sky, and white cloud, and still, no Presence anywhere up here. It makes me feel alone in a way I never feel, even though I am alone all the time.

I start back down the trail, still worrying about Aaron and his mother in an odd way I can't seem to shake.

On the last big switchbacks to the trailhead, I am practically in a run because I want to get to a phone and call Aaron before I forget to, which is what I always do in situations like this. Because isn't that what people are supposed to do? Worry about a friend's ailing mother, like they're supposed to worry about their own mother, not wish her dead, if only for the sake of her own belated peace? My own poor mother was always so sick, made crazy over time by pain that never ended and a slow, burning rage over her whole miserable lot in life. Unlike Aaron, unlike everybody, I suppose, all I ever wanted for her – after finally giving up on a cure like all the adults had – was a quiet and peaceful death, putting her and the rest of us out of misery.

At the trailhead, the parking lot is empty but for Aaron's truck. I drive back to Flagstaff under a gigantic marching band of cumulus clouds. There will be great thermals today for hang-gliding.

In town, I pull over and turn on my cell phone to call Aaron.

I have a voicemail, from Shelley, who tells me to meet her at the Flag Brewery at 5.

Before she is halfway in the bar, I notice the big dark circles under her fierce black eyes.

"So," I just blurt it out, with the first sip of beer, "you and John."

"Yes," she says, her tanned, angular face clenching a moment. "We split up. No big drama. Just time to go our separate ways."

"I know we weren't all that close," I say. "But do you mind – if I ask –"

"Not at all. We're all pushing 40, so this won't be a big surprise to you. Even if came as a bit of a surprise to me."

We sit and drink in silence, deliberate on her part I think, because she wants me to guess.

I am guessing it is even odds between: John cheating on her; or she deciding that she wanted to have kids after all – even though all three of us talked about never wanting kids the last time we were hanging out, and I was telling them that my own marriage finally ended over it. And neither guess will feel good coming from me or anyone.

"I give up," I finally say. "What was the surprise?"

"John decided he wanted to have kids."

"Huh," I almost spit the last of my beer onto the bar.

"Yes," she mutters. "That's about what I said, when he told me down at the bottom of the Canyon that day. 'Huh.' It was a long fucking hike out after that."

Our glasses are empty, and the bartender comes over and starts to say something, sees that she's crying and pulls up.

I nod *Yes* and he goes to pour us two more in fresh glasses.

"But it's ok," she sniffs, gathering herself. She seems not exactly self-conscious, maybe just a little stoic, or maybe something else I can't read. "I only cry about it every few hours or so now."

I have no idea what to say, so I say nothing, and we drink in silence for a long few minutes.

"So," I muster up some beer courage, thinking it's a good idea to change the subject, and actually wanting to say what's on my own mind. "I learned this really awful thing last night, right here at this very bar, about a close friend of mine. A guy I've been climbing and camping and skiing with for years."

"What's that?"

"His high school and college girlfriend died in an avalanche – up in Alaska – on some trip they were on. Like – seven years ago."

"And he never told you about it?"

"Nope. Not in all these years, of going through first responder, talking avy shit all the time, always dealing with gear, snow, safety stuff. Not a single word."

"That's – interesting," she says. "How did she actually die? Was it his fault?"

"Doesn't sound like it. His buddy, who told me about it, said it was an avy on some little scout-out, right near camp, triggered by an earthquake. Totally random."

"Hmm," she says, sipping her beer and looking at it off in space. "Like Alex Lowe's death."

"Yes," I say. "Exactly."

"And he never talks about it."

"Nope."

"Survivor's guilt is weird," she says. "And people – well – I guess they all have their ways."

"I guess."

We drink in silence for another long minute.

Then she turns to me and says, "Did you hear about Conrad Anker? And Alex Lowe's wife?"

"Hear what?"

"They're together now."

"You're kidding?"

"I don't think anyone would kid about that. They were married in April."

"Huh."

"Yeah," she sighs. "Like I said – people have their ways."

"I guess."

She turns to me, her eyes wet with more tears. "Yes, they do, Jack. Everybody is just trying to find a way to heal themselves. Isn't that why we're all up there in the mountains?"

Welcome Home

It has been twelve hours since we met up at the bar, and I still can't stop thinking about Shelley's words and tears as I drive north out of Flagstaff at dawn, back to Dudeville in Aaron's truck.

But at least I remembered to call him and leave a message before I left: "Hey man, I'm thinking about you. And I hope your – uh – your mother – I hope she's ok."

A couple hours across the aching sprawl of this red rock desert, I run through the last of Aaron's jazz, blues and klezmer CDs, which all sound alien and weird out here, so I switch on the radio. It's all Navajo drumming and wailing, fading in and out of angry static, then Jesus, then more Navajo drumming and wailing, then more static, before I give up and just listen to the roar of the truck and rhythm of the tires on the sun-blistered road.

I've been thinking I would camp somewhere halfway back, the same plan Aaron and I had when we geared up for the trip down to Arizona. Maybe find somewhere off the highway in southeastern Utah or southwestern Colorado, near a big mountain with clear skies and an empty trailhead, and call it an early night, then run up the mountain at dawn and have a good hard talk with the Presence.

But the weather out over the desert this morning is starting to turn dark and angry, threatening a rain that won't fall but won't clear, a series of high, charcoal-brushed storm clouds blotting out the sun and turning the red rock all purple and black. So maybe the Presence does not want to have a good hard talk with me.

Or maybe I just want to go home and stretch out in The Treehouse. (Even though I really shouldn't call my house that anymore, because that's Jill's name for it.)

Which is what I end up doing. Because every time I slow the truck down in front of someplace I might stop, hike, eat or just sit still for a minute, a strange uneasiness wells up in my gut. So I just keep driving, faster, back to Dudeville.

Eight hours later, I finally turn north up into our canyon. But I don't go straight back to The Treehouse, because I'm wired and hungry after the long drive, so I head straight to Ullar's.

It looks like rain has been passing through while Aaron and I were away, helping crews put out the fire north of town. The streets and storefronts all look damp and the air is clear again; but there is a haze of gray ash drawn across everything, like a shroud.

And Ullar's is half full again, with a couple dozen people I don't know in hiking and biking stuff, three dogs I do know, and Maggie behind the bar pulling beers and pushing burgers in between pages of *American Alpinist*.

Up on the TV, the Tour de France is in full swing, Lance crushing it already of course. He is a blade of yellow in a clutch of bright blue near the front on a big flat stage, all of them flying down the road at what looks like 45 RPMs against the trickle of tune-check notes and hoarse patter of the Grateful Dead in between two songs that never really seem to begin or end.

Maggie comes back from the far table, shakes her head, and changes the music to some new old-school country – bendy steel, boomy bass, crisp guitar, Wilco, Son Volt? – nope, a woman, more crying than singing.

"Who's this?" I ask her.

"Lucinda Williams."

"Wow. She's good."

She pulls me another beer, and smiles, a joke coming.

"So what did the Deadhead say when he ran out of drugs?"

"What?"

"This music *suuucks!*"

We chuckle as she puts the beer down in front of me and goes back to the *Alpinist* and I go back to Lance and the Tour.

"Hey you guys."

I look over and Kelly is flying through the door and up to the bar next to me, her mess of dirty blond hair everywhere, her faceful of sun even brighter red than usual, her eyes bloodshot. She is supposed to be down in Chile, on the same trip that had started out in Argentina, the same trip Jill had been on.

"Aren't you – "

"Where's your buddy Aaron?" she cuts me off.

"Back east. We were just down in Flagstaff. He had to fly back there."

"Why?"

I'm not sure what I should say. "Some family thing. What's up?"

"Nothing," she says, which is obviously, exactly not true. "And don't pout about it, for God's sake!" she snaps at me, like I've somehow offended her.

"Whatever, dude," I mutter.

"What do you need from Aaron, honey?" Maggie asks her.

"Just needed to ask him about something," Kelly says and turns to go, then turns back to me. "Sorry for getting in your face, man. I'm just beat from all the travel."

"It's all good."

"If you say so." She turns to go again, then back to me. "And by the way – you really should call Jill back."

"Yeah? I figured by now, I'd be about the last person she'd want to hear from."

"Well you figured wrong," she cuts me off. "Just man-up and call her. Alright? Dude?"

I Think It was Psalm 121

"Kelly doesn't mince words," Danny shouts back, over the grunge rock blasting in his Non-Hippie Bus, after I tell him the story the next afternoon, on our drive over to Leadville and Mount Elbert. "Maybe you should call Jill."

It's the very tail-end of mud season: there's mud everywhere, the skiing is shit, the hiking is worse, and Dudeville is lousy with tourists; so it's the perfect time to get up Mount Elbert – the highest peak in Colorado and all of the Rockies – without anybody around to bother us.

I just as quickly want to change the subject I just brought up, but the pulsing of the grunge and the sudden jarring of the drive does it for me. The forest service road up to the trailhead is turning rutted and muddy, the Non-Hippie Bus rocking back and forth as it labors up the hill.

The aspens are bursting with bright lime green, maybe more so from that last bowl of weed. But they are still less vivid than the wild sunflower gold of last September, when we were up here to climb Mount Massive from the same trailhead. As Danny focuses on threading our way up the steepening road, I look out at them, strung in glades and meadows along the rushing creek that drains this spine of the mountains running due north and south. This is the very epicenter of the Colorado Rockies, and it looks to be all ours today.

The road braids into the trees at the edge of the long creek meadow wedged into the canyon between Massive and Elbert. This will be our home for the afternoon and evening, right at the trailhead, where the forested wilderness starts.

We both sag with a little disappointment when we spot the bright colors and cloud of smoke up ahead: a big group is already camped at the upper end of the meadow, the best spot, where the mountains close right in over you.

Danny cuts the music, turns the bus around, and idles us down to the other end of the meadow, and parks.

We jump out, scout a spot for our tents, and pull gear, a ritual we've done a hundred times, every now and then in the dark, under the pounding of a hailstorm, against a screaming wind. This afternoon, the weather is perfect and our camp is up in minutes.

When we're done, Danny pulls out his sleeping pad and wanders off into the center of the meadow. He sits down facing the mountain – the pyramidal peak already in shadow at the top and bathed in fading golden light at the bottom – and starts meditating.

I wander over to the creek to wash up, check out the view, clear my head, maybe take a picture.

Sitting on a flat rock, I listen for a minute to the water braid through the boulders and the birds settle in for the evening. The weaving rhythms of the creek and dancing melodies of the birds swirl together into a natural baroque, a kind of chamber music without walls, a wild Vivaldi. As I sit back on the rock and listen and nod, everything around me slowly darkens to sepia from all the orange alpenglow spilling down the canyon.

"Hey man."

I look up, and see a wiry, bearded guy in a black fleece coming down the creek, carrying a water filter and armful of nalgene bottles.

"Hey."

"Thought I'd invite you guys over," he says. "If you're down."

"Cool, thanks. Maybe."

He turns to go. "Oh, and it's not much of a party with our crew. Least not on this trip."

"No?"

"Up here for a memorial service for our buddy, Dave," he says. "We summitted Elbert this morning and scattered his ashes."

"That's a bummer."

"Yeah, big bummer." He turns to go again, hesitates, then turns back to me. "Dave skied it a bunch of times, all seasons. Even did it on teles a couple times. One of his favorites." He looks up at the mountain looming over us, the sun fully behind it, all in shadow now. "He was frickin' hardcore." He looks back at me and shudders. "Anyway. We got plenty of food and beer. And Dave was all about sharing. Making new friends, dancing to the music, know what I mean?"

"Sure."

He turns to go again. "So like – in his honor. If you guys are down."

I watch him walk back in the sudden dusk to his friends, now gathered around a burst of campfire sparks in the fading light.

Back at our camp, Danny has our own little fire going, and a pot of tea. He's put out our camp chairs and is sitting in one, reading his battered copy of Whitman by headlamp.

I pour myself some tea and sit next to him, and watch the last of the alpenglow fade to black as tiny rivets of stars pop out of the darkening sky. Everything goes dark, except for our little fire, and Danny's headlamp and the big campfire at the other end of the meadow.

A Memorial Service. Like at Broken Circle Ranch up in the Tetons. A year ago with Jill.

She was back from her first ski season in Alaska and working in the Tetons that spring, crewing on some film and guiding backcountry skiers out of the Broken Circle Ranch. She called me because one of the three women who had built and run the place had died that winter, and they were having a memorial service.

It was all a little sad around there and made her think about time passing, she said. And if I'd ever thought about coming up and checking out the Tetons, that would be a good time.

Maybe it was the sweetness in her voice, or maybe I was just lonely, but I didn't really think about it much; I just went.

"And besides," Jill had added, with what sounded almost like a purr, "she was one of the original hardcore Betties, long before anybody called them that. And since you say you're fan..."

Jill wasn't kidding about that. Ruth was 88 when she died, the second of the three women to go, all of them skiers on the 1948 US Olympic Team. After the Olympics, with more energy than money and not feeling exactly welcome in most of the rest of the world, Jill said, they carved the ranch out of the wooded canyon at the bottom of Teton Pass.

They ran it as a working dude ranch: horses and hikers in summer; skiing the rest of the year. And for decades, the ranch also served as a sort of sanctuary for young women from all over the west who, as someone at the service politely said, "didn't exactly fit in back in their small towns." The three women were cowboy terse and rawhide tough, judging from all the recollections and jokes shared at the memorial service, and from how Nance still seemed despite her age.

The service brought hundreds of people, long since scattered all over the west and west coast, back to the ranch. What I remember best from it: no one cried, and everyone laughed, sometimes nervously, as if Ruth were not really dead, and was going to come around the other side of the barn any minute, and yell at all of them to get back to work.

"This was Ruth," recalled an angular guy about my age, turning a weather-beaten cap around in his even more weather-beaten hands. His story was about needing a place to practice for the Olympic biathlon, the old-school, old-world combination of cross-country skiing and shooting. "She's out on the porch one afternoon fixing something. I walk up and ask her 'Mind if I practice shooting down in the lower meadow?' She doesn't look up, doesn't really even act like I'm there. I figure that means no. So when I start to go, she still doesn't look up, just barks at me, 'Make sure you pick up all that damn brass.'"

"These were lives fully lived," recalled one of the many tough-looking older women, dressed up in bright western wool, gingham, denim, and a cowboy hat, who'd come of age on the ranch. "And lived way off what was the grid – the grid of what women did back then – when they built this beautiful ranch."

"They were lives fully lived because they helped others find their way," recalled another woman with a river of platinum hair flowing out from under her cowboy hat, near the end of the service. "And not directly, but through these mountains. Through taking care of the land, and teaching others to take care of it. Through what they did by example."

I was mesmerized by all of it, by all of them. But it was the tail-end of my very first year living out here in the west, and everything was an adventure, an antidote to the dull, noisy, crowded grind of life Back East. That ranch and those people were a giant living piece of western art to my hungry eyes: the great mountain pass looming up over the place; the real cowboys and cowgirls who worked it; the fecundity of a working ranch surrounded by gardens and pasture, ripening with summer and sweat and horseshit; the piercing eyes and weather-sculpted faces and sturdiness of those people. They shook your hand hard, held on for a moment and said almost nothing, and looked you right in the eye. This was nothing like Back East, with its horde of grovelers and evaders, liars and pretenders, sniping lawyers and petty bureaucrats. It was a foreign country more actually American than any place I'd ever been.

"This was the first place I ever felt safe," a woman our height but well into her 60s, with fierce blue eyes peering out from under an old straw hat, told Jill and me. "The first place I was ever judged for what I could do, not for what I was. That's all Ruth and Nance and Joanne cared about. The ranch, the horses, the weather. This place was hard, but it was fair."

"That's still this place," Jill said to her.

"Good," she smiled at her, "I can see that."

She turned to say *Hello* to someone, and Jill turned to me.

"I'm really glad you got to see all this," she said, reaching out to hold my hand. "Because of what you're always saying about your work. Or what used to be your work. This is mine."

"And you want to give this up for MBA school?"

"I don't know, dude."

And she really didn't know. But she was all of 25 at the time, like so many of those women at the ranch who'd fled small towns and found sanctuary in all that hard work and wild country. But they had all moved on too, to school, careers, and family, just like Jill would one day.

I am pulled back by Danny's voice.

"Wanna go check out those guys?"

I look up and see Danny squatting down and poking around in our little fire. But he's mostly looking past it, at the campfire at the other end of the meadow, which is raging now and encircled by a bunch of people.

"It's a memorial service for their buddy," I say. "Some guy named Dave. Used to be pretty hardcore, I guess. Some dude down by the creek told me to come over."

"Maybe we should."

"Maybe."

He watches them a minute, but then plops back down in his chair and goes back to Whitman.

Which is fine with me, because all I want to do is go back to the Tetons for another few minutes.

After the Memorial service up there, Jill had a few days off and I had nowhere I needed to be. So we spent the next morning sorting through climbing and camping gear, and the next afternoon hauling it up into the heart of that impossible upward explosion of a mountain range. Jill had been up there twice before – with NOLS (the National Outdoor Leadership School) in college and on a film shoot the year after that – and she knew the right people to connect with on one of the guiding services. That plus some timing luck, and we were able to tag along on their permits and hang out up there for three days.

The trip was brutal, and amazing, and a chance to learn some serious mountaineering skills. We camped in the crux of the range, on a vast bulge of broken rock piled up between the Grand and Middle Tetons, in a constant, screaming wind. We had to lash Jill's tent to the sharp fins of three boulders, and still it shook all day and all night in the wind. But the views! From up there you can see why it's called "Jackson *Hole*," because it really is a long, oblong-shaped, dark green hole, the size of a city Back East, knocked out of black mountains in every direction. (Unlike anything Back East, however, that sprawling flat space is nearly empty, except for the town of Jackson down at one end, with its cowboy art and "Indian" crafts, spas and oxygen bars, fancy wines and elk carpaccio.)

By day, Jill and I were literally learning the ropes – or re-learning in her case – from the guides we'd tagged along with. But the really interesting thing I learned on that trip was how to piss, while on all fours and with a nylon tent slapping at my ass from every direction, into a nalgene bottle. Because the entire rockfield up under the saddle between the Middle and the Grand drained down into the camp's water source, every time you had to go – including in the middle of the night, guided via headlamp – you had to hike across the shifting rocks in all that wind, and go into the next drainage over. I also learned how to stay out of the way, in that little backpacking tent, while Jill squatted to pee into her own nalgene bottle. We also learned how to keep very close track of what was in each of our four blue nalgene bottles until morning.

Jill and I never made it to the top of the Grand, nor anyone in the group we were with. Weather blew in the night before the summit bid, and half the group bailed without trying. But the guides wanted to try anyway, and so did Jill and I, even though there would be no view at all, just the inside of a gusting cloud. So we geared up at 4 AM, and worked our way up the mountain, through the foggy drizzle blowing sideways through our headlamps. We worked our way up, one slippery and barely visible step at a time, as the dreary morning light filtered into the cloud. And then the rain came, and then it was freezing rain, the rock getting wetter and slicker by the minute.

Finally, the lead guide shouted over the wind what I've heard Aaron say dozens of times since, and I've repeated to others and myself dozens of other times: "Sorry, kids, but summiting is optional, and returning to the trailhead is not. We're done. The mountain has other plans for today."

That night, bone-weary and three days ripe, Jill and I – and Kettle, who'd been at the ranch while we were up the mountain – checked into a fancy hotel in Jackson, but not without some negotiation. She always wanted to camp somewhere, anywhere, especially after a few days without Kettle. But I always had the cash and did have what Jill liked to call my "bourgeois weakness" for occasional physical comforts. (And, unbeknownst to her, part of my old, careful, buttoned-down corporate self loved to flaunt that I could just check into a fancy place on a whim, looking and smelling like a dirty mountain hippie with an embarrassed, eye-rolling 25-year-old Betty girlfriend, always to the overly polite mortification of the people at the front desk.) Jill and I finally just chalked up my "bourgeois weakness" for physical comfort as another awkward age thing, and decided to compromise by staying in a dive motel. But they were all booked, and the nicest places in Jackson didn't allow dogs, so we booked a room and snuck Kettle in through the back, where he happily curled up in the middle of his own king-sized bed while we went out into the streets looking for something other than fancy wine and elk carpaccio.

Danny's voice again, jolting me back. "Think I'll go check those guys out."

I look up to see that our fire is almost out, as Danny pulls himself to his feet, leaving his book in the grass.

He disappears into shadow across the meadow, toward the group gathered around the fire.

I should go over and join them – to honor Dave, I guess, he did sound pretty cool – but I'm not feeling social. I'm feeling like an asshole, actually, because every good memory of my time with Jill now makes me feel like that. And maybe Dave wouldn't want an asshole like me around. Maybe Dave had a sister or best friend just like Jill, who was also cool and who also got screwed over multiple times by some selfish jack(ha!)ass like me.

After our time together up in the Tetons, Jill went as far away as ever, to the Himalayas for the summer. And that kind of distance and time should have finally ended it. But it was 2000 by then, and Y2K hadn't ended the world, and instead had seeded Internet cafes into every corner of it.

Jill found one soon enough and sent me an email saying that I just might want to come visit and see the greatest mountains in the world.

I thought about it, alone up in The Treehouse, for several days.

Then, one night when I must have just been drunk and horny enough – or so I've convinced myself since – I emailed her back: "Hell yes, I'd be down for that. The Himalayas? Let's go big!" I even booked flights for August, for what would be my first trip halfway around the planet.

And then Amy the Rebound Girl showed up in Denver again, and I was definitely drunk and horny enough – self-evident, no convincing required – to say yes one more time. She was, after all, my age and still alone, and full of her own bourgeois weaknesses, and every bit as broken as I am.

That night, she made me work for it, the worst thing she could have done, because by the time I'd convinced Amy the Rebound Girl of my good intentions and apologized for whatever it was I'd ever said or done wrong, I started to sober up. When she saw that, and saw me starting to pull back, then *she* had to work for it, talking me into it by saying she'd re-thought it all and decided she really didn't want kids after all. It was the same old shitty drama, for the third go-round, but all compressed into one stupid night: we got drunk and slept together; right afterwards I regretted it and told her I felt nothing; and the angrier she got, the more I just looked at her and laughed. But I wasn't laughing at her so much as I was laughing with relief: now I couldn't go to the Himalayas, because I couldn't lie to Jill and she would never put up with the truth.

Which I could communicate only via email.

Which she replied to via telephone, a day later.

In the middle of the night my phone rang, and it was Jill, calling from halfway around the planet, and I could barely hear her. She wanted me to know she was tired of being pissed at me, and wondering about me, and trying to read between the lines of my email, which I thought had been clear, and told her so. And yet she asked, just for the record, if we had a commitment.

I told her, as plainly as I could, "No we don't."

She said she just wanted to know – because Brandon was on that trip, and she was done being a fool.

And she really was done, and so was I, and that was it for a year. Danny ran into one of the Betties who had been on the same trip, and she said that Jill and Brandon were a serious item, going out of her way to let him know just how serious, because she knew Danny and I were friends and it would get straight back to me.

And we really were done.

Until I ran into her at Ullar's last March. She was back in town for Hillary's wedding, en route from her second winter up in Alaska and first down in Argentina. She was in Dudeville for a few days, as always just passing through, swapping out gear, catching up. All the Betties who were in the wedding had skied up that day on the big snowfield to the right of The Lady, and were back in Ullar's drinking shots to toast Hillary and whoever the guy was.

Jill cornered me at the bar, and wanted me to know that she wasn't mad at me anymore.

But all I could say – because something about it did hurt somewhere, I guess – was a sort of snotty "so how's Brandon?"

"He's fine."

"My offer still stands," I said, repeating something I'd told her a year earlier, when she first brought him up. "I'd be honored to play guitar at your wedding."

"There won't be any wedding," she muttered, avoiding my eyes.

"Sorry to hear that."

"Fuck you!" she exploded. "That's bullshit. I hate you! Why are you even here?"

"Hey, you two," Maggie was right there. "Take it down a notch maybe? Or maybe a nice little walk around the block?"

I don't remember what happened next, only what happened after that: Jill and I were out behind Ullar's, yelling at each other; and then, somehow, we were making out.

The inside of her sweet, wet, giving mouth was as familiar to my tongue as my own mouth; her strong, slender hands fit inside my hands; everything just fit, felt good, felt like home.

And then we were back up in The Treehouse.

She stayed with me for the next three days, for the drunken festival that was Hillary's wedding, and then she was gone, off to Argentina this time.

But maybe this time, I thought, I really would visit her.

She just gave me the sideways look that last morning, and said, "Yeah, sure. Whatever, dude."

But I did mean it that time. At the time, anyway.

And then Freak Girl happened. Or I let her happen. Who knows.

All I do know is that I made the biggest damn fool out of myself possible. And not only did all that happen, but it happened after more email plans with Jill and another set of plane tickets, right when I was supposed to be flying down to Argentina. On what I didn't remember at the time was her birthday.

I am snapped back by a metallic slide and slam.

I look up and see a headlamp rummaging around in the Non-Hippie bus, Danny looking for something in the back.

Another slide and slam, and Danny walks over, invisible beneath his bobbing headlamp but for loose hair flying out into the light.

"Hey man," he says, "you gotta come check these guys out. It's a big deal. And they have a serious spread going." He holds up a bottle of wine. "We oughta bring something to honor this Dave guy. He sounded fricking cool."

"Ok," I say. "I'll be over in a minute."

I hunch over the last of the coals of our fire, and watch Danny disappear into the darkness of the meadow.

A moment later, he re-appears in the silhouettes gathered around the blaze of their fire. It looks like eight guys over there, and Danny makes nine.

So why not make it an even ten, I think, and pull myself to my feet and slowly walk over to them.

The guys are all ages, all fleece and mostly beards, and three turn out to be women. One says she's Dave's sister, another a college roommate, and the third – it's quickly plain – is a long ago ex-girlfriend. There is an old, empty camp chair past the far end of the fire, covered with pictures and filled with flowers, little stones, a couple pieces of old climbing gear, and a small, worn-out old folk guitar.

They stand around the fire, telling stories about Dave. Some wild, others intense, a few that are hilarious, none of them sad. They're just stories: about Dave and his ferociousness in these mountains; Dave and his love for music; Dave and his "little problem with women" (which makes them all laugh nervously, and look over at the long-ago ex who doesn't laugh); then back to Dave's ferociousness in these mountains.

"He was obsessed with them even more than most mountainfreaks."

"He was addicted to the rush, the adrenaline."

"He was always good for a throwdown. No matter how much of a hurry you were in, Dave would just pull off the highway when he saw a couloir he liked, strap his skis onto his pack, be up and down it in a few hours, and then be on his way."

"To Dave's throwdowns!" someone toasted, and they all raised their beers.

Then a long silence, as they stand around drinking.

"Remember that Psalm he was always reciting?" someone finally asks.

"Oh yeah," says another. "I think it was Psalm 121."

"I remember that," the ex-girlfriend says. "He'd always say it on the summit. Or when we'd get in some tough headspace on a climb.

Or every time he'd climb out of the tent in the morning, up at some big beautiful basin or cirque."

"How'd that go?"

"Psalm 121?" she says. "Um – I should know this, because he said it all the time." She closes her eyes and takes a big deep breath, and everyone stands silent, waiting. "'I lift my eyes to the mountains. What is the source of my help?'" And a few of them nod, and join in, "'My help comes from God, the Maker of heaven and earth. God will not let your foot give way – your Protector will not slumber.'"

And then silence and some sobs.

"What was the rest of it?"

"I don't know."

"Something about Israel not sleeping, and the sun not striking."

"He sort of mumbled the rest to himself."

"Yes, he did," she said. "And then he kept climbing."

More silence, then Dave's sister, looking up at the silhouettes of mountains all around us. "But not the last line. He always said the last line out loud. 'God will guard you,'" her voice cracks, but she forces it out anyway. "'God will guard you from all harm. God will guard your soul, your going and coming, now and forever.'"

Then a long silence, everyone staring into the fire, half of them weeping.

I feel a shudder pass through me, maybe from them, or from who knows where.

"Kind of messed up that he died in a car accident," someone finally says.

"Yes."

Dave's sister looks back up toward the mountains. "He should have died up here. This is where his spirit was."

"His spirit is up here now," Danny blurts out, and everyone looks over at the unfamiliar voice. "He left a piece of it every time he came up here. You guys are awesome for bringing the rest of him back."

"Amen, brother."

"That's exactly what Dave would have said," his sister says. "That and 'chill the fuck out you guys! And check out the curves on that mountain over there!'"

There are a few quiet chuckles.

"He'd be like, 'I'm up here forever now, you guys. And we all die. But these mountains?'" She looks up at the shadow of the peak towering over all of us like a giant pyramid in shadow, backlit by a wash of stars, the orange flicker of Mercury arcing west over all of it. "But these mountains –"

Her voice fades away, and we are enshrouded for a moment in silence, all ten of us looking up at the great vault of sky, the mountain, Mercury, and all those stars. Standing here with these others, I think with both fondness and awe of my many encounters alone on top of these mountains. The Presence was here long before any of us got here. And it will be here long after we are gone – all of us and our bloated selves and our little stories – glorified, exalted, and sanctified by the very fact of its unknowability, patient as cosmic time. The Presence continuously unfurling out across these mountains gives scale to the power of time and geology for the whole world, utterly indifferent to us; and in that utter indifference, it enshrouds all of us, and all the world, in peace.

"Amen, sister," someone finally says.

"Amen," we all say.

Serac

Sometimes these mountains seem not only *not* indifferent, but deliberately cruel. These sentiments, muttered for decades over countless *post mortem* beers at bars like Ullar's, are the modern echoes of our old pagan superstitions and fears; they are a way to deflect blame for our own complacency and arrogance, climbing where and when we should not.

Which is what Tyler was doing today, and why we are out here now, trying to save him.

We scramble up the trail on Bachelor Ridge as the last of the storm blows out the north end of the canyon, leaving behind a mean, howling wind. *Why are you up here, damn fools!* the wind seems to mock us. *I already got one of your friends, get down now.*

Danny and I were heading back to town from a quick training hike and some bouldering practice up on Powell's Peak when we got calls on our cell phones about the rescue party heading up after Tyler. A hiker coming down told mountain rescue she'd heard him screaming from the other side of the Jones Couloir. Tyler's girlfriend confirmed that he'd gone up there this morning to test some new climbing gear, on what had started out as a bluebird day.

We were all up there somewhere when the summer storm barreled in, with rain, lightning, and hail. Danny and I were bouldering around the bottom of Missing Arm when it hit. We grabbed our gear and sprinted into the trees, the hail like sharp little rocks, shards of ice not falling but shot from the sky.

Back in town, Aaron's boss Gregor was rounding up everybody with rescue skills; Aaron and two others were the first up the mountain with a backboard.

Now, Scott and I are half an hour behind them, scrambling up the rain-soaked trail with a radio and back-up emergency gear, fighting a wind that seems to scream louder every time I think about the helicopter over in Aspen, on its way, we hope.

Just as we get to the top of Bachelor Ridge, where it opens to the backside of the cirque, the radio over Scott's shoulder crackles with feedback and we can hear another crackling way down in the couloir. Scott and I lean down in and try to see: Aaron and Gregor are down there somewhere, their radio crackling off the rock walls.

Scott yanks the emergency poncho out of his pack and wraps it around us and the radio against the wind, so we can hear what's going on. The wind is howling down the couloir, and Aaron – his voice intense and a little addled but still measured and precise and deadly serious as any voice I've ever heard – has to say it several times.

"We have a visual on him from here," Aaron's voice crackles through. "If he is stable, we will bring him back up on haul ropes. ETA to the ridge, 90 minutes. Recommend Aspen Charlie to LZ below Jones Couloir, if able, over."

"Aspen Charlie, roger, over," a voice crackles over the high-pitched whine of a helicopter somewhere out there.

"Scott and Jack, roger, over," Scott replies into our radio.

A few minutes later, we've set up a long top rope and climbed down into the top of the couloir. We can see that they've reached him down near the bottom, one small human form in a heap on the snow, and two small human forms hunched over him.

Aaron radioes back to everyone in detailed technical language the simple message that Tyler is seriously injured. He has an open fracture to his lower left leg, deep lacerations in both arms, and has been bleeding for three hours; he has lost a lot of blood, is going in and out of consciousness, and they need to get him out now. They have him on the gurney, attached to either side of the couloir, and radio us to send the rest of our top rope down the couloir.

We send the rope down, and hold it steady while they attach it.

"Clear to send gurney," Aaron's voice crackles into the radio, barely audible over the wind rushing up the couloir and drowning us with its howl. "Clear up top, Scott and Jack?"

"Jack and I are clear up here, over," Scott radios back.

"Clear down in the LZ, Danny and Leese?"

"Clear in the LZ, over."

"Dig in, guys," Aaron radios, then his voice half off the radio, "Hang in there, Tyler. This'll be a piece of cake. Just a little sleigh ride." Then his voice booms back into the radio, "Lowering now, Danny and Leese."

Scott and I brace ourselves with all our weight and strength into the rockband lining the sides of the top of the couloir, connected by a second belay rope. We are vigilant for too much or too little tautness in the rescue top rope; but the tensioning is perfectly steady – because Aaron had set perfect anchors on either side of the lower couloir – as they ease the gurney down to the bottom of the narrow tongue of snow.

Scott and I watch the gurney slowly disappear over the lip.

"Clear of the lip," Aaron's voice crackles on the radio.

The rope goes slightly more taut, pulling at Scott just below me, a moment later pulling at me. The dead-weight tug of the line sends a shock of adrenaline through my entire body, and I brace harder against the rock – so much harder that I could pull all of them back up the couloir, or break my own legs, break the rock, break the whole damn mountain – but not so much of a tug that we need to pay out any more rope, I note when I finally look down at my distant feet to realize that I haven't actually moved an inch.

"Approaching LZ," Danny's voice, barely audible, crackles on the radio.

"Roger that," Aaron's voice.

"Ten meters. Five. Two. Got him and clear!"

"Clear!" Aaron screams up the couloir, not bothering with the radio.

"Clear," Scott radios back.

Our rope goes slack and my body with it, the adrenaline flushing away and air rushing in, as I realize that I can't recall breathing for the past five minutes.

Back up on top, we pull the loose rope and belay rope, and don't bother coiling them, just stuff them into my pack and scramble back down the trail.

As we are breaking off the ridge, right around treeline, the wind – as if suddenly bored – stops. Scott races straight down into the woods, but I can't help but look out across the canyon, at the last of the storm crowding its way out like an uninvited party guest, leaving a broken arc of a rainbow behind. *How dare you be so goddamn beautiful right now* is all I can think, and run down the trail after Scott.

I catch him and we hurry through the wet green woods, down to the trail that crosses this one and cuts over to the little moraine lake below the couloir. I am winded but can't think of slowing down or stopping, which makes this, in a bizarre, bitter twist on normal, exactly like any other day out on the mountain with Tyler.

Because Tyler is the man: indestructible, indefatigable, a little insane, everything I'd be if I could take all the energy I waste on rumination up here and put it to kinetic use. Mahogany from the sun, with sun-bleached hair and hard blue eyes, his jaw always a little clenched, Tyler is normally impossible to catch up here. I didn't know any of that on my first trip with him, but I learned fast and hard.

I had met him the night before at the trailhead, in a driving mix of rain and snow as Aaron and I pulled in. He was standing there in hiking shorts and thermal underwear in the sleet, putting up what could not really have been a three-man tent. It was my first spring in Dudeville, and my first big mountain ever, not that I was telling these guys that; to them, it was just another mountain on another day in Colorado.

All night, I tossed and turned in that crowded tent, listening to a waterfall of rock tumbling down the mountainside across from us, a grinding of giant stones and water I could feel through the ground, through the tent, into my bones.

We were set to wake before dawn and climb up the ridge, across a dozen or so little couloirs, and up the Crestone Needle, the centerpiece of the Sangre de Christo Mountains. I had no idea who this Tyler was, but Aaron was doing all of it with a broken bone in his foot. *So how hard could it be?* I remember telling myself. Besides, there was no way I wasn't getting up this mountain with these great guys. (As Jill likes to say, I'm the guy who "just shuts up and gets it done.")

But it turns out that Aaron did know better, and didn't want to push his foot, because they had a two-week backpacking trip coming up. So he turned back for the trailhead, right after we made the ridge in a clearing, freezing dawn, where we could finally see west, in between the long walls on either side of us, mountain running north and south.

I'd been counting on Aaron's bad foot to keep the pace makeable by a greenhorn with two good feet. But after he turned back, Tyler just took off.

I started after him, watching him leap back and forth over the little frozen couloirs, making his way steadily upward with each. It was a harrowing, high altitude ballet: Tyler danced with gravity as the mountain tilted, the couloirs narrowing and deepening with ice, all of it dropping straight down at a perfect 60 degrees to a graveyard of rock, two thousand feet below, huge piles of broken granite half covered with glittering ice.

Looking down at the icy rockpile – through a frame of vision turned by the then-unfamiliar altitude from steady oval to woozy blob – is what made me freak out.

I froze, on the spot, unable to take another step.

I waited a minute, tried to move, could not move. Because my entire body knew that with my next step – onto what looked like wet rock but would surely be black ice – I would slip, stumble, and fall, ragdolling off the mountain, down, down, down, and in three minutes from that moment in time I would be down there lying in a broken heap on that pile of frozen rock, dying a slow, painful, horrible death.

"What's the matter?" Tyler said, after doubling back to check on me.

"I think it's the altitude," I mumbled.

"Definitely the altitude," he said. "You sound like you're loaded. You want to head back and catch up with Aaron, or wait here for me? I'll be up and down in maybe 40 minutes."

"I'm good here," I managed to say.

He was off a moment later, and I found a rock to sit on.

And then I waited.

And waited and waited and waited. And how long could it take? I had no idea, because I was drunk with the altitude, fuzzy and funny just behind my eyes, caught in the drunk's is-this-my-body waking dream state. I was afraid even to stand to warm myself, knowing that when drunks stand up with a bellyful, they sometimes fall down. Which would not be a good thing up there.

But the buzz started wearing off soon enough.

And I was alone on the side of this dangerous mountain with a terrible hangover.

And where the hell was that guy???

It may or may not have been 40 minutes, or 20, or 120 (I had no watch on, yet another mistake I learned from that first mountain), but just about the time I'd convinced myself that something terrible had happened to Tyler – that he'd slipped and fallen somewhere between there and the summit and was down on that pile of rock, dying a slow horrible painful death, and I had better hurry back and tell Aaron – *Pop!*

There was Tyler's head, bouncing out from behind a rock, then the rest of him, bounding down, a huge grin on his face.

"I just love a quick summit," he said, stopping when he reached me, guzzling some water and not in the least bit out of breath. "And that altitude buzz that has you all high right now?" he giggled. "It always makes everything all fuzzy and nice."

I am snapped back by an odd vibration and deep humming, the sudden roaring of a helicopter.

Scott has stopped up ahead, where the trail opens into a glade and intersects with another trail.

I nearly run into him, as the bottom of the helicopter arcs around only a few hundred feet down the trail from us, out over the tops of the trees.

We hurry down the cross trail, our pace intensified by the roar of a flying machine so odd in this pristine air. The trail opens out into the upper basin, circles the moraine lake, and climbs up to the bottom of the couloir.

As we come out onto the last ridge above the lake, we see that the helicopter cannot land. It hovers and sways in a roar over the snowfield below the couloir; and out of its open door, two guys lower a gurney, down to the tangle of busy color on the snowfield. From here I recognize them all: Aaron and Mike, who'd rappelled down their own rope, after lowering Tyler, Danny, and Leese.

Scott and I run down the trail into the little basin, filled with the echoing roar of the helicopter. Just as we pull up to them, they are moving Tyler – covered in blankets, his face the color of ash, with smears of dried blood on his nose and left cheek – from the backboard over onto the gurney, and tying him in.

Aaron stands back, points to Scott and me, and gestures back up the trail we'd just run down, mouthing, "Meadow! Meadow!"

Scott tears back up the trail and I chase after him.

"What's this about?" I shout to him.

"I think we're backup," he shouts back.

"For what?"

"In case something goes wrong. With getting the gurney up. And the helicopter out of here."

As we run back up toward the little clearing, I cannot help but stop to look back.

Aaron gives the thumbs up, and Danny and Mike and Leese guide the gurney into the air. Then it spools up, quickly, cleanly, with one rotation, straight into the helicopter.

The helicopter hovers a few seconds, and then swoops down over the little lake before digging into the air and finally climbing upward, passing just over the last band of rock and out of the basin.

I think I am still running back up this trail, but the whole thing sounds and feels like it is happening all around me in slow motion with a deafening surreal roaring, a terrible dream.

And out of that dream, half an hour or maybe only five minutes later, Aaron, Danny, Mike and Leese are marching up the trail and into the meadow, where Scott and I are pacing, having sorted out all the gear, coiled and re-coiled the rope, paced some more.

"What the hell happened?" Scott asks, when they're still twenty feet away.

"Looks like a serac came down on him," Aaron says, pointing up the mountain. "With him. On him."

From here, you can see the long tongue of snow still lining the cavern of the couloir.

He hands Scott the binoculars around his neck.

"Oh shit, man," Scott says, staring through them and then handing them to me.

From down here, it looks like a small scattering of rock across the top of the couloir, a few sharp pieces sticking out of the snow like knives at random angles.

A few minutes later, we are all hiking down slowly, in silence, except every ten or so minutes when Aaron or Danny or Mike or Leese blurt out, as if someone had just asked, "He'll be fine ... Tyler's tough ... He'll be OK ..."

On the way down, I think about that word: *serac*. It's an effective one, because it sounds like it would hurt – a penetrating object, a knife, a serrated blade – but it also sounds in a weird way like a name for a piece of art, but maybe just because it's French. Like so many French climbing words, it was first applied way up in the highest, hardest reaches of the Alps, where the towns are connected by gondolas and *all* of Dudeville is above treeline. Leave it to the French to give such crisp, artful words for such harsh and occasionally deadly things: serac, cornice, moraine, col. They do sound like art, or kitchen items, or good stiff brandies, not pieces of geology that break off and fall on people in the killzones above Chamonix.

It takes a solid hour to get back to the trailhead, and nearly half an hour for all of us to convoy back to mountain rescue HQ in town, where I know we'll sort out all the gear; and we'll all murmur that Tyler will be fine; and we'll have the first of a hundred conversations about what happened to him up there. And no one will want to go home until we have news about how he is doing.

When we get to mountain rescue, the small, gear-stuffed warehouse-like building at the end of Main Street, it is buzzing with people who'd heard the news and want to help.

I carry in a big pack full of rope bulging out the open top, drop it on a bench, and turn to go.

And there she is, standing right in the middle of the room, staring at me.

"Hey," Jill says to me, her voice wary, almost a whimper, but her eyes on fire.

"Hey," I say back.

"Are you OK?"

"I'm pretty rattled," I say. "The helicopter got him up at Jones Lake. We had to lower him off the couloir. He's hurt pretty bad."

"Yeah. We heard. We were on standby down here, if they couldn't fly him out, and he ended up coming down with you guys."

All around us people are unloading gear and helping Aaron and another guy sort it out in silence. Everyone looks lost in their own thoughts, flattened after their own rushes of adrenaline. One by one, they are heading out the door and back to wherever they were five hours ago or, more likely, over to Ullar's.

Jill doesn't move. She just stands there between me and the open door, leaning a little forward at me like she wants to hit me – and she should hit me – but it could just be the angle of her climbing boots.

I notice that the whole place is suddenly almost emptied out, the fluorescent lights buzzing.

"So," she says.

"So," I say.

"So are you ever going to call me back?

"Sorry about that, I just –"

"Just – no. No more bullshit."

"But –"

"No more bullshit, please. And don't call me, if you don't want to call me. But you owe it to me, this one last time, to tell me why."

"But if I'm not calling you –"

"I don't understand you," she snaps at me.

"There's nothing to understand."

"Oh yes there is. But I'm done trying."

"So what do you want?"

"I just want it to not be so weird," she says. "We live in a small town, Jack."

"But you don't really live here."

"Well you don't either."

"I live here more than you do," I protest.

"Well I lived here first!"

"'Well I lived here first,'" I try imitating her tone. "Listen to you – you sound like a little kid. Act your age!"

"Look who's frickin' talking!" she bursts out laughing. "Why don't you try acting half of yours?"

"Why don't you both try that somewhere else," Aaron passes between us with a clipboard, on his way over to a bench piled with medical supplies. "You kids are usually funny. But not today."

"Everybody's heading over to Ullar's," she says. "And I want to go, but I don't want it to be weird."

I watch Aaron working through the supplies.

"Look at me!" she snaps again. "I'm talking to you!"

"Ok," I finally say, transfixed by Aaron's counting of bloodied gauzes into a white plastic bag. "Just – let's not try to figure it all out today. Today's been a little intense."

She looks over at Aaron, then back at me. "Yes it has," she sighs. "See you over there anyway? I promise, no more intense. Today. But I do want to talk."

"Ok," I say, feeling aggrieved, even though I know she is right, wanting only to get out of there.

I grab my pack and turn to go.

And there is Deputy Dog, standing in the open doorway, Tyler's bloodhound, looking up at me, his sad little old man's face full of worry.

An hour later, Aaron walks into Ullar's and the place – half-crowded but weirdly hushed, except for a litany of pain from some skinny woman with a guitar on Austin City Limits – goes suddenly and completely silent when Maggie mutes the TV.

"I just got off the phone with Gregor, who flew to Vail Valley Hospital with Tyler. He's in surgery now, to deal with the open leg fracture and clean out the other stuff. He's lost a ton of blood, but he's in stable condition. He is one tough son of a bitch, as you all know. So let's just hope for the best. Gregor will call over here when he's out."

There is a big collective exhale, and suddenly the bar is buzzing with talk and the singer-songwriter's next heartbreak. Aaron walks slowly over to the bar, looking as exhausted as I've ever seen him. He crumples onto the stool next to me, grabs the beer Maggie already has there for him, and takes a long swallow.

"Uhhhh," he lets out a long groan of a sigh, a pent-up, belated, terrified groan of an I've-just-seen-death (again) of a sigh.

"Sorry, man," I say.

He doesn't say anything, just puts his hand on my arm on the bar for a minute, as if to check that I'm physically in one piece, then takes another long swallow of beer.

We drink in silence for several long, weary minutes.

"I don't know if this helps," I finally find something to say. "But you were a rock star up there today."

He looks over at me and starts to say something, but his eyes go blank, faraway, right at the edge of gone. Maybe that's the "thousand-yard stare" of a combat veteran I've always read about?

Then he shakes his head, snapping back to here and now, and puts his hand on my arm again. "Thanks, man," he says. "It does help."

By the time he's into his second beer, Aaron is not only back in the room, but he's talking fast, telling me more of what Gregor got from Tyler during the transfers. He replays the whole rescue again, sifting the details, tallying the how's and why's, and all the not-next-time's we will all need to remember.

It wasn't the storm, Aaron says Gregor told him. Which makes sense, because Tyler would know never to be in a place that exposed in any kind of storm.

It was the culmination of other factors. Day upon day of snowmelt, combined with nights not cold enough for hard re-freezing. The high angle of the summer sun and square slant of its rays before the storm blew in. The instability of the rock in the upper couloir, through cycles of freeze / melt / freeze / melt, sitting in what looks solid but is really a suspended slush-bath. The sluicing beneath all if it of ten million gallons of water around ten million rocks. And then, with just the right amount of water trickling down behind the uppermost rock, and a sudden wind, and...

WHAM! The mountain just fell out from under me, Tyler said.

According to Gregor, according to Aaron, Tyler had been working the ridge, practicing easy class IV and bouldering moves along the edge of the gendarmes – rock sentries that line the ridge, yet another oddly *apropos* French word for what's up there – when it happened. He said he'd been having a grand old time up there on a beautiful day, and saw the storm coming in, no problem; he was on his way off the top, no hurry; he had all his gear together and on his back, no worries.

But as he was passing the top of the Jones Couloir, just a few bootstomps and handholds on a good day, he said he noticed streams of water coming out of the seams in the rock that hadn't been there on his way across earlier. And while he was staring at it and reaching for it and his boot was toeing up onto it, he said he remembered thinking *Hmm, that's weird* – and then it collapsed under his boot and his hand, the whole of the rock face dropping out beneath him and before he could do anything he was suddenly airborne off the ridge ragdolling down the couloir with his backpack full of gear. Even with no ice ax at the ready, he managed to kick and claw with his legs and arms, snaggling off some speed, he said. But he just kept dropping and falling and then bouncing off the rocks near the bottom thinking he was going to fly off the cliff at the very bottom and he was dead and that's the last thing he said he remembers.

Aaron finishes the story and we drink in silence.

Danny comes in, with Deputy Dog on his heel, and leads him over to the fireplace with Kettle, Buddy, Tashi and another dog I don't know. He checks the water bowl, then joins us at the bar.

"Hey man," I say.

"Hey," he says, and starts in on the beer Maggie has in front of him.

The three of us drink in silence.

Up on the TV, the singer-songwriter is still crooning, waltzing along with a sad, weeping fiddle. And over by the fireplace, the dogs are all down on their bellies, their heads on the hearthstone, looking from person to person, confused, worried.

Jill is over at one of tables with some people I don't recognize. Every now and then we make eye contact, until she finally gets up to leave.

"Hey there," I say, walking over toward her, halfway to the door. "I do want to talk. I'm really sorry for not just calling you back."

"You should be. So meet me back here then," she says, like an order from a boss. "Tomorrow." Then her voice cracks, "Ok? Please?"

The phone rings and Maggie kills the TV, the place suddenly deathly quiet again.

"It's Gregor," Maggie shouts, even though everyone in the room is listening.

She hands the phone to Aaron.

He listens, nods, says "OK" several times, and hands the phone back to Maggie.

"Tyler's out of surgery," Aaron turns and says to everyone. "It was gnarly, but we all knew that. They put eight screws and two plates in his tib-fib. His knee cap was shattered, so they replaced that. He lost a lot of blood, so they had to transfuse four units into him, so far. And he's stable. The good news is there's no sign of any nerve damage or infection. So he's going to be ok. Banged up for a long while, but he'll be fine."

The bar erupts in cheers and high-fives, but only for a minute. It feels like everyone is forcing it – it's the first time Jill and I have ever high-fived while not on top of a mountain – everyone still terrified of what happened up there today, seemingly at random, to the very toughest among us.

I walk back to the bar and catch a last glimpse of Jill as she lingers at the door.

Tomorrow, she mouths and points at the floor.

I nod *Yes.*

Bye, she mouths, then turns and hurries out.

Danny and Aaron and I sit and drink our beers in silence.

"Fucking serac," Aaron finally mutters.

"Fuckin' bad day on the mountain," Danny mutters.

"Fuckin' A," I mutter, because it could have been any of the three of us up there, counting on the other two to save him, and I have to mutter something.

The End of Something

So what exactly am I supposed to tell Jill, I wonder, when I awaken to the sliding glass door bang of Danny coming in my house and going straight to my hot tub.

It's a perfect summer morning, and there's nothing I'd rather do than go out for a hike with him – and the very last thing I want to do is drive back down into town later and deal with Jill. But it's time, or way past time actually.

After she and I mixed it up, yet again, those few days around Hillary's wedding, I promised, yet again, that I'd meet up with her, this time all the way down in Argentina. We had made a big plan and, yet again, I didn't show up. Standard stuff after two years of go-rounds with her. (Well, maybe a little worse than standard, as she reminded me with the "Fuck you, I hate you" email afterwards that it was also her birthday; and maybe she would have made other plans – in a strange and beautiful country full of mountains, desert and coastline – than hang around in a hotel near the airport, waiting for me not to show.) So yes, she has good reason to seem more pissed about this than the other times.

Maybe I should make up something truly outlandish about why I bailed on her this time. Rebound Girl showed up in Dudeville that week, and we've decided to make a go of it. Or, I met a tourist – you know, someone my age, someone with teenagers even – and I was giving up the mountains so I could run them around to soccer practice every weekend. Or, I finally realized that the reason I can't commit to a woman after all those years of a dead marriage and the past two years of on-and-off with her is because I've discovered, in this extended midlife crisis, that, well, I'm gay.

I try to crawl out of bed, fighting the gravitational pull of shame, dread, and a brand-new kind of self-loathing: anything besides the humiliating truth. (Though the truth, on the other hand, has the special advantage of driving her away, once and for all, in complete disgust.) Because the truth is that I blew her off, in Argentina on her birthday no less – along with an entire hemisphere full of new mountains – because the weekend before, I was tracked down and bedded, after nearly a year of pristine celibacy, not by Rebound Girl but by a dreadlocked white girl in tutti-frutti cowboy boots.

By goddamn Freak Girl. With the big hoop through her nose, and the goofy little blond dreads, and old boots dribbled and drabbed with a dozen colors of paint. She was bouncing on the rail next to me at the String Cheese Incident up at Steamboat, in that mad, drunk, stoned, ecstatic tribe. It was my first good sweat, not alone on a mountain but in the middle of a crowd, in a very long time. I suppose I knew in the back of my mind that Jill and Argentina were only days away; but I wasn't thinking about that, really, only that it had been a very weird day.

I fall back into bed and piece that day together up there: how it started out so shitty, and ended up so weird; how I ended up falling into bed with Freak Girl.

I'd been out mountain biking with Samuel and Cynthia, Danny's "high-drama married friends" – as he always called them, for reasons I was soon to discover – from college. It was way too early in the season for mountain biking up there, which we should have known, and we lost the trail almost immediately in the mud and snow and winter downfall.

And so what should have been a two or three-hour workout ride turned out to be an all-day ordeal: dragging our mud-caked bikes across pastures ankle-deep with melting snow and cowshit; Samuel and Cynthia screaming at each other about the route; each of them sniping about how lost the other had made us. I instantly recognized, from as far back as my parents and every other miserable married couple I'd ever known since, that they were not fighting about the route: they were sniping about how miserably unhappy they were with each other. And it wasn't so much that they were just yelling at each other: they were trying to annihilate each other, just like young, healthy, outdoorsy versions of my parents, and all I wanted to do was get the hell away from both of them. But when we finally found our way out through the snow and the mud and the cowpies to a rutted forest service road, and I could fly well ahead of them, as rotten luck would have it my tire blew out almost instantly, a flat that threw me off my bike and into the muddy, spiky brush. And it was the kind of flat that my spare tube couldn't fix – a big deck screw through the sidewall of the tire – something the duct tape and dollar bill trick could barely fix. So I had to walk/roll my bike the five miles back to town, while Samuel and Cynthia peddled along behind me at their leisure, still screaming at each other.

We crawled back into the campground outside of town just before sunset, freezing cold and covered with dried mud and cowshit.

Without a moment's thought, I gave in to my "bourgeois weakness" and got a hotel room next to the show.

The String Cheese Incident was staying there, along with half their wild crowd from the show. And my room – a big suite, the only room left – turned out to be the perfect place for Danny and Julie to hold court after the show. (Not that I had much choice in the matter.) A bunch of people they knew were in and out all night; and I barely noticed when a freaky looking girl with little blond dreads and big sparkly diamond-colored eyes drafted in on some of them.

We were all crammed into the main room of my suite, beers everywhere, the bong going out on the deck. A young hippie guy had brought a guitar and could play it pretty well, and his buddy was carrying his own beat-up old guitar like a fashion accessory and couldn't play it all. So I did what I never do, maybe because I'd overcome the frustration, weirdness and exhaustion of the day with massive doses of coffee and weed: I picked it up and just started playing it, along with the hippie guy, and people got right into it.

The guitar was chewed raw in places and covered with stickers for old punk and skate rat bands, and I thought it would sound like crap – which is mostly why I picked it up, to verify that it did – and it sounded warm and clean and good, like very old blue jeans for my old hands.

"Play that thing!" Freak Girl yelled at me.

I drove the guitar harder, started chopping at it like a madman with a drum, banging out some old punk songs I used to do – and it turned out that Freak Girl could *sing*.

I felt around on the strings for the pattern of a song I hadn't thought of in 15 or maybe 20 years, since the dying gasps of what had been a band before I renounced my vow of extended poverty and grew up. (If only temporarily, obviously.) I silenced the guitar a moment, counted to four, and then exploded into a quick, tight, minor-keyed rhythm.

The hippie guy was right there with the chords, and Samuel leaned over the coffee table and drummed in perfect time.

And then Freak Girl – I still don't know how she did this – found words for it, words that worked, like a rapper, except it was more of a folk-punk thing, like Ani DeFranco, but with an actual melody.

Freak Girl finished a two-verse cycle, took a huge chug of beer, and just as the angry slash of guitar chords came back around to the minor root, she jumped up on the couch between Danny and Samuel, threw her head back, and sang out:

Gotta bleed for me honey
How else will I know you care?
Gotta cry for me, little honey
How else will I know you're there?
Gotta die for me now, die for me loud
Die for me on this little dare of ours
Cuz how else, little honey
Will I know you were even here?

And we played on and rocked it out, everyone in the suddenly crowded room clapping in time to the music.

Freak Girl's lyrics got darker, then silly, then crumbled into bebop.

A few others took a stab at the ad lib, none of them any good at it except Freak Girl – until there was a security guy at the door who told us to keep it down (I guess they'd been trying to call) – which is no small feat in a hotel where String Cheese and their crowd is staying.

The rest is a bit of a blur, back and forth between the crowded room and the half-crowded deck and the bong, until the suite started emptying out, and Freak Girl was still there, her big diamond eyes all full of *Fun!* and *Yes!* and *Let's just do it!*

And so we did it, all that night and all the next day.

I am jolted back by the big bass drum of a sliding glass door.

Danny is rummaging around in my living room, then I hear his voice on the phone. Which is odd, because he usually kills a solid hour out in the hot tub before he does anything else. He is never in a hurry, and I always am, which is one of the reasons we get along, I think: we each want a little of what the other guy has, maybe.

He was definitely not in a big hurry back in Steamboat on that trip. He was off in the love bubble with Julie, and I was settled into the hotel, so I stayed on for a few days.

Freak Girl was just passing through from Boulder, she said, off to look at grad schools in Utah, with nothing to do except sing old songs, drink beer, smoke weed, and screw around. And she was outlandish, which was part of the fun, I suppose: odd dabs of hippie and punk and mountainfreak; the little dreads popping off her head like antennae; the big silver hoop through her nose that she could touch with her long tongue; the rainbow hemp and old jeans, and tutti-frutti cowboy boots. She was a whir of theatricality, playing to my straight man with all her funny voices, hooks from songs, shticks from old movies. And she knew all the classic blues-rock songs I used to play. She'd learned them, she said, from (ugh) her grandparents.

"They were really young! And really cool! Really!" she added quickly, when I involuntarily mouthed the word *Grandparents???*

Best not to think about any of that, especially given what I have to go do in a few minutes. And I know I should get up. But whatever

Danny is doing on the phone out in the living room sounds a little intense.

I roll back over, wishing I could sleep, wishing I didn't have to deal with Jill today, wishing I could un-do what I did with Freak Girl, or at least forget the whole thing. What a damn fool I made of myself. If Jill ever knew the full horror of why I blew off Argentina, it would definitely finish off this thing, finally and forever.

Without really thinking about it, I assumed that Freak Girl was just an overgrown kid lost in her mid-20s, maybe a year or two younger than Jill when we met two summers ago. But I decided it was better not to do any of the math on her. Her actual name was Ariel; but the only other Ariel I'd ever met was an Israeli guy who worked for me Back East, a chubby engineer with hair sprouting from his nose, ears and knuckles, so the name wasn't so hot for me. Freak Girl, by contrast, was crazy hot for me, or so it seemed at first; but I think she may have been that way for whomever, whatever, whenever – the female version in particular, or so she said, if only because she thought that might excite me more.

Not that I didn't have enough data right away that she was trying way too hard: she was instantly and persistently in a state of vocalized orgasm, from the first minute of contact. This odd feature – which Danny has since described to me as "auto- and perma-coming" – would rise and fall but never stop, not even for breath it seemed. All her howling and yelping and *Oh Godding* was inspiring and gratifying at the outset, but quickly grew monotonous and numbing, and then strange, cat-in-heat-like creepy, to the point where I was certain they weren't orgasms at all, just some gratuitous reflexive acknowledgement, an erotic notarization.

Each morning up there in Steamboat, I told myself, would be the last – time to get the hell out of town and away from Freak Girl.

Then, out in the morning sun, she would look over at me with those big bright eyes that just said *Fun!* and *Now!* and *Tomorrow you can go back to getting old and dying.*

Each of those days I knew in the back of my mind that I needed to get back, that the window on getting to The Treehouse – for my passport and skis and gear – was closing, closing, closing, and then . .
.

Bam! Suddenly it was the weekend and Argentina was come and gone. I'd blown another thousand bucks on airline tickets to somewhere exotic I'd never go (kind of a punishment, I guess, not trying to get a refund or credit from the airline); Jill would never speak to me again; and I was still in Steamboat with Freak Girl. In the middle of all that, my computer modem blew up, like they always do; there were none to be had in all of Steamboat of course; and someone was always on the hotel computer doing their own email.

And so, I blew it. I couldn't reach Jill, not that I tried very hard, to let her know what was up. And that was that.

I drag myself out of bed and go out into the living room.

Danny is sprawled out on the floor in his underwear, with credit cards, slips of paper, my phone, and his calendar. His blond hair is a big, matted, wet-brown mess, the purple and pink streaks all but gone.

"Hey man," he says absently, working on the calendar.

I pour a cup of the coffee he's made and watch him leaf through his calendar. "What's up?"

"Heading to Portland next week. Just booked the flights."

"Really?"

"Yeah," he sighs, "Just to hang out, you know. With Julie."

"Good," I say, "you should do that."

"Just for old times' sake."

An hour later – after smoking a bowl with Danny I probably shouldn't have and fighting the urge to run off with him on his hike (with, oddly, only gratuitous encouragement from him because I think he likes Jill after all) – I head down into Dudeville.

It feels like I am driving to my own execution. Another perfect summer day in the mountains of Colorado, the sun climbing into a bottomless blue, drenching the aspens and evergreens with bright lemony light, the greens all turned up – and all I can see is that dark, cold, driving rain back in Steamboat.

"Nah, I hate that place," Freak Girl said, when the skies opened up and I started in to the big brewpub on the main drag.

We'd been out seeing if maybe some of the local stores had a modem I could buy.

"Come on," I said, "just for a quick one – to wait out this rain."

Her face went dark for the first time since I'd met her, but she finally shrugged and followed me in.

A beefy guy in a Vikings sweatshirt was working the door. He was giving everybody the once-over before letting them in, carding only the people who looked like you would card them, so I started past him.

"Hold on there, buddy," he put his hand up like a traffic cop.

I pulled out my ID and he studied it.

"Sorry, dude," he said when he handed it back to me. "The light's really working for you in here."

"I'll take it, dude," I shrugged, as I went by and started into the bar.

I was most of the way to the bar when I realized Freak Girl wasn't following me. When I turned around, I saw her standing next to the bouncer, waving me back. I walked over, and the bouncer was sitting on his stool, ignoring her, already carding somebody else.

"What's up?"

"He won't let me in!" she yelled, more at the bouncer than me, who ignored her. "I forgot my ID!"

Then she started toward the door, flaring with anger, a bizarre little temper tantrum. "Fuck you all!" she screamed back into the bar. "I just forgot my ID!"

The bouncer looked over at me.

"What, dude? She forgot her ID. She's with me."

"That doesn't matter."

"Why not? You can't just let her slide?"

"No."

"Why not?"

"Because she's 19 years old."

"Oh," I said.

Something like bile flooded my mouth, the whole world going dark as the street outside, curtained suddenly with pounding rain.

"That girl," the bouncer laughed at me. "She's been trying to lie her way in here for the last six months."

Right about then I'm guessing, the light in there stopped working for me. If he had checked my ID again, all it would have said was *Dirty Old Man*.

Back in the dark and rainy street, disgusted with myself and furious at her, I told Freak Girl I was checking out of the hotel and driving home.

"Like – tomorrow morning?"

"No – like now."

She grinned, *Cool! Fun! Let's go!* then saw what I meant and her smile turned into just as big a frown. She searched my face with those big bright teenager's eyes – like I'm Jerry Lee Lewis and we're just going to pack off for the UK or something – and all I could do was mumble: "By myself."

"Really? But – we're rocking it and – "

"Yeah, sure. And it's been great fun. But you're nineteen. You're a goddamn teenager! Which makes me a dirty old fucker."

"But –"

"It's time to move on."

"That's cool, dude," she shrugged, not missing a beat, ever the little hippie rapper. "You know what they say up here." She grinned at me and shook her little blond dreads, like someone who really was in high school a year or two ago, like someone who could be the freshman roommate of my ex-wife's and my daughter, if we'd had one the year we met. "You don't lose your girlfriend, you lose your turn."

The whole thing made me want to retch right there on the street in Steamboat and it makes me want to retch right here in my truck, down off the hill already.

I force myself to turn right, onto the main drag into Dudeville, and not left and west and free of this crappy little business I have to take care of, finally and forever.

I drive by Ullar's, as slowly as any curious or nervous tourist has, and park a good block and a half away. It takes every ounce of strength not to hit the gas and keep going.

I am barely out of the truck, and there's Kettle, running up to me, his tail whipping the air. He gives me his usual quick lick and head butt, and turns and runs back.

And there is Jill, out in front of Ullar's on the bench made of old skis. She's wearing her old white ski hat, the one she had on when we met two years ago right in here, pulled way down onto her forehead.

When she sees me, she jumps up – not into her usual question mark, looking at me sideways, wondering what I'm thinking – but into a half-squat, like she's at the top of a run, bracing herself for the drop.

"Hey," I say, our usual greeting, but she says nothing, just stares at me with hard, reddened, burning eyes.

I know she is going to tear into me, not that I don't deserve it, haven't always deserved it.

But she looks truly angry at me for the first time in all these round-and-rounds. All the playing house up in The Treehouse, then gone again, farther away each time, then right back here, never any promises made to each other – which is what I thought mattered – but never any promises the other way either, which I suppose to her has been promise enough. More than two years now, like the seasons of the mountains: snow, mud, sun, and snow again. Never once did I say what any of it meant, but never once did I actually let her go, tell her to go away and never come back.

She turns and walks into Ullar's, Kettle on her heels, me dragging behind.

Now has to be the time, I remind myself again, to make it as plain as the sky is blue and Ullar's is empty: *we are done.* And if that doesn't work, I'll have to drive a stick right through her heart, and tell her exactly why I didn't go to Argentina: *because I ended up in Steamboat shacking up with some random, pretentious little goofball who wasn't old enough to drink yet. Because, you know, why not?*

Which would make me the Asshole of Life, which I am anyway, but only in my own mind and maybe with a few Betty friends of hers. But then life, as they say up here in Dudeville and everywhere else, will go on.

I follow her down to the far end of the empty bar, as far as we can get from Maggie, who is hunkered down with the pile of Sunday's *Denver Post* down at the other end.

There is a documentary about the old west on the TV, the air heavy with dust and yet another singer-songwriter with an acoustic guitar and a broken heart who sounds like she wouldn't be old enough to drink either.

Maggie quickly pours us beers without saying anything or even looking at us, then gathers up the newspaper and takes it into the back room.

I hadn't noticed yesterday, but Jill is darker than ever from the sun. Her skin is mahogany against her white t-shirt and tan hiking shorts, her ski hat flecked all over with little black pills and lint. She has pulled it down over her eyes, all the way past her brows; her braids, still wet from a shower I suppose, stick out the back at odd angles. Her green eyes are darkened, red around the edges, harder than ever.

"So."

"So."

"Argentina was good?"

"Argentina was good."

We drink our beers in silence for an eternal minute and a half.

"So, Jill. I know I should have called you back. I just felt like shit –
"

"Blech!" she almost spits the beer back into the glass. "You *should* feel like shit."

"But –"

"Just stop. Before you start."

"No, I want you to understand –"

"You blew me off, dude. Again. What's there to understand?"

"I know, I know," I say, then take a long swallow of beer. "And it was on your birthday."

"Birthday, whatever," she mutters. "I don't care about that."

"Sure, you do. It was totally lame . . ." and I have no idea what I was going to say when I look over and see a cold, dead-hard seriousness to her eyes.

"You don't understand," she says, her voice turning hard, brittle, anguished.

"What don't I under–"

"I was pregnant," she cuts me off.

I take a long swallow of beer.

"I was going to have an abortion."

Another long swallow of beer.

"I had a miscarriage."

And because there is absolutely nothing I can say, I take another long swallow of beer.

We sit in silence for how many minutes I don't know, staring at the bar, drinking.

A pale sickness wells up behind the beer on a stomach empty but for coffee. And I was just thinking that Freak Girl made me the Asshole of Life?

Maggie is back to pour another beer, then disappears into the backroom.

She tells me the rest of it in a blur – because she had access to anything you could need on a big guided trip and was with Kelly and a couple other Betties, she was looked after so she didn't need to tell me, and I didn't really need to know, not technically – and all I can do is sit here in horror and hate myself. And wonder: what would I have done, if I had known? Would I have shown up in Argentina, not to play in the snow, but shown up for her and that whole nightmare? Or would I have failed? All that I know – all that we all know – is that I did not show up. That she was left to deal with it without me. That I *am* the Asshole of Life.

She finishes telling me what I think are the last of the details, and we sit in silence, gulping at our beers.

The singer-songwriter's heart is still breaking, over and over, one song after another of unrelieved longing and sadness, with fiddle and mandolin breaks.

I feel like crying, if I knew how with somebody else around.

I am finally about to say something, though I'm not sure what, when a big group of people barrel through the door in biking gear.

Maggie is back behind the bar. She switches the music to the boisterous bounce of a bluegrass band, which makes Jill sigh and roll her eyes sideways, and makes me feel like crying more.

I finally blurt it out: "I want you to tell me the whole thing."

"And I want to tell you the whole thing," she says, looking wearily at the group of cyclists all high-fiving each other over something. "In private."

Five minutes later, I'm driving back up to The Treehouse, with Jill right behind me in her own truck. She said she needed food, and that talking it out – in private and over more drinks – would make it easier. I heartily agreed, at least with the more drinks part.

But Kelly is home, she said, and in a really weird, touchy mood.

So we headed up the hill in separate trucks, after both saying upfront what had to be said and repeated: no hot tub, no bong hits, no nothing. And if she gets too drunk to drive herself back, she can crash in my guest room.

Up at The Treehouse, we make a big wrong-end-of-the-day breakfast and strong bloody Marys, and head out onto the deck with all of it, just as the sun is dropping behind the ridge on the other side of the canyon. As we worked our way through our now familiar cooking and drinkmaking routine, she's been telling me everything else about Argentina: the people, the shoot, the mountains. But I haven't really been listening. I keep dreading the rest of the story, like a bad piece of news you know is coming at the end of the meeting, which makes the rest of the meeting seem annoying and pointless.

Out on the deck, sitting in the two weathered lounge chairs like we have so many nights over the past couple years, the stars start to come out.

After a long silence and half the Bloody Marys, Jill finally tells me the story, which isn't much of a story at all.

"I was sick to my stomach every morning," she says. "I couldn't climb or work, and half the girls on the crew took one look at me and knew."

They all Bettied around her of course, and figured out how to deal with it in a Catholic country, which was essentially the same thing that rich and middle class people do in all Catholic countries, and rich and middle class Americans do in redneck states: they came up with the cash and dealt with it in secret, in abject terror of someone finding out.

I should be listening more patiently, I suppose. But because this was like any other piece of bad news at the end of a meeting, I was more interested in figuring out how it happened so it won't happen again.

"I don't know," she finally says. "But I know it was you, if that's what you're thinking."

"I'm not thinking –"

"Because I didn't screw around on you," she mutters into the last of her drink.

Of course she wasn't, I think, because that would have made all of this so much easier.

All she could figure out, she says, was that we must have had a condom failure back in March, the week of Hillary's wedding. Because that's all it takes: one condom failure. Among how many hundreds? But wouldn't we know?

Neither of us could think of how or when or why.

"Because sometimes they just fail," she says. "That's what they told me at the clinic. It's just a numbers game."

"I guess."

"Too bad you never got the vasectomy you were always saying you were going to get, huh?"

"Well..."

"Mister I-Never-Want-to-Have-Children," she mutters at me, "So-Badly-I-Left-My-Wife."

She is right about the vasectomy which, for some reason, I just never got around to.

"So," I try to clear my dry throat, not wanting to talk about this because she is exactly right. "That morning – you and the girls..."

The morning she was supposed to have the abortion – or what would have been my third day down there, but for my being The Asshole of Life – she says she woke up even sicker than she had been every morning on the trip.

I am trying to listen, but I keep going blank, drifting off to the stars popping out of the sky.

"It only felt like a really bad period," I hear her say. And that she "went to the secret doctor anyway. And it was gone."

Then I hear her start crying.

I am snapped back, as if by a cold hard slap across my face from all those stars, right back here on my deck next to her. Right back next to her tall, lean, strong, giving body, all hunched over, weeping openly.

"I'm sorry," I say.

"Not as sorry as I am," she weeps.

I reach over to comfort her, to pat her on the – what? hand? shoulder? knee? – and she slaps my hand away.

Then she clenches her fists and bursts into full-blown tears, a deathly wailing not at me but at everything.

I don't know what to do so I don't do anything, just sit back and stare at the stars, and feel her hand reach for mine. And then we do something we've never done in all those round-and-rounds over the past two years: we just hold each other, for a very long time.

Her sobs slowly dissipate, and she goes limp in my arms.

The whole re-telling of the horrible thing, along with three Bloody Marys on top of the beer from Ullar's, has wiped her out.

A few minutes later, without saying anything, she gets up, goes in the house, and stumbles off to my guest room.

I make sure she has what she needs for the night, then say "good night" and shut the door behind me.

I grab a fleece and go back out onto the deck to watch the stars and figure out how to feel about all of this. But that would require some privacy and some quiet; and unfortunately, there is neither back out here on the deck.

Instead, the Presence is out here, staring down hard at me from somewhere inside all those stars. And before I can settle back down on the lounge-chair, it says in that voice I know all too well: *You made promises to her.*

No I didn't, I give the answer I'd give anybody.

Your body made promises to her.

I am not my body, I say, remembering something Danny once said.

Or was it? From one of his road-trip parsings from the Yoga Sutras, or that British novelist, or Kerouac, maybe. Or wasn't it something I came up with myself? Conjured most likely in the presence of the Presence. That's right: last summer, when I was out on that grueling, gut-busting, mind-flattening solo backpack, all vertical and not another soul, up and over the Never Summer Wilderness. *I work this hard back in my body because I am NOT my body, never was,* I remember saying to it. *And inhabiting it down here in the world is strange, frustrating, terrifying. That's why everyone flees their own body – with food, alcohol, work, drugs, gambling, sex, risk, adrenaline. I'm just borrowing this body of mine, taking it out for joyrides.*

I am not my body, I say again to the Presence. *And my body is not me. Those are all just tests.*

For now, yes, it answers. *But she is on that ride with you, whether you like it or not. And you failed the test.*

So I AM the Asshole of Life, I say back.

But the Presence says nothing, answers only with an angry scatter of stars across a suddenly cold black sky.

I have nothing to say back to the stars, except what I said to Jill: *I am sorry.*

And I am sorry. But beating myself up doesn't do me or anybody I hurt any good, any more than just running away does. And I really do have to do something else this time.

Because I am not really my body; I am just taking it out for one very long and complicated test-ride. That's why all the risk and adrenaline and adventure, trying to shock myself back into this body, and really feel the contours of the test-ride.

But all these random people, I suppose I should admit, are on the same test-ride with me: Jill, Danny, Aaron, Amy the Rebound Girl, maybe even Freak Girl.

Or not. I don't know anything anymore. I know only that my body is sinking toward sleep, even though I am not tired.

The stars are hard, icy, silent; and even now, in the height of summer, at this altitude the air turns a steely cold at night, crawling up from the canyon and engulfing the deck and The Treehouse.

I am slapped awake from the chill, get up, and stumble off to my empty bed.

Christmas in July

But the sun does always rise, and across a flawless blue sky – in the middle of July, in the middle of Colorado – it feels like the sun will keep rising forever.

Aaron and I are following it up the mountain, hiking up to the same backcountry hut outside Aspen where I'd spent a week two winters ago with Danny and the crew.

We are trying to cram in as much training as we can before the big fall climbing season and our attempt to drop in and snowboard down The Lady. And rather than another quick run up or down any of the mountains around Dudeville, or another day up on the rock practicing rope work and rappels, Aaron suggested we do more LSD – a long slow distance hike with full packs and an overnight up near treeline.

Before I could suggest the Flat Tops, or Eagles Nest, or the Raggeds, or any of the dozen other wilderness areas where we can go long and big and not see many people, he said, simply, "Polarstar." The name is charged for me with color, light, music, and something like what I think people mean when they say "Christmas magic" – if I believed in such things and didn't hate Christmas – and I practically threw the rest of my gear into his truck.

As we drove out here, Aaron told me there had been some unusual weather data coming into the mountain rescue system from up at the hut, and he wanted to go check the instruments – an oblique way of saying to go check that nobody had messed with the place. Polarstar is one of a dozen or so huts strung throughout the central Colorado Rockies, built by the 10th Mountain Division to practice for combat over in the Alps during World War II, and now used by skiers in winter and hikers in summer ever since.

Two winters ago, at the last minute, I was lucky enough to be sitting alone at the bar in Ullar's when Maggie got a call that a coveted spot on her hut trip had suddenly opened: someone had decided at the last minute to go home for Christmas. Today, at the exact other end of the cycle of seasons, Danny is off in Portland with Julie and so it's just Aaron and me.

We drove most of the way to Aspen, then turned off the highway and up a dirt road, up ten curving, bouncing miles to the trailhead.

Ten minutes up the trail, this particular mix of blue spruce and lodgepole pines all look familiar; but they are taller, especially along what I remember as a narrow snowtrail now melted back to dry ground.

"So how's your mother doing?" I finally ask Aaron, our first time alone and off in the quiet since he got back from Boston two weeks ago.

"She's alright," he says. "She'll be fine."

I know those aren't the same answers, but I also know that's all he wants to say, so we hike on in silence.

"Thanks for asking," he says, long after my mind has drifted back to the trail, trees, and sky.

"Sure," I say, and we leave it at that and push on in comfortable, familiar silence.

Despite deliberately heavy packs, the hike flies by at three times the speed of our winter trip, when I was dragging the same pack with a snowboard lashed to the back, trying to keep up with the rest of them on their telemark skis.

It was my first full winter Out West, and I was still hauling a snowboard everywhere I went. Aaron, Danny, Maggie, Kelly and the others had been on these long hauls in deep snow and knew better, all of them on those backcountry skis I'd never seen before – with free heels that allowed them to whisk up the snow trail. All of them except Maggie's tourist pickup, of course, the big, strong, friendly guy from Wisconsin, and what was his name?

I sure got to know him, if not his actual name, by the time we were this far up the mountain. Our snowboards were weighing us down, our snowshoes sinking into the light powder past our knees. But Big-Hearted Wisconsin Boy and I were determined to keep up: him because of Maggie; me because I was the new kid in town and ten years older than everybody else, and would rather die up here of heart failure – then as now – than let those ten years show.

Like everything my first year in Dudeville, that trip up here was the purest antidote to everything I'd known Back East. I had always hated Christmas because it was the time of the great confrontation: I am an orphan; I have no family; I am alone. Even when I was married, even though I had a sister running around somewhere out there, even though my parents hadn't done me the favor of dying yet – I was completely alone in the world, and Christmas was the garish, ubiquitous mirror on all that. Everything the color of fresh blood and fake forest green, all of it draped in fake gold and silver tinsel and accompanied by that icky, saccharine music everywhere you went, Christmas was always a gnawing reminder of how fake and forced the world really was, and how completely alien I was from it.

My wife and I had fled our families in those first hard-ass years, which was our first step out of their respective hells, but it turned every Christmas into a bitter confrontation with the void surrounding us. She responded by cleaning every square inch of whatever apartment or house we were in, while I climbed every square inch of its walls – right up to the last year of our marriage, the first after I'd discovered snowboarding.

That last year, we drove up to Killington and I tried to show her how to snowboard. But it went even worse than my attempt to get her down into the Grand Canyon a few months earlier. It turned out – I've since come to witness from chairlifts over cruisers all over the country – just like every dude-shows-wife/girlfriend-how-to ski/snowboard situation: whatever is not quite right between them, under the pressure of a few bone chilling and crushing hours, breaks to the surface and somebody starts screaming. She hated everything about snowboarding, and spent most of the day on her ass, freezing, frustrated, and snapping at me.

The next day she took a real lesson from some junior Betty snowboarding instructor who looked like she was still in high school, and that only made her more frustrated. By the end of it, she hated everything about snowboarding – even more than she hated hiking in the Grand Canyon, she let me know, in case it wasn't obvious enough.

She spent our third and last day up there getting drunk by herself in some bar wreathed in Christmas colors and music, while I frantically tried to explore the rest of that sprawling playground of a mountain.

On the long drive home, my wife was so vocal with her hatred of everything about snowboarding – the physical pounding, the cold, the dudespeak, the whole mountain scene – that I made the mistake of suggesting it may just have been Christmas biting her in the ass one more time. Which made her only more bitter and withdrawn, and we drove the rest of the six hours back to our nice new empty house in a smoldering silence.

The next morning, I woke up early and crawled out of bed to see new snow thick as cotton falling soundlessly onto our nice new empty lawn. It made my feet itch and twitch and burn, and it was at that precise moment that I made a vow to myself: I would be going back to Killington the very next Christmas, because I knew we would be split up by then.

Which is exactly what happened. One year later, I was dancing with all that freedom on my snowboard, and too exhausted (almost) to notice it was even Christmas, but for the minor funk of early drunken dinners alone at the bar, surrounded by all those couples and young families. And on Christmas Eve of all nights, I found the perfect distraction from the rest of the holiday: the proverbial Nice Jewish Girl from New York. By Christmas morning, I knew just how nice, as she quickly morphed into Amy the Rebound Girl.

I spent the rest of that trip and every other weekend that winter up there with her and the wild crew of twentysomethings who'd moved into the ski house she'd salvaged from her own dead marriage. She was hot, drunk, horny and, best of all, Jewish. And along with the Wall Street wild boys who rented rooms from her – two more Jews, a South African surfer who killed it on his snowboard, and a crazy Russian drunk who liked to fly down the mountain at full speed until he crashed into something, every one of them indifferent to the holiday – she was all the non-family I needed to laugh off the forced, fake, intrusive, cloying bilge of Christmas once and for all.

How funny to look back at all that now, from up here in the high-altitude wilds of Colorado. Little did I know then how tame Killington, for all its steeps and swagger, really was, all inbounds, safe and stratified, a few days' distraction from the constant push, shove, grovel and grind that is life Back East. It was rush hour in ski clothes and sunscreen: lines, crowds, traffic jams at the base, three deep at the bar come happy hour, and Christmas crap everywhere.

That whole snow circus was a world away from Christmas in Colorado's Polarstar hut, a rugged A-frame in a cluster of towering, snow-blanketed spruce up near treeline. Up here, I discovered with a pounding heart and soaring spirit, there are no crowds, no lines, no traffic, no noise – just one very long, very hard hike up this trail, through what felt like bottomless Rocky Mountain powder.

For that Christmas up here, it was another non-family, but a much more interesting one: Aaron, by himself of course, and now I know why; and Maggie, cooking and opening beers for everybody, a busman's holiday for her; and her Big-Hearted Wisconsin Boy, who spent the whole time chopping wood, fixing things around the hut, and tuning everybody's skis and our snowboards. Danny was packing bowls and holding court, of course, with his *femme du jour*, a classic tourist pick-up (newly divorced and busting out, etc.) And Kelly was another last-minute fill-in, and she was more edgy and jumpy than usual, trying to get over some guy who'd dumped her just in time for the holiday. Who else? Gregor from mountain rescue and his older Betty wife, who mentioned a few dozen times how happy they were to be empty-nesters for the first time that Christmas; they were the first ones up and out every morning and last ones in every night. And some Betty friend of Aaron's from the wilderness project and a beast of a Betty friend of hers, both emphatically lesbian but emphatically not together; neither of their families, each made it clear when asked, wanted their lesbian daughter home for the holiday.

Kelly kept giving me The Hairy Eyeball – as if I were giving her Bedroom Eyes, which I wasn't – and then asking me about Jill, who I was doing my best not to think about. But mostly she was entertaining us each night after dinner, around that great pine slab of a table, with stories about all the guys who had tried and failed to bed her, all the idiotic things they had done, egged on after each one by Danny to tell another.

On that first night, Kelly told us about the orthopedic surgeon / NFL team doctor from Back East who kept hitting on her at some knee surgery seminar over in Telluride, where she got "a big fee for doing a ski celebrity Q&A" with what she called "all these geeky doc-jocks."

"The NFL dude got into a chest-thumping argument with the rest of them about 'the fallacy of the pristine knee,'" she said, while he pawed hers a little more in front of them than she thought necessary.

As part of the gig, she said she had to go out skiing with all of them the next morning. The NFL doc-jock – who had been talking smack at dinner and breakfast about what a great skier he was – jumped on the first chairlift with her and said the rest of them could have their blue cruisers but he was "a big double-black diamond guy from way back."

So she said fine, and dropped in to the first double-black diamond they came to, a classic Telluride elevator shaft lined with head-high moguls. The doc-jock followed her down, and didn't make it three moguls in before he crumpled, ragdolling and screaming before sprawling out in the snow halfway down the headwall and clutching his own knee, "which was a shitload less pristine than the night before," she said, when the ski patrol came and splinted his leg, under his detailed instruction of course, and carted him to the bottom.

The second night, she told us about the knucklehead gym teacher from Boulder who decided the ideal first date with a professional extreme skier would be to go backpacking up in the Maroon Bells. Very romantic views, and the most photographed mountains in Colorado, where everyone who doesn't live in Colorado thinks Coors beer comes from, thanks to their perennial appearance in TV commercials shot nowhere near the industrial gray river town just outside Denver where it actually comes from.

Kelly of course smoked the knucklehead the first half-mile up the trail, and had to keep waiting for him at trail junctions. After the last one, all the way around the backside of the Maroon Bells, she said she got too cold and sweaty, and just pushed on ahead to their site, and set up their tent. By the time the knucklehead stumbled into their high altitude camp two hours later, he decided the best way to re-man himself for the big romantic evening ahead was to challenge her to a contest of push-ups.

"Seriously?" Danny blew out a cloud of pot smoke and we all laughed. "Oh, that dumb bastard!"

"Yes, seriously," Kelly said. "And if you think that was dumb, he even said, 'Bet I can go two-for-one on you.'"

Kelly said she was disgusted enough not to argue, just dropped and start doing push-ups, there at 11,000 feet. And somewhere between 25 and 30, she asked the knucklehead if she should stop, and that was the end of their big romantic evening.

The third night Kelly told us about the outdoor company climber guy – no, the other kind of climber, the corporate kind I used to deal with – a big up and comer at some gear manufacturer in Salt Lake City. She said she thought he was an okay guy for the first few dates, if a little too corporate and pushy and in love with himself – until she discovered the desperation of that love one night when he took her to "a dinner party at his boss' boss' cozy little 10,000 square foot ski cabin up in Park City."

The guy was all about "laying it on thick for the Big Boss, the company founder," she said, "with his hot new Betty girlfriend." She went along with the whole thing because it might be good for a laugh, she said; and even if it wasn't, it would be a chance to meet more gear company people if nothing else. But when the guy came to pick her up at the hotel for the party, he barged into her room – not to hit on her, she said – but to check out what she's wearing. And to suggest upgrades: better colors, a different logo, maybe a nicer sweater over the whole thing.

"The fucking poser!" she said, as Danny burst out another cloud of pot smoke and laughter.

And then finally – because Kelly apparently needed to look even more "outdoorsy" than she already does, with her fierce eyes, strawberry blond hair, hard rock shoulders and tree trunk legs – the guy pulls a move so weird she had to say exactly what happened twice before any of us actually got it.

As they're standing on the porch to the Big Boss' house, right before the guy knocks on the door: "He reaches over and grabs my cheeks, between his fingers and thumbs, and pinches them, hard – OUCH! – for like, five full seconds! And I'm like 'What the fuck, dude?' And he says 'Oh, but it makes your cheeks so rosy red!' Like really? Like my face isn't red enough already from the sun, dude? And he's like, 'Aw, come on! It'll make you even hotter. You know, like make-up – but it's all natural!'"

I am slapped back by Aaron's voice.

"What's so funny?"

I didn't realize I was laughing until Aaron asks me why.

I look up to see that we are already pulling up onto the ridge at the first trail junction. Last Christmas, it took us half a day in the waist-high snow to get up here; today, maybe an hour.

"Just thinking about Kelly," I say, "and those funny stories about dudes she told on the trip up here."

"Oh yes," he laughs. "All the manly suitors to the throne, lying broken along the trail." He carefully lowers his pack to the ground and says, mostly to himself, "Poor girl."

"Poor girl? What do you mean?"

"Aw, nothing," he says, going through the top of his pack and pulling out an energy bar. "Just that it's tough to be so – tough – if you're a woman."

He starts to pull his pack back on, but I'm not ready to leave. I want to stand here and drink in the view, and not only because this first big view of the day makes me thirsty for a can of cold piss from a factory down near Denver.

Off to the west, way back up the valley past Aspen, the very mountains I was just thinking about from one of Kelly's stories – the Maroon Bells, with the sexy sway of their hips, the suggestive tilt beneath their red and black striped skirts – hover and beckon like in a dream. Even if they hadn't long ago been turned into just another set of big tits for beer posters, they would still be the most photographed mountains in Colorado because they look exactly like what every dude's inner frat boy might reduce to just tits: they are Goddesses, hovering, sparkling, vibrating, enrapturing, all things even the best camera cannot capture.

But I fish my camera out of my pack and try anyway, while Aaron downs some calories and water.

"Shooting a beer ad?"

"That's funny."

"Try as they might," he says, coming over and standing next to me and looking out at the Maroon Bells and the panorama of mountains surrounding them and tumbling to the west. All of it is still bathed in orange-yellow with the morning light. "They still can't spoil this."

"Fuckin' A," I say, Dudespeak for "amen."

We pull on our packs and take the trail turning to the east. It drops a bit, then zigzags back up a gladed basin toward the hut, back toward treeline. We hike past open meadows that two winters ago had been great tilted lakes of snow, endless blank expanses of perfect white. Now, they are braided with rushing creeks and greening willows, and garnished all around with wildflowers.

I remember the slog through all that engulfing powder, trying to catch up, the temperature dropping. And I remember very clearly thinking: *If my world ends right here and now, it would be the perfect time and setting, because I died of hypothermia in the most beautiful place in the world, not rotting in some hospital, or trapped in some crumpled rental car, or shot by some junkie or redneck holding up a convenience store off I-95.*

It was a little drastic to think that way, especially at age 38. But it also happened to be Y2K later that same week; so we had the added bonus of joking the whole trip about the stupid little world below us collapsing into anarchy and apocalypse which, as far as I was concerned, was long overdue anyway. We were as far off the grid as you could get, with sun to power the hut and melt the endless snow into water, and an acre of firewood to power the stove.

"Y2K? FTW!" Danny kept chanting, raising his beer every time someone brought it up.

Every night was a big party around that big table, a holiday of our own making. Big-Hearted Wisconsin Boy had brought a few red and blue ornaments, and he cut down some pine boughs and tried to make it look like Christmas around the hut. But the rest of us grumbled "Who cares!"

"But what if this is our last Christmas?" he said, almost seriously, like he was actually worried. "What about Y2K?"

"Y2K? FTW!" Danny shouted from across the porch, and raised his beer and we all laughed.

And there was that little part of me that thought: *Yeah, who cares? FTW, forever. And then I'll never have to live through these past few weeks of Christmas nonsense – the blood red and fake forest green and tinsel and all that hideous, sugar-cookie music everywhere – ever again.*

But sitting out on the porch of the hut, with its steep-timbered walls the color of gingerbread and its frosted windows glowing, the sun going down behind the snow-draped trees and just enough cold dry wind to dust everything with a glitter of snow – it really did look a lot like Christmas, idealized, as if we were inside a snow globe scene so enormous we couldn't see the glass.

Over dinner that first night – Christmas Eve, I guess it was – the party grew quiet, when Gregor's wife said something about how it used to be when their kids were little.

Big-Hearted Wisconsin Boy said that it sounded like what his family would be doing right then, back at their house by the lake.

Then the party grew somber, when Danny's *femme du jour* said it was her first Christmas without her husband and his family. And in a voice that convinced no one, including herself, I imagine, she said, "isn't it great – just to be sitting around relaxing?"

Then the party grew sour, when one of the Betties said she'd actually been thrown out of her house on Christmas Eve, her freshman year, when she came out to her parents.

Her voice trailed off, filled in with a long, sad silence.

Then Danny shot up from the table, and I half expected him to say "FTW!" again. But instead, he bounded over and threw his arms around her, a little awkwardly – gave her an actual bear hug from behind and put his head down on her shoulder – and said: "Well, you're here with us now! And we – love – you!"

He rocked her a minute, and she started to burst into sobs. "I'm sorry," she fought back the tears.

"It's ok," Danny rocked her harder. "Besides, my base layer is waterproof."

Laughter all around broke the sudden sourness of the mood, but not for me: I could feel it turning into one of those touchy-feely round-robins – like one of those bullshit get-to-know-you exercises at the beginning of a work meeting – and I got a little squirrelly, wondering which version of my family and holiday history would be the least horrifying to offer up before we moved along to the next person.

Maggie turned to Aaron. "So why aren't you home for Hanukkah?"

"Because Hanukkah is bullshit," he said. "A minor holiday. I go home for Passover and Yom Kippur. Hanukkah's for kids, to make up for the Christmas thing."

That's a good one, I thought. I can tell them I'm Jewish, or half-Jewish anyway, which my grandmother used to say could actually be the case. (It's why we had no records of anything a generation back on that side and why everyone hated us, she liked to say.) Hanukkah's bullshit, I too can say, or at least half-say, and that's why I was there, and had nothing more to share.

"What about you, Jack?" Maggie asked me.

"What about me?" I asked like I hadn't known it was coming.

What could I possibly say to this room of mostly strangers? That my mother was a borderline Catholic who converted to Nihilism? And that my father – notwithstanding his mother's musings on some sad, vanished Jewish past – had reportedly accepted Jesus Christ as his personal whatever on his last trip through rehab? That Christmas was the one time a year when the family came together to get drunk and tear each other to shreds?

How to tell them that my immigrant grandfathers had long since worked themselves into early graves, and that my aging, raging grandmothers spent the holiday sniping at each other and my parents: about food, candles, the music, the tree, too many presents, too few presents, the neighbors' lights, our lights, America, the cost of everything, going to Mass, not going to Mass, heaven, hell, the Holocaust, and why does your son drink so much, and if only your daughter "wasn't so goddamn crippled" maybe then he wouldn't drink so much – all to an endless looping of "I'll Be Home for Christmas" and "There's No Place Like Home for the Holidays."

How to tell them that my sister and I learned early on that the best way to deal with Christmas was to run from it as far and fast as we could in that little town. She would flee for the home of that year's best friend. And I would flee for the woods and whatever snow fort I was working on – until I was fourteen and could flee to the local ski area, after discovering that you could turn Christmas into money by shoveling snow, hauling wood and digging out cars. I was done with the family Christmas nightmare for the same reason I'd gotten married so young: I really was an orphan, whose parents hadn't done him the favor of dying yet; and every third or fourth Christmas that my wife and I would go pretend with her parents or mine, it put us into deep dark winter funks that would run well into January, a crash-reminder that family, for the two of us anyway, was just a fancy code word for pain.

"Yeah, Jack," Kelly said, in a tentative (for her) way that made me realize Jill had told her that I don't talk about any of that. "What *is* up with your family?"

I wanted to say what I always say when someone pushes: "I don't like to talk about that with anyone." But that was the worst stink I could have let out into the close air of that warm, cozy hut. So I took a long breath and decided it was easiest just to tell the lie.

"My family?" I said, avoiding a dozen curious faces. "They're all long gone. No more family."

"And how about you," Maggie quickly moved the conversation along to the other Betty.

I looked up and the other Betty was talking, but Kelly and Danny and Aaron were all staring at me. I knew they knew it was more complicated than that, and Aaron especially seemed to stare right into me, or maybe it was just past me. So I let him know I didn't want to talk about it by looking away. Because that's Aaron: no bullshitting him with simple blow-off answers, the exact opposite of everything I learned in my work world. For him, it's as if every detail is life-or-death, like out on a climb: if you lie to him, you're putting everybody around you at risk.

Maybe that's why I like him. And maybe that why it's sort of been bothering me lately that, while he never bullshits me about anything, he doesn't say a lot either. He lost his high school and college sweetheart to an avalanche? And he never even mentions it?

I look up the trail and he is a few paces ahead, like he has been for a few thousand hours since that trip up here two winters ago. We've talked about it a little since then, the contrast between the closeness of his family and the absence of mine; and I know he finds it fascinating, but never pushes on it too hard, which works for me.

"There it is," he says, stopping in the middle of the trail.

He points across the meadow at a tall isosceles triangle of burnt orange wood. The hut, with it steep angles and big porch, glows in the summer sunlight, sitting half-hidden in a cluster of burly, ancient spruces spiked blue-green with new growth.

I hike up alongside him and the sight of the place – its heavy winter dress swapped out for summer –- startles, bewilders, and finally bewitches, like the mix and match of any other dream.

"That was a good time," he says.

"Yes it was."

"Piece of work in all that snow."

"Yes it was," an involuntary groan leaves my body with the memory.

He turns and grins at me. "It got you on teles though, didn't it?"

"Oh yes," I laugh, remembering all the grueling post-holing I was forced to do on that Herculean haul up the same trail Aaron and I just summer-buzzed in less than two hours.

At the other end of the year, it took nine solid hours of plunging into the snow behind Big-Hearted Wisconsin Boy, under the crush of that overloaded backpack, digging out, plunging in again, crawling out again – the rest of them skinning up through here across the snow. While they waited for us, Kelly and Gregor and Aaron even hiked up a few side slopes and skied down, then whisked on across the snow and up the trail before we could catch our breath.

It was two days after the shortest of the year, the temperature dropping as fast as the sun, the little water left in my blue nalgene bottle frozen solid. And I remember looking up from right here on this same trail, as the flicker of light from the hut finally emerged from the darkness, thinking: *Ok, so I won't die out here – which would have been fine – but how easily I could have, and how thin the margin a few miles out of bounds in winter, how thin the margin we inhabit on this planet.* It was the exact same thing I'd learned a few years earlier at the bottom and top of the Grand Canyon: the margin we occupy between heat stroke and hypothermia, between life and death, is really just a few dozen degrees Fahrenheit and barely any degrees Kelvin, and our lives relative to the life of the planet round to absolutely nothing.

Aaron bursts up the trail, faster than usual, at almost a Tyler pace. He looks as energized by his memory of those days in the hut as I am.

We pass through a towering stand of old spruces, the trail curving back toward the hut. The meadow drops out in front of us, the distant ridge opening back toward the Maroon Bells and dozens of other peaks. They look like freeze-frame waves on a roiling sea, shadowy black silhouettes now in the flood of midday sun, the same way they were shadowy white silhouettes in the winter nighttime sky.

I remember this same view from those mornings and nights in the hut. Best of all, I remember it right before bed that second night – Christmas Night, I guess – when Big-Hearted Wisconsin Boy went out to get more snow to melt into water and a moment later came running back into the hut.

"Hey you guys!" he ran in yelling. "There's something going on! A fire I think! Come check it out! What do we do?"

We all rushed out onto the porch, under a sky so full of stars it was more white-pink and powder-blue starlight than black.

"A fire?" Aaron said, running to the edge of the porch. "Where?"

"It was right there!" he pointed over the trees. "Right there, I swear, I swear I saw –"

He was cut off by a sudden explosion of pale pink and tangerine light, a flashing rush of color across the tops of all those mountains, and then suddenly a burst of bright fuchsia and flaming orange from the behind the trees. And yet, all those stars beyond the fire, still visible? Through what had to be smoke? But there was no smoke, just a surging, flaring, slow motion explosion of color and light across the sky.

"That's the northern lights!" Aaron said. "Hell yeah!"

The flaring and flashing grew until it filled the whole vault of sky above us, like high thin clouds but with color instead of cloud; and then it started pulsing, like a great heart pumping, clenching and unclenching, like the very light of creation.

"Fuck *yeah* hell yeah!" Kelly said.

And a dozen of us just stood there for I don't know how long, like children, wordless, gawking.

"We should sing a song," Maggie finally said, looking from one to the other of us. "Don't you guys know any Christmas songs? 'Midnight Clear?' Anything?" She looked at Aaron. "Any Hanukkah songs?"

"Worthy of that?" he pointed at the sky. "No."

We stood and watched as the color gyrated, twisting into a great mobius strip of light and color, still silent.

Slowly, it started to dissipate, retreating back to where it came from beyond the mountains, leaving behind the same white-pink and powder-blue dustcloud of stars.

I look back from the stars, the night sky, the snow, and see Aaron halfway to the hut.

I hurry after him, under a backpack that feels like air compared to what the same pack felt like with my snowboard on top and the trail collapsing under even my snowshoes.

I finally catch him right as he's pulling up to the hut. Even up here, the snow is long gone, except for muddy heaps of permanent snow banks from the long winter, highest where I remember there had been an igloo.

We walk around to the front, and stop dead in our tracks when we see the ATVs.

There are four, covered in mud, and a guy sitting out on the porch, dressed in camo hunting coveralls and camo hat. He has a goatee and big belly, and he's drinking a beer and cleaning a gun.

"Shit, man," Aaron murmurs to me, as we walk up. "Let me handle this."

"All yours," I murmur back.

We walk up closer to the porch, stopping maybe ten feet short.

"Hi," Aaron says to him.

The guy just stares at us for what feels like a minute.

"I help you with something?" he finally says.

"We're up here to check the weather instruments." Aaron points at the gaggle of metal and wire on one corner of the roof, running up to an antenna, the wind gauge spinning slowly in the breeze. "The data stopped coming in from here."

"You from the goverment or sumpin'?"

"Not exactly. I'm with Mountain Rescue in Fremont County."

"That so," he takes a drink of beer. "Well ain't no one up here needs any rescuing."

"Got it. Just wanted to check the weather instruments," he says again, and points at the gauges. "We lost the feed, and –"

"They look fine to me."

"But –"

"We got this cabin for the weekend," he says, pulling the gun across his lap.

My ears ring, and there is an odd metallic taste in my mouth. Bad adrenaline, the unfamiliar, agitating kind, flushes my body. Time slows, even more than with good adrenaline, to a near-stop.

"Ok, got it," Aaron says a moment or full minute later, I can't tell, lifting his hands halfway into the air, his palms out. The back of his right hand pushes against my chest, telling me to step back exactly as he does. "No need for trouble."

We back away slowly, staring at the guy who just stares back, twenty paces down the trail. Then Aaron turns slowly, and I follow, and we scurry back the way we came.

Ten minutes down the trail, the bad adrenaline has turned into speed, neither of us saying anything, Aaron's face red and jaw fixed, my arms and legs still on fire with activated but undeployed punches and kicks.

We are well past the big open meadow and into the thick of the trees when Aaron finally starts mumbling to himself, replaying the encounter, I think, but I can't make out most of what he is saying. Something about "the frickin' Kill-the-Earthers...everywhere in

Colorado now...everywhere Out West, ever since they closed the range...it'll never change."

He is right about that: it will never change. This is why they just divided all of Rabbit Ears Pass down the middle. One side is pristine, full of wildlife, and quiet but for birdsong and the wind through the trees, with a few hiking and cross-country ski trails leading off the pass into the woods. The other side is a mess of snowmobile tracks in winter and ATV tracks in summer going in all directions, that side of the parking area littered with oil cans and cigarette butts.

Thinking the great American cultural divide would be different up here in the American outback is like thinking anything back in Washington DC would ever change. Each side has their own version of reality, and each is certain their side is right and the other is wrong. (And of course the Kill-the-Earthers are obviously wrong and we are right.)

We hike off the adrenaline and anger at a furious pace, and before long I'm not even thinking about it anymore. I'm back to thinking, of all goddamn things, *what a great Christmas that was* – and to meta-thinking, *what an odd thing out of my mind's mouth, that is!* A great Christmas – but maybe only because it was my first not-horrible Christmas.

Or maybe not quite my first not-horrible one, after I discovered snowboarding and Killington, and how to run away and exhaust myself on that gigantic playground of snowy steeps.

Even the first one up there with my wife wasn't so bad, if only because I knew what was coming but for the first time could see what would be coming after that. Which it certainly did, in a drunken frenzy of après ski sex with a stranger on Christmas Eve the next year, when I met Amy the Rebound Girl at the bar in the Wobbly Barn.

Those first few days cut loose up at Killington were all solstice short, the light never more precious, my sudden freedom a miracle I thrashed around inside with an almost maniacal fury. I was up at dawn every day, the first guy up the first chairlift. The mountain would fill soon enough with swarms of people, liftlines and long waits, loudmouths and jackasses; but I didn't care, if only because I didn't know better yet. All I wanted to do was ride, to whip my snowboard around on that giant frozen skateboard park, suddenly full of an adolescent swagger I'd never had, freed at last from all those awful adult chores, the deathly grip of my horrible parents, the sadness of my marriage.

I would squeeze every run I could out of those days, and discovered that it was all about timing the chairlifts. They stopped running at 4 PM, so how could I get on that last chair on the highest lift to the very top of that mountain, to the top of the glades, for one long last endless ride down the empty trail? Yes, it was all as mechanized – and I was just as selfish – as those Kill-the-Earthers in our hut today. But I didn't know any better back then, nor would I have cared. All I knew and all that mattered: I was free, finally and forever; I wanted all of it to myself; and I would have all of it.

From up on top of the mountain, on trails suddenly emptied of people, the mountains of Vermont all around me so big back then – ha! how easily we recalibrate – I was always the last guy up that last chair. As everything around me turned soft orange with alpenglow, I'd start down the big empty mountain by myself, loose and worked by the day but still strong. Gathering it all in, then picking up speed down the empty trail, I'd gulp in the biggest, cleanest breath of my life and say to myself: *Look at me! I am 35 years old, I have survived all that bullshit, and now I'm prospering, unembarrassed, unapologetic, and utterly, completely HERE.*

Huh.

Now that I think about it, maybe that was the Presence, all the way back then. I just didn't recognize it yet, hadn't named it because I didn't even think to name it; I knew only that it felt incomprehensibly and indescribably good to be alive, for the first time in 35 years. I was breathing into the full measure of my body, something I'd never done before, and my breath was connecting me with something beyond my body, something like infinity.

I am brought back by Aaron's voice.

"To hell with the Kill-the-Earthers," he says, as if he's finally shaking it off himself.

I look up and see that we are already coming down to the trail junction on the first ridge. Aaron is a few paces ahead, up on the ridge where the trails meet, pulling off his pack and grabbing his water.

"Redneck assholes," he says, between gulps.

I pull up next to him on the ridge and drop my pack.

"But you know what," he says and we look out at the Maroon Bells, hazy now in the blast of midday sun. "I'm not going to let them ruin our day." He takes a long drink of water. "It's not like we didn't know somebody would have the hut – that we'd be finding our own campsite anyway, well out of sight of it." He pulls his pack back on.

"So what are you thinking?" I ask.

He nods up the hill, up the continuation of the trail we'd started up three hours ago.

"I'm thinking *Mountain Gazette*," he smiles.

I get it and smile back, and we say in unison: "When in doubt, go higher."

Wagon Ruts & Interstates

Not that I think it will undo any of the damage I caused or relieve any of the pain I inflicted on Jill over the past two years – though I wouldn't know, as I never worried about that before with Amy the Rebound Girl or even my ex-wife – but I have a weird compulsion, like a deep muscle ache, to set things right with Jill before she is gone for good. For some reason I don't understand, I need to show her that I really am sorry, if for the first and maybe last time in my life.

And it seems like the only way to do it is to prove it: to prove that I can make, and finally keep, a promise to her. Also – and maybe for the exact same incomprehensible reason? – I want to end all this round and round with her, finally and forever, as friends. With this one last chance she seems to be giving me, I am determined, with all the fury I bring to a new mountain I'm about to climb up and ride down, simply to show up for her and take nothing in return.

All of which was supposed to be easy. Just help her drive her truck, Kettle, and her gear, books and clothes to grad school in Sacramento. I learned, via Danny and Kelly of course, that Jill decided on a graduate program in environmental science instead of business school – the very first thing we ever talked about two years ago – though as serious as I now know she is, especially for her age, I can see her dealing with MBA school just fine.

So enviro grad school in California is where she's heading, two years after that random howdy-do in Ullar's, and I'm heading there with her, who would have guessed. But roadtripping is something we've always done well: take turns driving, watch the scenery go by, pick music to match it, and point out the occasional roadside oddity. One of us drives while the other reads out loud, something paired with the landscape – Abbey, Ambrose, Crane, McPhee, Momaday,

Muir, Stegner, Whitman, Williams – just like on all my trips with Danny or Aaron.

And like with them, Jill and I are going just as friends. Separate tents, no messing around, some side hikes and maybe a few climbs along the way. A good long drama-free road trip will be the perfect way to defuse all – or at least most, much, some? – of Jill's anger at me which, for some reason, I seem to want, or need, or crave.

But already, the trip is turning out messy, if only directionally, which has made me a bit bitchy, if only in my own clattering head. What was supposed to be a road trip west from Dudeville to California sent us east to Denver first; then north to Cheyenne; and now up here on the wind and sun scorched plains of Wyoming, hounded by gigantic 18-wheelers in the wide ruts of the Interstate.

Jill needed to drop a bunch of ski gear off with a friend down in Denver and pick up some other gear from another friend in Boulder. And as long as we were down off the Front Range, she said, why not head up to Laramie for a quick visit to a third friend who just moved there from Alaska with her geologist husband who just got a job with an oil company. Cool?

Yeah, sure, cool – especially because all three friends, and the husband, seemed to know all about me. And the third, halfway into her pregnancy, could barely disguise her dismay at seeing me hanging around with Jill. But at least everyone made nice, especially the husband, who told me about an interesting new natural gas technology he was working on. And we made quick enough time on all three stops to get west out of Cheyenne, just before sundown last night, and set up camp far enough down a back road that we could barely see or hear the Interstate.

Now, we are up with the sun, finally heading west in Jill's overloaded truck, running back toward I-80.

I'm driving, and she is staring out the window at the sun-blanched country, when she says, "Oh, goddamn."

"What?" I slow down, check the mirrors, look over at her.

"Those deer fences," she says, pointing at the long skinny line of crude poles lashed together and running for miles alongside the road outside Laramie. "Somewhere out here. On one of those fences. That's where they left him to die."

It takes me a few seconds to realize that she is talking about Matthew Shepard, the gay college kid from Laramie who was murdered out here. A couple local pieces of shit dragged him out of a bar, somewhere in town, beat him not quite to death, then dragged him out here and tied him up on one of these fences to die long and slow through the night.

It was an Old West version of a crucifixion, a brutal, sadistic, public killing meant to mark your territory and terrify whoever was your enemy. Because they would surely hear about it from whoever would find him and live to tell the tale: the local tribe; the settlers; the invading tribe; the distant tribe hunting too close nearby; the bluecoat soldiers; the Mormons; the Chinese; the Mexicans; and whoever else happened to be that year's "Other," which really meant that year's "In the Way." Except this didn't happen in the Old West; it happened three short years ago, and there are the fences to prove it.

Matthew Shepard was strung up and left to die because he was the worst kind of Other: a gay man. It was the same summer I moved west to flee the crowds and jerks and bigots Back East, because like so many I too just wanted – like so many Kill-the-Earthers who move out here too, I suppose – simply to be left alone.

"Fricking human jackals," Jill says a minute later, slumping down in the seat and staring out at the string of fences zipping by her window.

Another few miles of the fences, and we are finally out on the Interstate, where there is no history, only the liquefaction and conversion of distance into time.

There is a fierce crosswind, and it tosses Jill's little truck back and forth between the ruts like a rickety wagon. It is a drill I know from hours in my own little truck, or Aaron's, or Danny's Non-Hippie Bus: both lanes of the Interstate are double-bottomed out with wide troughs, good grooves for channeling the giant tires of 18-wheelers; but in cars and small trucks, you pick one or the other trough, until you're bored, then you pick the other one.

After a few miles of that, I've switched three times, and Jill finally rolls her window up against the screaming wind.

"Book or music?" she asks.

"Your call."

"After that little morning pick-me-up," she mutters and points at the deer fences still whizzing by, then goes to dig behind the seat for a book. "How about we finally deal with this?" She holds up a copy of *Bury My Heart at Wounded Knee* that she's had in the truck since our third or fourth road trip, a book we've both heard is the definitive text on the horrors perpetuated on the tribes out here, but have never had the fortitude to open.

"We definitely have the time," I say, pointing at the sign *Rock Springs 201 / Utah State Line 308* zipping by.

"Yes," she says and scans the waves of brown, wind-whipped grass. The landscape is devoid of people and scorched by the sun, broken only with long strings of wire fence, a billboard for guns or junk food or gas, shouldering into the wind, an occasional rusty silo or tangle of idle drilling equipment. "And this looks like as good a place as any."

She starts reading the book, but it is so heartbreaking I can barely follow it. She has to stop every five tear-stained, blood-soaked pages to cry, and I feel like I want to cry with her. The "Indian Wars," they called them, in the years after the Civil War. The bluecoat soldiers were the last to survive the slaughter, with the last of the surviving graycoats mixed right in, all of them too broken to return home; so they took their arms and their wounds west. West, to the Cheyenne in Sand Creek, out on the plains of our beloved Colorado, the men off hunting, the women and children massacred at dawn by bluecoats led by an evangelical madman general. Northwest, to the Nez Perce, wanting only to be left alone in the mountains of Oregon, flushed out by the bluecoats and driven across three states, only to be captured in blizzard 19 miles from Canada and freedom. And southwest, to the Navajos, herded into every last canyon of the southwest by the bluecoats and eventually starved out or hunted down like dogs. The conquering Lakota, Commanche, Apache, Arapaho, Ute, and all those they had conquered – the Pawnee, Shoshone, Assiniboine, Hopi and Cree – the names of the tribes come one after another like music, the way wind through a stand of trees, or water running over rock in a creek, can sound like music; but this music darkens as it unfolds into a long, slow, steady dirge, one people after another are rounded up, penned in like animals, starved and subjugated, their children stolen and sent off to "schools" Back East.

Halfway into the next story, Jill starts crying so hard she has to stop reading. I look over just in time to see her cover her eyes with her strong, lean fingers, the tears running down her suntanned face.

Yes, it's horrible, I think, and choke back my own tears, trying to steel myself with other books I've read about the broader arc of history and conquest. What chapter in the steady march of "civilization" is not horrible?

The heinous human history of the American West is one of simple domestic colonialism, the classic arc of invasion, swindle, dispossession, dislocation and genocide, with germs, booze, and the wanton destruction of the critical food supply thrown in to hasten the inevitable. It was the same old crushing advance of capitalism and civilization, packaged and sold to one kind of perennial American sucker as "Manifest Destiny" and to the other as "Christian progress."

Then as now, there were treaties, and land contracts, and corrupt bureaucrats, and of course the messy sham of due process, all designed, rigged and controlled – then as now – by the dominant and self-serving power structure to control everything in its path. Then as now, might makes "right," or right of possession anyway, and possession is indeed nine-tenths of the law. The group with the bigger numbers, deadlier technologies, faster means of transport, and biological immunity to what they are carrying with them always wins. (I learned early on in my career that for all our happy chatter about entrepreneurs and start-ups and such, these exact same rules apply to business life, with lawyers and lobbyists serving as the modern equivalent of deadly technologies and biological immunity.)

Go ahead and try to stand up to the bluecoats, I am thinking, but would never say to Jill, who is still quietly weeping into her hand as the brown landscape whizzes by her window. *Back them into a corner for a minute or two, because you're such a ferocious warrior. Sign the treaty you can't read and they don't mean, and let me know how it works out for you. Might DOES make "right," because might also happens to control the the cops, the courts, the banks, and the history books.*

None of this is actually news to me. It's just brutally sad in its human particulars, made more so because it was written in so much blood on landscapes I have come to love as much as I can imagine anyone loving any landscape. Before it was overrun, shitted on, and stolen from them.

Jill finally wipes her face, and holds the book up. "Can you handle anymore?"

"I can. Can you?"

"No. But it feels wrong not to."

"How?"

"To at least honor these poor people, all their suffering. If we don't read about them..."

And we say in unison, "they die all over again."

"Yes."

She clears her throat and goes back to the book.

Yes, I know all that and am not surprised, I suppose. And I cannot help but trace it forward to some of the more ruthless and vicious things I've seen, perpetrated by the corporate version of the bluecoats on anyone who was in their way. People in power take what they want, and they rationalize that taking by demonizing their victims.

But what I didn't expect, in Jill's sweet and now straining voice, were the particulars of the cruelty, the escalating savageries, the visceral vindictive pleasure that so many who fought to destroy the tribes obviously seemed to take in inflicting pain. I've seen the modern equivalent in business: a few lawyers and corporate middle management psychos who have gone over the edge. But their sadism usually splashes back on them, eventually, professional networks and "small town" industry effects limiting their damage, at least over time. But there seemed to have been no limits to human cruelty out here in this empty place – and still no limits, like with the murder of Matthew Shepard – only ruthlessness and annihilation.

If such recurrent savagery were not necessitated by the barren harshness of this landscape, then it certainly had to have been inspired by it. And it just as certainly seems to have left behind the stains and scars of that savagery. Because this bare and desiccated land, salted by tears long since dried up, now wears its horrific history like sackcloth, covered in dust and ashes, withered, empty, dead.

Thank God for the fuel warning light, which just came on. Because as we are riding the left rut into the sprawling industrial wasteland that is Rock Springs, Wyoming, the stories Jill has been forcing out, much of them through more tears, have filled me with a gnawing anguish. Accompanied by the numbing wind and pounding of her truck back and forth across the ruts of the Interstate, my nerves are worn raw and I'm actually relieved that we are nearly out of gas and need to get off this miserable highway.

While I am filling up the truck and Jill is off with Kettle for a pee, I trace the foothills on the other side of the Interstate as they rise and melt into a long line of high mesa tops to the south. How much better just to buck the Interstate and disappear somewhere up in there? Out of all this wind, high above all the sorrow down here.

I hear Jill back behind the truck, loading Kettle.

She comes around to my side of the truck and we stand for a moment in silence, looking at those mesas to the south. They are hazy with dust, dissolving into horizon, the sun arcing over them from the east.

"I've kind of had it with all the damn trucks," she finally says. "And we do have a bunch of days to get there."

"Yes we do."

"Why don't we just blow off the Interstate?" Then she nods with her head, "and go that way."

I burst out laughing.

"What's so funny?"

"You always could read my mind."

After several hours of back roads – several hours of up, over, and around low desert hills somewhere southwest of absolutely nowhere – we make camp, a campfire, and a big dinner in a vast meadow ringed by wildflowers and horizons of mountains in every direction. We had set up both our tents in case it rains; but it looks like another night we can just sleep outside on the tarp, apart, Kettle nestled between us.

When we're finished eating, and I'm making tea and pouring out a couple shots of Irish whiskey, Jill tells me she has a surprise: two hits of Ecstasy.

I'm not so sure that is a good idea. The time we did Ecstasy in Telluride turned out a little weird: too much fun, too sweet and nice, and then way too heavy, like I could see right into Jill and she into me. But everything was weird back then, so maybe this is yet another chance to make something else turn out right.

We pop the X with a "here's to you," then drink the shots and settle in with the tea around the fire.

A few minutes pass, and nothing.

And then, exactly as before, after a few more minutes of sitting there with her and Kettle by the fire, the same sweetness and niceness about everything descends, like lulling music all around that you can't actually hear, but it's there, and it sounds wonderful. It's the same sweetness and niceness about where we are, who we are, and everything we are doing, and isn't it lovely?

Jill's face turns rosy red in the glow of the fire, and the dusk lasts for what seems like hours, rosy red just like Jill's face. And I notice the same color spreading now across all the hills, long streaks of orange and red along the ridge to the west, like we're in a watercolor painting we can't actually see, accompanied by sweet dreamy music we can't actually hear. And over there is Kettle, that wise little man: he sits on the other side of the fire and stares at us, like of course we are all here together, and what else is there in life but a full stomach and a good fire and the three of us.

Jill goes to get him a treat and some more water, and she can't stop smiling, and my face hurts because I know I am smiling. But this can't just be the X, because it's what I really mean, really feel. And then I start to notice – and not for the first time, but it always seems like I am noticing this for the first time – the way Jill babies Kettle, like he's a little boy, not the wise old man I think he really is. And then, of all crazy-ass things, while I am watching them, I feel it rise up inside me as suddenly and surely as it does on any mountaintop.

The Presence.

Laugh all you want, I hear that small still voice, the one that sounds like my own voice but isn't, say to me. *But if you ever did want a baby, you would want its mother to be exactly like her. Healthy, strong, capable, kind. Can you not see Jill like that? With a beautiful little baby in a sling inside her coat while she cross-country skis into town?*

And as fast as it welled up right here, the Presence dissipates, and is gone.

Maybe it was the X this time.

Except that I know the difference.

I look up and Jill is still over at her truck with Kettle, futzing with more gear.

In the void left behind from the Presence's sudden appearance and departure, I know the X is really messing with me now. Because I keep seeing all of it unfurling like a tapestry of blue skies, rainbow fleece, and smiling faces: Steamboat Springs and the bike and ski trail along the Yampa River, surrounded by snow-capped mountains; all that fresh air for Jill and the baby; the old house where Julie was living when Danny and I met her, maybe even Danny and Julie right around the corner; and me back to making money by telecommuting or consulting or whatever; and Jill working up at the resort teaching skiing, not like all those miserable soccer moms out in the godforsaken suburbs, but Jill, the same hot, ripped, young, smart, cool Betty that she ever was, and now a mama bear too, but with a kangaroo pouch, on cross-country skis...

And what a goddamn fool I am!

Damn drug! Ha!

I shake my head and start to force myself part of the way back. But I can't help thinking: *Wow. What the hell was that?*

And as I come all the way back, Jill is standing across from me, smiling sheepishly.

"Can we just lie down?" she says. "Not for sex. I know it's the X, but I just want to hold you."

And I just want to hold her.

So we practically run over to the tarp, and crawl under the old Indian blankets she has piled up. It isn't at all about sex; it's just the X. I know this because her body isn't throbbing or quivering; it's just a big puddle of warmth against all that cold.

At some point we fall asleep, I think; or maybe we don't sleep at all, just float around in the silent music of the X. Or maybe it's a weird dream I'm having: Jill skiing along the Yampa River, a baby tucked into her coat, her eyes emerald like the river, flowing past the mountains, flowing south and west toward the Colorado River, then on past where it meets the Green River, and then down into the Grand Canyon, and gone.

Jill and I don't say much as we wake up and make coffee and breakfast in the dry, quiet chill, just after the sun breaks over the hills to the east, lighting up the opposite ridge the colors of sherbet. If there is an Ecstasy hangover, it is a sweet melancholia, a lingering sadness.

When the coffee finally kicks in, we pack up in a few quick, efficient minutes. We've done this so many times now, we don't have to say a thing and it all gets done – food, dishes, tents, gear, Kettle – and we are off down the road. We decide to go back to *Bury My Heart* later, and just listen to music for now.

All of Jill's CDs, heavy on the folk-rock, femme-rock and grunge, are with us; and they all seem to work this morning, especially the songbird harmonies and acoustic jangle rhythms of the folk-rock, perfect for an Ecstasy hangover.

Twenty or so miles down the road, we see a brown sign for a historic site and *Pioneer Trail*.

Before Jill can slow down, we bounce across a dip in the road, and in either direction, two parallel breaks run off into the sagebrush.

Jill stops. "Feel like a side hike?"

"Always."

We park and study the two sets of ruts that run east and west from the road. We're not sure which way to go (they both look interesting), when Kettle decides for us by sprinting west (of course). It is just a spur off a cutoff of the Oregon Trail, connecting it, I would guess from the *Road Atlas*, with the Mormon Trail.

I stand there next to Jill, my eyes following the ruts off to the horizon, and I try to imagine the tens of thousands of exhausted, sunburnt, disease-ravaged people who dragged themselves through this cracklebrush. I cannot.

"Wow," I say. "Can you imagine?"

"I was just trying to," Jill says. "And nope."

We start out along the ruts toward Kettle.

Both troughs are still deep as our knees 150 years after they were made and 130 years after they were abandoned. They rise and fall at the lowest possible breaks in the landscape, cutting left around a ditch, right to avoid a hump, through the sagebrush and cactus and cheatgrass and off to the horizon. How all of this must have looked to them, day after day, month after month, through howling wind, scorching sun, freezing rain, shattering hail, mountains ahead, always more mountains ahead, wavering over the hotplate of the earth, with attempts at names as harsh – the Bitterroots, the Sawtooths. Then the burnt lava fields, waves of frozen rock, and then the fires.

This was real hardship, I think as we hike along in our perfect gear, *these vast and hostile spaces without pity. Would this be why you – local native or invading native, bluecoat soldier or redneck settler – slaughtered your enemies so mercilessly? Because you were utterly terrified of all this wildness? Because your enemy was the only thing out here you could make bleed?*

Jill and I walk and eventually start to talk about exactly that: can you imagine? Can you imagine if we were stuck out here, for days, weeks and months on end, with all the violent weather, everybody exhausted, sick, terrified?

"No wonder so many of them went crazy."

"No wonder so many of them of them died."

It's a wonder any of them made it, I think, remembering what Aaron and I read in a history of the west on another trip: the trails had something like a 20% mortality rate. And while some isolated emigrant parties were ambushed and kidnapped or killed – sometimes horrifically – by the natives out here, the typical emigrant never saw a single native or bluecoat during their entire crossing. Rather, they died from the flu, or dysentery, or a snakebite, or a misfired gun; they died during childbirth or from drowning at a river crossing; or they died from any manner of infection and fever served up by carelessness with an ax, campfire, knife, or sawblade.

Jill and I hike up the two dusty wagon ruts to what we think might be the top of the distant ridge we were looking at last night. It takes half an hour and the sun is still low in the sky but already we are hot and sweaty.

The ridge turns out to be just a long rise and break in part of a ridge running in both directions to the northern and southern horizons.

From up here, we can see more and more of the same desert, the two ruts undulating across it with the rise and fall of more and more ridges, off into the dust-brown blur of the horizon.

"Can you imagine?" I say, as much to myself as to Jill.

"No," she says. "It's a miracle of luck that *any* of them made it."

"I was just thinking the same thing."

A jingle up ahead, and Kettle comes tearing over the next ridge, back toward us.

Without saying anything, Jill and I turn and hike back the two ruts, to our truck and our gear.

Over lunch in a whitewashed little town south of Salt Lake City, we study the *Road Atlas* and both sigh over what we see is the only obvious way to Sacramento: Interstates, blazed at odd angles across Utah and Nevada, before piercing the Sierra Nevada.

Jill suggests it might be fun to try to get there without taking any of them, and I know it would be: avoid all the Interstates, all the way there, even if it means going way out of our way, which we both know it means. We have several days set aside for this trip, which ends no later than in three days, when she drops me off at the Sacramento airport to fly back to Colorado.

"Seriously?"

"Why not?" she says. "We have the time. It'll be cool checking out places we'd never go normally."

"If you're not in a hurry."

"Deal?" she asks, and goes to high-five me.

"Sure," I say.

I go to high-five her back but we end up linking fingers to seal the pact and I quickly pull mine away. Her grasp is strong, warm, familiar, and it makes something in my chest flutter faster than I can let her fingers go and shoo it away.

Back in her truck, we also realize that we will need more drive to get through *Bury My Heart at Wounded Knee*.

After we worked our way down off the high prairie, doubling back a bit to drive south through the aptly named Flaming Gorge, we kept saying we should stop for a big hike or to make a big meal. But every time we finished a chapter, it was one more story, just one more, and by the time we pulled into the sprawling grid of Salt Lake City, Jill was cried out and I was emptied out. We decide to go back to music.

We drive in an easy silence, out across white salt basin and then red rock desert, then up and over more mountains. Making a steep ridge, we see larger ones looming up ahead, gathered around a licorice-black basin.

"We should hike up one of those," she says, studying the *Road Atlas*, then looking over at me and smiling. "Like their Wheeler Peak!"

"Really?"

"Must be named after the same dude," she says.

We are both thinking about the other Wheeler Peak in New Mexico, our first big mountain – no, wait, our second big mountain – which is like saying our second "date," if we'd ever had such a thing. But they were definitely mountains, not dates, because she essentially moved into The Treehouse with me after the first one.

"Wheeler was our second peak," she says. "Sunrise summit, ski down. That was awesome."

"Yes it was."

"I guess you could call it our second date."

"If you can call it that," I say. "After you moved in with me."

"Duuude!" she punches me on the arm.

"It *was* awesome," I say. "We rocked that mountain pretty hard."

"We rocked the trailhead pretty hard too."

"So..." I need to change the subject fast. "Is Wheeler the highest point in Nevada?"

She laughs and shakes her head. "You guys and your size thing. Who cares? Look at it!" She gestures at the great shadowy hulk of the mountain through the windshield. "Let's hit it up."

A few hours later we are setting up camp in a sun-blanched, wind-scoured campground just outside Great Basin National Park – no dogs allowed in the park, so we have to figure that one out – in the shadow of "the other Wheeler Peak," as we're both calling it.

The mountain stands alone astride the harshest desert I've ever seen, a sentry over an ocean of black and brown basin, an earthly void.

The next day, we wake up in the middle of the campground in our two tents. The day is already hot as an open oven and getting hotter.

We know we can't leave Kettle in the truck for as long as it would take to hitch a ride into the park, do the hike, and hitch a ride back. And we can't find anyone among all those settled into the campground whom we'd want to ask to look after Kettle for a few hours. It's all tourists with squirming kids off to the next place on the checklist; or Kill-the-Earthers, who give us the hippie-hater look as we walk by (because nothing says hippie like a bald, wiry 40-year-old guy and tanned, athletic 27-year-old gal in hiking shorts and t-shirts); or old, fat, half-pale/half-sunburned waddling RVers ("Home! Don't leave home without it," as Aaron would say, when we're stuck behind one). Our first and last choice would be the campground owners, who have dogs of their own, even if they are shitty little yapperdogs. But when we walk by their site near the entrance, they are blasting right-wing radio out the front of their trailer and screaming at each other.

Kettle finally gives us the look, after our lap around the campground: *Please don't leave me with any of these people, unless you really need to, and you don't really need to, especially in this heat.*

And Kettle is right. The day is heating up fast – too hot, too fast for the hike to be anything but a hard chore at this point – so we just break camp and head west.

Out across the actual great basin west and south, and about 10,000 times the size of Great Basin National Park, the day just keeps getting hotter. I keep my eye on the *Engine Temp* gauge, which is ok for now, only to notice the *Outside Temp* rolling upward with the miles – 105, 110, 115 – until the empty, blistered, tar-squiggled road feels like it's melting and the great pan of the horizon ahead turns to liquid silver.

Whatever silky, folky femme rock CD Jill was trying to play over the road roar finally ends, and Jill pulls out *Bury my Heart.*

For the next couple hours, she reads and I drive.

We finally pull into a sun-scorched town that looks like it was dropped from the sky like chopped onion onto the skillet of the desert: Tonopah, an oasis of civilization, with the elemental promises of shade, water, and silence, after the dry, hoarse, roaring of the truck's engine under this brutal sun.

"I think I might be good with giving in to your bourgeois weakness," she says as we drive past a Best Western.

"Really? Without any fight at all?"

"Just this once."

The motel lobby is chilly and stale, like cheap ice cream with a vague smoky, sweaty aftertaste.

When the old lady tells us what she has and for how much, I'm about to say "two rooms" when Jill says "one with two queens would be great, right?"

I just nod and know it won't be any weirder than the last three nights camping together.

We unload in the room, which smells exactly like the lobby, but the cool air still feels great.

Kettle climbs up on one bed and watches us unpack.

Jill goes in to the bathroom and shuts the door and takes a shower.

I stretch out on the other bed, drinking in the cool, foul air, and fall asleep.

Later that night, the heat breaks a bit, and the sleepy little town flickers awake with neon against all that surrounding darkness. A couple blocks from the hotel we find a Mexican place. We drink big margaritas and eat huge platefuls of fajitas. Next door is a honky tonk – we can hear the band fire up before we're done – that sounds like all of what's happening in town tonight.

We head over and the little place is packed. Must be everyone in town, we guess, drinking and dancing and sweating. Because we can walk back to the motel, we drink more margaritas, each going more easily down my throat than the last, still parched from the day, the road, the whole trip.

The band is all bounce and shuffle, skittering steel guitar and fiddle, Hank, Buck, George and Dwight, from western swing to 12-bar roadhouse blues, all delivered by a husky singer, well past the 100,000 mile mark, with a booming, whiskey-stained voice. The dance floor is filled with denim and gingham and hair that was once big hair, and slick new cowboy hats on heads that look like they wear real working ones the rest of the time. And everyone seems to be smiling at Jill and me, the new kids in town.

One of the older gents, a string bean half a foot taller than us in a big white hat, comes over and asks me – in gestures over the band with his brown, sinewy, weathered hands – if he can dance with Jill.

I look to her and she shrugs *Sure* and goes out onto the dance floor, all six feet of her and six-six of him, and the whole place makes room. The song ends and she comes back, some dance still in her step, and tries to drag me out onto the dance floor.

I really don't want to, but for the singer barking into the microphone: "Now what kinda fellow wouldn't wanna dance with his sweet young gal?"

And so, glistening red I'm sure, I let Jill pull me into the sweaty crowd, if only to make them all stop looking at us, as the band launches into the zip-twang of a western swing number.

Jill and I dance for the first time since Hillary's wedding, and it feels fricking great.

Back out in the street, the air is cool but the pavement still pulses with heat. Jill and I walk slowly back to the motel and yes, I want to reach over and hold her hand, just to touch her, but we both know where that is going and so I don't and we don't.

Back in our hotel room, I lie awake on my bed, listening to Kettle sleep and Jill breathe in and out in the other. She isn't sleeping either, I can tell, not for awhile anyway. But eventually, her breath slows, and I am left listening to my own breath, trying to synch it with hers and fall asleep.

I wake up to sun through the door as Jill is taking Kettle out. I am fully awake by the time she comes back and goes into the bathroom.

She is in there forever, taking a very long shower, which she never does.

She comes out wrapped in a towel, her suntanned body glistening red, especially her face. She avoids my eyes.

"Hey," I say.

"Hey."

"Bit of a hangover this morning?"

"I guess that's what it is," she says. "A little. Fun night."

"Yes."

I take my own long turn in the shower, realizing why it might have taken her so long.

I am looking forward to getting back on the road because the sex vibe in this room is making me a little queasy. And I'm wondering, for the first time since the detour through Cheyenne, if this whole thing isn't some fool's protracted errand. Why exactly am I driving her all the way to Sacramento? To make up for things I can't fix? To fix things I never should have broken? Or to break them one more time, because she is so beautiful and sexy and present? Yes, my body made all those promises, and for a damn good reason, even if I didn't.

Back out on the road, the hot morning sun is exploding upward into a harsh blue sky, turning everything into liquid fire west of Tonopah.

Half an hour out of town, with Jill driving, I go back to *Bury My Heart*, my throat parched already, trying to choke itself shut as I sputter through one heart-shattering page after another over the roar of the truck.

Finally, it ends, in 1890, on the Pine Ridge reservation, with the last of the Lakota who'd held out against the bluecoats, dying on the floor of a church a few days after Christmas, or out dead and frozen in the snow.

We drive on in sobbing silence for several minutes.

Might may make right, I know the saying goes, because it controls the cops, the courts, the press and the history books; but it is still wrong. And if there is a universal lesson from that belated (to me, anyway) history book, written in the tears and blood of millions of mostly anonymous human beings, it is this: eventually new books will come along and tell the real truth about history, even if it takes a hundred years.

We drive on in the silence of our shared sorrow, and I grope for whatever bitter triumph there might actually be in that long and horrific story. There is one, even if it's wholly pyrrhic, a triumph of will and determination and defiance as real as the rest of it. Given the harshness of this landscape, and the sheer numbers and raw greed of those coming west, the long view of the history of the American West has to marvel *not* that the tribes were broken, nearly wiped out, and herded so quickly onto the reservations – but that they lasted out here as long as they did. The bluecoats may have had all their obvious technical advantages, their guns, germs and steel; but they also had the advantage of this merciless landscape, which offers no margin for failure, no shelter for the weak, no mercy to anyone.

And then, as if to prove that exact point, there it is as we crest the top of a long steady rise – the Sierra Nevada – one long continuous wall of mountain.

From out here across this heat-fluttering desert, the range is more hallucination than hard fact, a haze of gray and brown rock etched along the top with a long, jagged squiggle as far south and north as we can see. It hovers over the desert's shimmer of brown hard-pan like a dream – or like what had to be a very bad dream for anyone who'd spent six months getting to somewhere along the foot of this impossible range in a wagon.

It takes us another hour of driving straight at it, at a numbing speed, for the hallucination to harden into fact – for the haze to solidify into brown, black, and purple peaks and slabs with white flecks in their upper notches. And another half hour for all of it to tumble and crash, finally, in great waves of rock and forest down onto the last of the desert still in front of us.

And then we hit one of the great transcontinental T-intersections.

The Sierra Nevada, like much of the Front Range in Colorado and Wasatch in Utah, forces everyone and everything to take a hard turn north or a hard turn south. The road we are on runs straight up into the mountains, to Whitney Portal, a dead end at the foot of the highest peak in the lower 48.

Jill parks on the shoulder, the great wall of mountains looming over us now, leaning over and looking at the *Road Atlas* in my lap.

"We could always just go hike that," I point at Whitney.

"You need a permit," she says. "And we have Kettle."

"But it's the highest peak..."

Her eyes roll sideways.

"I know, I know," I say. "Guys and their size thing."

"But we still have a couple days," she says.

I follow her finger as it drifts south along the map, away from the obvious roads over the top of the mountains. There are no roads over the top until we would be too far south, still in the desert and practically east of Los Angeles, so her finger heads back north.

"Here," she says. "This one goes through Yosemite. Nice."

And so we head north, toward the first road that climbs up and over the mountains now towering over us to the west.

We drive through foothills toward Mono Lake, which reminds me of another book we brought: Mark Twain's *Roughing It*. I've already read parts of it, including what I remember to be a wickedly funny thing set right there next to that enormous sinkhole of metallic-colored water.

I dig it out, check with Jill who nods *OK*, and start in.

But I'm too distracted by the scenery, the mountains flaring to the left, the desert sprawling off to the right, the intense light and heat.

And the story feel archaic and strange, like it's from another time and place, even though it's set right here. Or maybe the sarcasm and the silliness is what makes it feel out of place in the very place where it is set, and this book is best read and heard in another time and place, when this place is just a memory. Either way, my voice keeps drifting off and I can tell that Jill isn't really listening anyway.

"That's ok," Jill says. "It's funny, but kind of hard to follow out here with all this going on," she gestures out at the landscape, which isn't in the least bit sarcastic.

I put the book down and she puts on music, a big crashing, plunging grunge guitar, perfect for the wild landscape.

When we get to Mono Lake, we turn left, up into the mountains, and run smack into a snarl of traffic, cops, fire trucks, and a blinking sign: *Wildfires Ahead. Road Closed.*

"Shit," we say in unison.

Jill tries to pull the truck around, navigating the demolition derby of cars, trucks, minivans, SUVs and RVs all turning around. The air looks clear, no smoke, no blue haze. I roll down my window: no smell of woodsmoke either, but maybe that's for all the idling cars.

We keep heading north, another half hour of chugging grunge guitars, but the next road up over the mountains is closed too: another blinking sign, more cops, another tangle of cars scrambling to turn around.

North again, another ten miles, and finally an open road, though it's not exactly open; we fall in behind a long, slow, steady line of cars, trucks, minivans, SUVs and RVs, probably all re-routed from the wildfires. We head up the steep hill in the procession, up a dozen long switchbacks snaking all the way to the summit pass, where Jill pulls over to let Kettle out.

The sky west over the high ridge is just starting to haze over with a blue that isn't sky and an orange that isn't sunlight, and the air is thick with the acrid tang of campfire from every direction.

We pull out some of the gear in the parking area, and make lunch out of the back of the truck, watching the continuous line of vehicles thicken, then stop. Within a few minutes, the road over and down the pass has turned into a parking lot.

Then a strange bird crying – but it's not a bird, it's a siren. Then a flock of sirens, from way down the canyon on both sides of the pass. They grow louder, and cops appear up the shoulders from both directions. One pulls up right in front of us and the others spread out around the now crowded parking area.

"Sorry folks," a lanky sunburned cop with a shaved head and sport wraps says as he pops out of his car, the lights still going. "But you are going to have to clear out of here, and head down east. Now."

"What's the matter?" asks a short fat guy, walking by with a short fat dog, dressed in an open shirt, wife-beater and panama hat way back on his head, an unlit cigar in his mouth.

"There may be a fugitive associated with the fires in the area west of here, and we need to clear the whole area now."

"But –"

"That's all the information I have," he says, getting back into his car. "Please vacate the area in the next five minutes, or you will be arrested and your vehicles impounded."

"Wow," the guy says to us, chewing on his cigar and staring at the Colorado plates on Jill's truck. "Wildfires and psychos running around the goddamn woods. Welcome to California, kids."

"Thanks," Jill says and I say nothing, hoping he'll just move along, but he stands there, chomping on the cigar, his dog pulling at the leash.

"It's all the goddamn methane gas they put in the air. Makes everybody crazy. That, and all the taxes we pay to support all the greasy Mexicans and their goddamn kids. Who wouldn't go nuts!"

I can feel Jill's heat rising, feel her biting her own tongue like it's my own; but neither of us say anything, which seems to disappoint him, so he moves along to the next people.

We finish up our lunch in a few minutes, pack up, and it's my turn to drive. I let out a long sigh, and half-nudge and half-fight my way into the long line of cars, trucks, minivans, SUVs and RVs heading back down to the desert.

It takes us an hour and a half to drive the 10 miles back to bottom.

The next road up and over the mountains – which leads up to the southern end of Lake Tahoe – is backed up all the way down onto the highway. We wait in the long line to turn left, but it is everyone we

ıst drove down with, plus everyone from the south, re-routed, trying
ɔ get over the mountains.

"Well this sucks," I say, not that this wasn't obvious to Jill, who is
rowning at the traffic.

"More like sucks *ass*," she mutters. "We probably can't find
nyplace to camp up there either."

"No?"

"Hell no," she sighs. "And Tahoe is kinda lame."

"Really? I heard it was beautiful."

"It is," she says, "around the north side, or if you can camp far
nough out. I did a couple gear company things around the lake, and
ɪ's super-touristy. Like one long Vail, with casinos."

"Oh, great."

"And probably way booked up anyway."

So we keep heading north, crawling over the top of the great
ɔlanched cowchip that is the half-developed Nevada desert. There are
ɪouses and traffic everywhere, baking in the sun and heat, all of it
ntensifying as we head toward Reno.

I am driving and now Jill is reading the Twain; and suddenly the
sarcasm and silliness work perfectly, in this traffic, with idiotic
ɔillboards going by and old west junk cluttered up in front of gas
stations and dingy convenience stores.

The book is one tale after another about greenhorn miners, two-
ɔit hustlers, gussied up gamblers and lawyers and fools, all of the
ɪumor dry and deadpan as this desert, the jokes as much on Twain
ɪimself as anyone – though it seems like the jokes are really on
everyone, especially those who don't know the jokes are on them.

We drive by another road up into the mountains, toward Lake
Tahoe, with a dozen signs and billboards for casinos. Jill and I just
look at each other and shrug "Nah" and keep going.

And faster than we can get through Twain's next yarn, we are
confronting the shiny black glass and brown adobe sprawl of Reno:
neon, casino signs, freeways, traffic. I keep nosing the truck
northwest, on commercial strips of utter sameness, the wearingly

familiar box stores and chain restaurants from coast to coast, and Jill goes back to Twain.

We crash one for the bathrooms and when we come out it's Jill's turn to drive and my turn to distract us with the Twain.

A few minutes up the road, she asks, "We're sticking with the no-Interstate rule, right?"

I look up from the book and see that we're pulling up to a light with four lanes of traffic, half feeding into lanes for *I-80 East Reno* and *I-80 West Sacramento*.

"Don't know why not."

"We do have two more days together," she says as we head straight and cross under the great rattling bellies of the ramps and the Interstate. "Before your flight, I mean."

We may have two more days until we have to be in Sacramento for my flight, but I can move my flight around easily enough. In either direction. Not that I would. But we do have to be down there in two days when her cousin's friend's stuff shows up at the place they will be renting near campus.

"Yes," I say, nodding toward the wall of mountains looming up again to the west. "And it would be great to pull some altitude, somewhere up there, with our big climb coming up."

"That's right," she says and speeds up through the traffic.

A few minutes later, we are rolling over more desert foothills; and in a few more, we are finally heading west, up into the mountains. I've stopped reading and Jill has loaded another CD, simple folk-rock guitars and harmonies, a good rambling rhythm for this road.

There is a big brown sign up ahead – *Little Last Chance Canyon Scenic Area* – and we look over at each other and chuckle: it's the name of the bar back in Dudeville where we'd gone with Aaron and the CPR dummy after we'd met at his clinic.

"How can we not?" I shrug.

"Just what I was thinking," she says and turns up the road. "Our first date. If we'd – you know – had one of those."

We make our way up the mountain and in a couple miles catch the back of a line of vehicles, half towing boats, just as the road narrows up through the canyon. But in a quick couple miles more, the road empties around a busy lake. Around the back of the lake, we have the whole road to ourselves. It narrows, steepens, and climbs the hill along one side of the small, steep river impounded to make the lake.

We pass an empty dirt road, then another and another, all of them leading up into forest. As we approach the next one, we look at each other and shrug *Why not?* and Jill turns up it.

The truck chugs its way up the dusty, twisting dirt road for a couple miles, until it suddenly goes to ruts and ends, right where the woods thin and the ground opens to rolling views in three directions.

Yes, we both nod. *This exactly.*

We park and let Kettle out and pull gear for the night. It is a nob of a mountain, too small for a name in the *Road Atlas*, but it feels big enough for us after all that traffic.

We set up our tents in case it rains, but we know it won't rain – that would be a good thing, with all those fires down south – so it will be another night sleeping under the stars, Kettle between us. The mountain is starting to feel like ours and ours alone as we're settling in, spreading out, and making dinner – until we hear an engine buzz grinding up the hill.

A truck pulls up and the bearded guy behind the wheel says "Sorry!" and turns around quickly and heads down the mountain.

As we sit and eat, we survey the mountains spreading out in front of us. All the way to the south, we can just make out the blue haze from the northern edge of the fire, but that's it.

After dinner, we sit in our camp chairs, drinking tea and Irish whiskey and smoking a big bowl, watching the sun set and the sky all around us turn a burning orange and then an angry red. It would be great to have a campfire up here, but of course we can't with the forest tinder-dry.

"All the smoke in the air from the fires," Jill sighs. "Tough way to get such cool special effects."

"Yes."

Then a long, easy silence, but for the wind through the trees and the birds settling in for the night, as we watch the stars struggling to come out. The sliver of a new moon rises through the last of the color and the haze over the first stars, the pot making everything fuzzy and buzzy with a silly, almost weepy sadness.

Just as I'm about to say something, anything – because all the silence, combined with the fiery red streaks across the smoky sky, is starting to enshroud us in gloom – Jill beats me to it.

"I don't want this to sound weird," she blurts out. "But what would you do if you were suddenly sick? Like really sick? And you're all by yourself?"

I know exactly what she means, but don't know what to say, so I stall until I do. "What do you mean?"

"I mean – you have no family, or anybody really close to you. And I know you're all down with your climbing bros. But that's just Dudeville, and everybody's just passing through. And you are too."

I hate talking about this because I hate thinking about it, which is why I almost never do either. But I can tell she's been wanting to ask me this for two years now, has finally worked herself up to it, and probably won't let me change the subject.

"I know if I got really injured out here," she goes on, "or sick – like with cancer or something – I could count on my mom. Or my aunt. Or my sister. What would you do?"

I finish the whiskey in my tin cup in a swallow and swish it around in my mouth, my head swimming with weed and the last of the blood red scrawl on the western horizon. And then the words spill out of me before I can stop them.

"I would just die," I say. "Period. End of story. Lights out. And I'd find a way to do so without anyone's help."

Even though we are shrouded in near darkness, I can see her hard stare, her mouth suddenly agape.

"You would just die. Just like that."

"Yes," I say.

I can feel her breath catch, stop, start again. "You're serious."

"Yes. I am."

"That makes me so sad," her voice cracks, as if she were trying to choke back tears.

"I'm sorry," I say. And I am sorry, not for what I said, but for saying it to her, out loud, the thing I never thought I'd say to anybody. "But you asked."

"Yes," she clears her throat. "I did."

"I know it's harsh," I say. "But I'm all alone in the world. Always have been."

"Except for the nine years you were married."

"Yes, except then. And maybe that's why I stayed married that long. My wife and I were all we had."

She doesn't say anything, picks up the bowl, lights it.

That was also the wrong thing to say, I suppose.

She takes a long toke, then hands the bowl over to me.

"And independent of all that –" I say, then take a long hit of the weed even though I'm plenty stoned and feeling suddenly defensive and expansive at the same time, and as far away from her as I've ever felt, and now I have to talk my way back, "—which is really just a matter of practicalities and logistics – the truth is I'm not at all afraid of the physical act of dying. Seriously. My life was total shit for 20 years. And then it was a total grind for fifteen. And for the last five years it's been great – heaven on earth. So why not go out on top?"

"You're serious."

"I am," I say, because I've said it all now and can't un-say it.

"And you actually think that way, the whole time you're up in the mountains? At the edge? With everybody counting on you? With me counting on you?"

"Of course not. I'm talking about me, not anybody else. I would never mess around with risk, or safety, or anyone else's odds up here. I'd sooner –"

"Sooner die? Than let somebody else get hurt up here?"

"No, I mean –"

She cuts me off with a snort. "You already set the bar pretty low for what that might mean."

Now she's angry, I think, but I can't see her face in the sudden darkness all around the camp site.

"That's not what I mean. And yes, I would sooner die than let somebody else get hurt up there. A lot of people are like that in the mountains. The mountain rescue crew? Why do you think they go out after people? It's like war. You do what you –"

"It's not war," she cut me off. "It's a sport. A revved-up hobby." She is definitely angry.

"Yes, but it's also about facing down exactly what we're talking about, and living through it. You know how safety conscious I am up here. How many summits have we done now? And you think Aaron would trust me on all those climbs?"

"That's true," she says, her voice finally calming and breath letting go. "So you *are* afraid of dying. For others."

I'm not sure what she means, unless she still means the cardinal rules of mountain safety. Just this past March, alone on the deck of The Treehouse back in Dudeville, I learned something she would find even more disturbing about what it might mean to stay alive "for the sake of others," but she can't mean that.

"Sure," I say. "For others."

We sit in complete darkness now, and a difficult silence. I think about those "others" for whom I'm apparently remaining alive, and what I'm really afraid of, and how this whole awful conversation got started.

"But what I'm more afraid of," I finally say, "and this was your original question – and yes, it does sound harsh – is being sick, disabled, hosed by life, dependent on someone."

"That *is* harsh, dude."

"Sorry, dude," I say. "But you asked. And that's the truth. Sucks to hear it, sucks to say it. But I really would rather die alone than be dependent on anyone."

"No wonder you..." she mutters and her voice trails off.

"No wonder I what?"

"Nothing," she sighs.

I realize how stoned I am, and that I can make her feel only worse, and that I better just shut up before I do.

We sit for a few minutes in a difficult silence, watching the sliver of the moon and a few more stars struggling to poke through the hazy black. And I think on how I got to such a harsh place. Maybe it was all those hours alone up in the mountains; or all those cold winter nights up at my house, with the wind howling down the canyon and beating on the walls and windows with sleet, or sandy grit from the road, everybody gone. It was exactly what I always used to crave – pure solitude – borne of freedom from any obligation to anyone.

I hear Jill get up from her chair and stretch, like she's ready for bed already. She switches on her headlamp, which sends a swath of dusty light through our camp site like a searchlight.

"Anyway," she says and looks over at the tents. "Long weird day on the road. And I think it's going to be cold tonight. We should probably sleep in the tents."

"Probably a good idea," I say.

I watch her in the shadow of her headlamp wander off to pee, come back, and grab a water bottle. Then, with a quick "good night," she slips into her tent with Kettle, glowing with her headlamp for a minute. Then another zipper opening and closing, and darkness, and quiet.

I shouldn't have said any of that, but she asked. I suppose she is still trying to figure me out, two years later and with only two days to go. So why not just tell her the truth? My truth, anyway, about the harsh place that rose out of rock like a remote mountain lake, rose to swallow me in its icy water on what could have been just another freezing night out on my deck in Dudeville last March, a few weeks before Jill came back for Hillary's wedding.

Three feet of a wet, heavy, freak spring snow had fallen in less than a day, and shut everything down. I snowshoed my way back and forth to town, not because I needed anything, but because I was bored and restless and wanted to exhaust myself. Then, as night fell, I got good and drunk out on the part of the deck I'd shoveled off. I was freer than any man had ever been and had everything I could need or want. I was completely alone, drunk not so much on the beer and whiskey as on the sensation of absolute physical and emotional freedom that I remember thinking would kill men back in the world, and could easily kill me, if I simply decided to let it.

I'd been reading in my mountain rescue manual about hypothermia: how its victims will be lulled into immobility, cross a line, and not want to move; how they can become belligerent as drunks when you try to move them, because medically they *are* drunk, their minds shutting down and a sweet euphoria setting in, the easiest kind of death I could imagine. This was exactly how Guy Waterman – naturalist, writer, musician, and agitator, the Edward Abbey of the New England woods – chose to die last winter. After an active, expansive, exuberant life lived on his own terms, his once tough body aging and failing, he decided to end his life by freezing to death alone, in a stoic, quiet dignity on top of his beloved mountain. Many of the aging natives chose to die the exact same way: when they still could, before the reservations, before the white man came and broke their will to live and die in their own way, when they were still free.

I sat out there on the deck of my house that night, the temperature plummeting and snow still falling, the sudden iron cold working its way down the neck and up the sleeves of my fleece. I started shivering violently but kept drinking anyway, just to see what would happen, just to feel a little bit of that other kind of drunkenness. Part of me reached out for it, while another part was watching myself reach out for it so I could stop my reach just short of grasp. The shivering became a shuddering, then a spasming down through my core; but I pushed on through it (I think), and the shivering did stop (I think), and I could feel the snow tumbling onto the back of my neck, no longer cold and wet but dry as dust, like soft lint falling on numb skin, a clicking sound as snowflakes fell on my head and neck and shoulders like hundreds of tiny hands, a benediction, nothing but peace without, peace working its way within...and...

Wham!

The part of me watching was snapped awake, a voice somewhere deep inside (the Presence, yet again?) yelling "Hey! No! Stop!"

And I was shivering again, out on my deck, looking around and wondering: *Was that it? Was that the real edge? Or a death dream? Was I jolted back not out of fear, but out of shame, anger, pride?*

The blessing of that falling snow – the peaceful clicking sound of sugar sprinkled across my void and The Void – may have been nothing more than a drunken dream at the shallow end of the long killzone of hypothermia. I'll probably never know. But I did have (I think) the option of dying right there and then, alone out on my deck in the snow; but (I am fairly certain) I could not allow myself to die there and then because (I believed at that moment) that the Presence would die too, which would be a terrible thing for me to do to the universe. Which is self-comforting nonsense. But what drunken stories spun before bedding down under a suddenly dark sky are not?

In the morning, Jill is up first, humming, making coffee, puttering around the back of the truck.

I crawl out of my tent into the first rays of the sun, and Jill says nothing, just smiles at me and points at the coffee. Everything is better, as if we'd never talked about any of that.

And how could it not be better, when you wake up on top of your own mountain, golden morning light streaming through the trees, and you look out on mountain after mountain awash in the same light, the sky to the west all lavender and blue? Hot coffee, still some good bread and fresh fruit, a great dog running around in circles, itching for a hike. It has always sounded stupid to me when people say "it doesn't get any better that this," because of course it does. But sometimes maybe "it" doesn't, not because "it" can't but because you don't need "it" to. Maybe there is no "it," only our perception of it.

This is the sort of thing Danny could go on about for hours, on a long ascent, or an empty stretch of road, or over a good cup of campsite coffee on top of your own perfect mountain. Which makes me wonder: what and how are he and Julie doing right about now?

After breakfast, Jill and Kettle and I go for a long hike down the trail into the next canyon, then back around and up onto the next mountain over. From its summit, we can see our camp: Jill's little truck and our tiny tents, flecks of color amidst all that green and brown. We bushwhack down into the canyon, find the trail back up and our way back through the trees to where we'd landed almost 24 hours ago when we were just poking around up here.

Back at camp, we talk about what next. We have one more night before we have to be in Sacramento, and we know which way we don't want to go – anywhere back toward Reno and the Interstate – so we eat lunch, pack up camp, and head down the mountain.

When we get to the paved road at the bottom, we turn left, going the other way, further in. We work our way slowly south, via a twisting, rolling maze of forest service roads. This is the very spine of the northern Sierra Nevada: no big peaks, but no parks and no people; just big rocks, bigger trees, dust everywhere, and rutted roads.

We follow the *Road Atlas*, but when the roads go to four digits or three digits and a letter, the *Atlas* is often wrong – something Aaron pointed out to me way back on that first trip with Tyler. And the *Atlas* is completely wrong down here, which is fine, as we know how to do this by compass. As Danny likes to say, "you are only lost when you want to be somewhere else." And Jill and I don't want to be anywhere else, until Sacramento anyway, and not until tomorrow.

I am driving and Jill reads more of the Twain. It's funny, but still city-funny, and doesn't work up here either, the rhythm all wrong for this narrow old road through a thick canopy of trees.

Jill stops an hour in, and puts on some music: a guy and a gal, a fiddle and a banjo, perfect for our slow-go up along these rugged ruts. The woods are closing in on us, in shadow already as the sun sinks behind the ridge to the west. We don't need the compass to know where we are now; we have the sun and the shadows of all these great trees, and if we're lost, we don't really care.

At the next break in the woods, we stop to let Kettle out, and it's one more great view: all mountains spilling to the west in a blue haze, the sun suddenly right there, a great ball of fire almost to the horizon, like a match hovering above so much tinder. A mile or so south and the road starts to get gnarly. The ruts deepen – the CD skip-skipping with every jolt of the road until Jill finally switches it off – but we keep going, knowing we can just camp anywhere, knowing we still have just enough food and water for the last night and morning.

An hour or so later, we are down to a crawl. The ruts are bigger and deeper still, the truck rolling back and forth across them, pitching us around inside the cab. It would be fun if we knew when it would end, and if it were not getting dark. We work our way slowly around a ridge and down into the shadow of a canyon thick with tall pines. The road isn't getting worse, but it's not getting better, we're hungry and tired, and I am starting to feel just a little bit bitchy. Jill is too, I can tell, by the way she turns the CD on and off, then skips ahead through each track, then changes it to another just like it, more guy and gal, mandolin and guitar this time, like we're both thinking *Ok, we've had enough of this road, and this music, and this would be a perfect place to get a flat tire, have to unload all the gear to get at the jack, then reload all the gear...*

Maybe we'd even have a big fight about something, like a bickering couple in some movie. Or like my parents might have done, if they'd ever gone anywhere. And wouldn't it suck if we somehow ended up stranded out here with all our gear and, by this time tomorrow, no food and water. Would that finally un-do us? Our first real fight, and a fight not about my being The Asshole of Life for standing her up once a year on one or another continent, nor about mountain safety and risk and death and responsibility for others on the climb, nor about cancer and dependency and the real meaning of life – but because we got a flat tire in the middle of nowhere and were both reduced to blood sugar bitches?

"What's so funny?"

I look up from the blurry grind of the darkening road and realize that I was laughing.

"I was just imagining us getting stuck out here," I tell her, which is exactly what I was thinking, which is nice for a change. "With a flat tire, and no food or water."

"Yeah, that's hilarious."

"I guess you had to be there," I say.

"Glad I wasn't."

Then a light pokes through the trees. And more lights, up ahead, and we both breathe a sigh of relief.

A hundred feet later, the ruts suddenly give way to a graded dirt road. We see several sets of lights, scattered through the thinning woods, and then suddenly, road noise, cars and trucks, the road widening into a big turnout.

In another hundred feet, there is a scattering of cars and trucks parked along both sides of the road, a few groups still out hiking, even though it is almost completely dark.

In another hundred feet, the road turns to pavement and there are cars, trucks, minivans, SUVs and RVs everywhere.

We drive by a long, crowded campground, dense with tents, vehicles, and people, and then pass a brown park service sign.

Donner Pass Campground
FULL

In another hundred feet, there it is, in its full rattling roar and incandescent blaze: the Interstate.

We cross under it and head south, joining a continuous line of vehicles zipping down a two-lane highway toward Lake Tahoe. I have the *Road Atlas* on my lap and we study every road sign, looking for a forest service road we can take west and back down into the woods.

But it's a blur of ski areas, golf resorts, houses and condos, all fenced in, all bounded by high ridges silhouetted against the deep blue early evening sky. No roads at all down that way.

So we keep heading south, in the dark now, through the resort sprawl of Tahoe, and turn onto the first highway heading west. The road runs down into the trees and undulates for awhile; but it is mostly heading down, unmistakably descending. Jill slows so we can read every sign and look up every darkened road for what might be a good way off the pavement and back up into the woods for our last night together.

We finally find a forest service road; and less than a hundred feet in, we're engulfed in trees and quiet. A few miles up a good dirt road, we find a little grove where people have camped but it's empty tonight, so we pull in.

Kettle and Jill head off into the woods to pee, and I stand in the sudden silence and look up through the canopy. We're obviously west of the fires because the stars are coming out, along with the new moon, through the breaks in the trees. It is almost a crescent now, its spherical face a blue-gray shadow.

Jill is back and we put on our headlamps and start pulling gear.

"Looks like it might be cold," she says, pulling out her tent.

"Yeah." I grab mine.

"Oh, don't bother with that," she says. "Unless you really want to. We've made it this far. We can behave."

I put my tent back in her truck, set up the camp kitchen, and make dinner while she puts up her tent and rolls out our sleeping bags.

The cold is coming on fast, and we are flattened from the long day of hiking and hard driving; so we avoid all the Big Questions this time, drink more whiskey and tea, smoke a bowl, and head straight into her tent. Kettle sleeps in a warm ball between us.

The moon has crossed directly over the gap in the trees, Jill's tent bathed in the soft glow of its milky white light. I do not fall asleep for awhile, and neither does she, I can tell. But we don't talk, just turn over, and sigh, and turn over again.

We awaken to find ourselves up on a high ridge, in a large grove of aspens on the very top of an anvil-shaped mountain. There is a long, tall, uniform wall of cloud to the west, running as far as we can see in either direction, like a perfect plateau of nothingness under the lavender blue sky. We shiver and stomp our feet over our coffee, and walk out to the very edge of the edge, looking for that first sliver of light.

And there it is: a sudden shaft of orange-yellow slices through the trees.

The sun is rising, unseen behind us and the ridge, unseen behind the whole massive upwelling of the Sierra Nevada.

But out across the void to the west, the very shape and shadow of the ridge we are standing on shoots out its silhouette against the watercolor orange and yellow light suddenly filling the cloudbank. It is morning alpenglow painted not on the face of a mountain, but on the face of the sky, all the way to some vanishing point, maybe all the way to the Pacific Ocean. It is something I've never read or heard about before, let alone ever seen.

"Wow," we say in union, then look down at the same time to see the same color crawling across our four feet. The forest floor all around us is suddenly bathed in the same golden light flooding from east to west and out to that vanishing point. "Wow," we say again.

Kettle runs back from his early morning patrol and stands next to us, watching the alpenglow surrender to full daylight, then urging us back toward camp for breakfast. We make a big one out of the last of our food, and eat it slowly, then Jill makes another pot of coffee.

I start breaking camp and Jill pulls out the tattered Road Atlas.

"This really is it," she lets out a long sigh. "Sacramento's just down the hill. As the crow flies, like fifteen miles. So maybe two road-hours tops."

I notice a dull ache in my chest, one that has been there without my really noticing it for the last day or two. Maybe it has been there the whole trip, or at least since we got west of Cheyenne.

*Kleinke * 316*

I've been thinking the whole time that it will be good when this trip is finally over. She can start her life from scratch in Sacramento, with no more trips through Dudeville and rounds up at The Treehouse between jobs; and I can go back to whatever life in Dudeville I've wanted all along. (Or think I've wanted. I'm not really sure anymore what that was supposed to look like.) But now, actually, suddenly – or not so suddenly but cumulatively and suddenly at critical mass – I am starting to dread it: the actual final moment when she drops me off at the Sacramento airport for my 5 PM flight. The end of it. Really the end this time. Forever.

"Or we could take the long way," she says, pointing at the *Atlas*.

I walk over in an odd daze, come up behind her, watch her fingers move south on the map, down into the national forest, almost all the way into Yosemite.

"Maybe head down here," she says. "Yosemite. The place is legend. Wanna check it out?"

"That would be great," I hear my voice say.

After we break camp, it's my turn to drive and her turn to navigate, and we get lost again, this time on purpose. We'd crossed the highway at the bottom of the mountain, back into the woods, and now we're feeling our way down another forest service road south toward Yosemite. The air starts to thicken with a blue haze, a barely perceptible scrim at first. Then it starts to roll in like blasts of campfire smoke, and we can smell it even with the windows rolled up.

The road swings around to the west, and even as the morning advances, the woods darken, turning more gray than blue and filling with another smell: dampness. The cloudbank we'd seen this morning off to the west has moved in, engulfing the sun with clouds and a low-lying fog that reaches all the way to the ghostly floor of the forest. Good for the fires, but it makes everything look creepy, dangerous, lonely somehow.

"Looks like rain," she says. "Good for the fires."

"I was just thinking that," I hear myself say.

The road curves in and out of the fog, mostly to what feels like the west; then it swings out onto a turnout, a large grove empty but for scattered trees and long mist-fingers of fog crawling across a carpet of pine needles.

We pull up to the edge and look out through the windshield, down onto the rolling checkerboard of an agricultural valley, brown and green and yellow corduroy fields, a highway straightening beyond into the gloom.

We both sigh at the same moment, look at each other and laugh, sort of.

"We should let Kettle out," she says.

We jump out of the truck, go around to the back, let Kettle out and watch him sprint away.

I turn back toward the truck and Jill is just standing there, all six feet of her, bent over like that old question mark, her tattered ski hat pulled down over her eyes, her emerald eyes soft and warm and wet with tears.

Then it just happens, in a sort of slow-motion, dead silence kind of way, the woods stopping, everything stopping, everything except her mouth, all wet and hungry and giving and good. And then she's grabbing me, and holding all of me so tight, and squeezing all of me so hard it's like she's breathing me in and out, and I'm breathing her out and in – and then clothes are coming off and I can't stand it anymore: I need to feel every inch of her skin on every inch of mine.

"Wait," she pulls back.

"Yes, you're right, we need to –"

"No, we need *this*," she says, reaching into the back of the truck and grabbing a sleeping pad. Then she grabs me by the hand and pulls me over onto the pine needles.

"But – we can't – I don't have a –"

"That's fine," she says as we crumple to our knees onto the mattress, "I had an IUD put in."

"Seriously?"

"I am *not* getting pregnant again."

"Are you sure?"

"Yes! Now shut up!" she says and grabs my head, and our mouths liquify into one mouth.

We crumple onto the camp mattress, shivering, clutching each other against the cold as shirts come off and pants go down, all of my regret and resolve gone as my mouth finds those sweet familiar breasts and those long strong tanned legs go up into the air, still hooked in pants down around her hiking boots. I jump through the hoop of her legs with my own pants down around my boots, my toes digging into the pine needles as I push and push and disappear into the pushing, the forest floor spinning and shaking, Jill pushing back with all that strength, all that old familiar moaning and groaning, right at the edge of screaming and grunting. And then there's another sound, a rushing roar all around us, up in the trees and all over the pine needle carpet, like a sudden rain – but it isn't rain, it's pea-sized hail! – and we are still pushing and moaning and coming, hail raining down like sharp gravel thrashing at us, but we keep going; and there's more and more hail, a thousand cold pinpricks all over my ass and legs, but Jill keeps coming, spasming, buckling beneath me, clenching her teeth against it but still coming as hard as she has ever come; and I hold her tighter and I come and her spasms finally break, and we both start laughing, and then she is crying and laughing, and the hail stops as fast as it started; and wow, what was that?

We don't say anything for the hour it takes to drive south in air suddenly thick not with hail or rain, but with smoke, acrid billows of it, and then a whole blanket of it as we cross a highway over onto a road closed a hundred feet up for fire, blocking us well north of the back way into Yosemite.

I guess it will have to be next time, I almost say, as Jill drives right up to the chain across the road I'd found on the map that would get us down there. But that would be exactly wrong: there will be no next time. And even if it weren't, it would be the wrong thing to say, right about now.

*DUDEVILLE * 319*

An hour later, we finally work our way down to Sacramento without going near an Interstate.

It takes less than an hour in town to find her new place and unload all her stuff. Her cousin's friend hasn't arrived yet; but there are boxes out on the porch and we move them in too. When we are done and Jill is in the bathroom, I look around at the little two-bedroom apartment, bare but for the boxes and pile of Jill's gear.

I try to imagine her life here. Soon this cold and empty place will be warm and cozy, full of two young women's new lives. But I will never see it that way because I will never see her again. So why can't I stop thinking about that IUD? What exactly was she planning?

I force myself to stop imagining any of it, because it fills me with so much pain and regret I can't stand it.

"Let's go," she says, grabbing my hand. "I'm starving."

We head back out, toward the airport, and pull into the first place we can find, a Mexican cantina.

She has to deal with finding her way around town later, so she reluctantly says "I wish, but no" when the server asks if we want beers or margaritas.

All I have to do is fly back to Colorado later, so I am dying for a beer or margarita right about now, but I know it would be a bad show of solidarity. Not that any shows matter at this point.

We eat in silence, awkwardly, under two shrouds of sadness that we take turns trying to break with small talk, which drives the other only further inward.

Or maybe what I really want to talk about is that IUD. Not that it's any of my business now. And what is there to say? I know it's a good thing: it means she really is moving on. What else do I think is supposed to happen? But I can't stop thinking about it, about how much it is bothering me, for some strange reason.

"What?"

"Nothing," I say.

"Bullshit. What?"

"I don't know," I finally say. "I guess I'm just curious – about what's up with the IUD."

"It's for birth control."

"No shit."

"So if you know all about it, why'd you ask?"

"I don't know."

The server comes back. Jill and I look at each other, and she gives me the nod.

"We changed our mind," I say to the server. "Could you bring us two margaritas?"

But the margaritas only make the silence and sadness even worse.

Half an hour later, Jill is supposed to be dropping me off at the airport curb with my gear and be on her way. But I still have a couple hours before my flight, so we park the truck and I say goodbye to Kettle, which tears my chest open in a way I never could have imagined any human, let alone any dog could do. Then Jill follows me in, helps me re-arrange and check my gear, and then goes with me all the way through airport security and out to my gate.

"For just one more goodbye drink," she says.

Which turns into one more goodbye drink for her, and a third and then a fourth for me. Because getting drunk is a good way of dealing with all this – because it's not dealing with it at all.

And so here I sit – my body does anyway, I'm not sure where the actual "I" really is – in yet another airport bar.

But this time, Jill is with me. And it's the mix and match of a weird dream I'm having, except that I'm wide awake and fiercely drunk. Jill is talking to me, but I'm having trouble following her through an odd mix of elation and euphoria that this whole bittersweet thing is finally almost over – even though there's a tiny voice in the back of my head telling me that the elation and euphoria came with the drinks and would wear off when they did.

Crowded into our corner down by the window, Jill's great height bent down into the space between us, she has one foot on the bar and the other on the bar of my stool. Her face is flushed and eyes misted over, and she stares at me from faraway, as if we were already a time zone apart.

This will be over soon, I keep hearing the words in my head, *and we can get on with it, and everybody will be fine. Just get through this.*

Jill is talking again, and I realize that she's talking about something *with* me.

"Yosemite," she says again, "would be cool to check out. And it's like an hour from here. And an easy flight for you."

"But I thought we were – you know – done. I thought –"

"This is it, yes, I know."

"So why are you talking about Yosemite?"

"So why did you ask about my IUD?"

"I don't know. I thought – you know. I don't know."

I realize she is drunk too, because she is looking at me in the same curious and hungry way she did in the window that first night at the Last Chance, the same way she did across the hot tub we poached in Breckenridge.

"Because look at you," she says, holding her hands out at me, as if I were actually something to behold.

But all I can think is: *What? Look at me??? Look at you! You're this young, hot, smart, totally together woman, and you are actually stuck on me? Old, selfish, lost, corporate drop-out, arrested adolescent me? After all this? What the hell is the matter with you?*

And all I can say is "What do you mean?"

"I mean look at you," she says again, her eyes filling with tears. "You're so – right there. You're driven, and you're smart. You're tough, and you're funny. But you're so fucked up. You are so – fucked – up!"

I do not know what to say or do; and it is the last thing I would ever mean to say or do; but it's the only thing I can do, if only to keep from falling backwards off a stool in an airport bar: I burst out laughing.

Then everything goes in and out: the look on her face, like I'd just slapped her; the others in the bar; the airport; the whole weird day.

Everything except what happens over at the gate, right before I get on my plane back east to Colorado, which I'm afraid I will never forget: people streaming all around us, and what may be the longest, sweetest, saddest kiss of my life.

Then everything goes completely blank.

I am jolted awake, in an airplane, by a hard landing in Denver. Everything out the window is flooded with blinding, metallic sunlight.

The elation and euphoria are gone, melted into the muck of a hangover at the wrong end of the day.

But at least, I realize as I come back into my tired, aching body, I'm sober enough to drive, all the way back to the mountains and up to a place I will never call "The Treehouse" again.

Bagging the Lady

Today is the day, finally, the first on a short string of days in late August. The last of the snow in the upper couloirs is settled; the morning temps are up just enough to soften it into skiable – but not unsafe – condition, before sunhit a couple hours after dawn; and the first new snow is weeks away.

The weather is perfect, not counting the afternoon thunderstorms that roll in on hot summer days, and it's supposed to be perfect for tomorrow. And so we climb, hauling all this damn gear for the big descent.

And I am terrified.

I've endured countless mornings an order of magnitude more challenging than this one – when it's below zero and still dark at the trailhead, the mountain is ripped by wind and a razor-dust of blowing snow, and every breath aches and every step hurts – and I've asked myself, over and over, *Why am I doing this? Why am I volunteering for all this suffering and hard work and misery?* But I eventually start to warm up, the sun breaks through the trees, the mountain opens out in every direction, and I know it was just weakness talking. Then I laugh it off, laugh at myself, and carry on and up with the day's plan.

But today? No. Today, fear and doubt are gnawing at me. And at Danny and Aaron too, I think. It's like a bad smell all around us that won't clear, no matter how far or fast we hike on ahead of it.

On most big climbs, we have the same running discussion – in the shorthand that comes with a couple years of doing this as a team – about perception versus will, about knowing when to turn back and when to push on. Is it weather, snow conditions, real fatigue, or just laziness? Is it lack of training for what we happen to be doing that day? Or is it really just weakness, masquerading as concerns about weather, snow conditions, real fatigue or specific training?

This is the best thing about climbing with partners who know you, or at least know what you can and can't do. Because the nagging part of the brain loves to show up and ask, at some point just after the start of the climb, *Why am I doing this? Why am I volunteering for all this work and misery? And what about the weather, this snow, the crappy sleep crammed in a tent with the wind going all last night?*

Today, that voice is nagging harder than ever, cutting right to the outsized heart of the whole mountaineering enterprise: *Is this even sane? What am I trying to prove? What exactly is the point?* Today, this long-anticipated, oft-discussed climb and first snowboard descent of The Lady feels, if not insanely self-aggrandizing and otherwise pointless, then at best (as our corporate lawyer used to say about various requisite administrative rituals) "perfunctory."

Last night, we took the conversation in Ullar's almost that far – *Why are we bothering? What is the point?* – each of us looking to the other two to bail all three of us out.

For Aaron, Tyler's accident has him spooked, and he said so flat out, and I mostly believe him.

For Danny, "it's just bad juju," he said, and he'll work through it – though I think it's something else, like maybe Julie, who always worried when we were out and made him call the minute we got back into cell phone range.

For me, it was the nightmare last week on Borah Peak up in Idaho, which I can't seem to find a way to tell them about.

Last night, when we talked our way that far to the edge of asking *Why bother,* and one of us would start to cave, the other two would hasten to change the talk back to gear, snow, timing, and trailheads.

So here we are, halfway up The Lady, doing what we've been talking about doing for almost two years. And there is a palpable, collective shame suspended in the silence all around this morning – that bad smell not passing but following us up the trail – for the doubts we did share with each other.

I try to shake it off, ignore them and stare straight down at the trail, cinch my heavy load tighter to my body and pull harder up the mountain. This, after all, is the upper couloir of The Lady, the great suspended snowfield that has taunted and seduced us, staring down at us for years. It is the great un-ridden wonder, a mystery unveiled and hovering in plain sight, not off on another continent with a big sponsored expedition Jill and a whole crew might be on, but just down the road at the end of our canyon.

At 13,451 feet, The Lady isn't even a Fourteener, which is why only a dozen or so people have ever climbed up the jagged ice and rockpile ridgelines to her summit; why only the great Len Davies has ever skied down and off of her; why no one has ever ridden her on a snowboard. The Lady is something still wild and dangerous and beautiful, sitting right there in our own backyard. For two years we've been talking about her, planning routes up, down and off of her, and building practice trips around how the whole thing would go: an easy day up to the bottom and a high camp; then a predawn climb up to the top and rappel down onto the snowfield as the sun is coming up; then those fifty forbidden turns; and then out.

In all those hours of all that planning, *Why bother?* never once came up.

So why has it now? The harder I work on the question without an answer, the heavier this load on my back and the more labored my breathing, to the point where I've almost broken out of the aerobic box.

I pause for a minute to catch my breath.

Better not to think about any of that. Better to think about the route, and measure out my breaths, and inventory all this damn gear one more time.

Aaron has the climbing racks.

I have the ropes.

Danny has the kitchen and tent.

And strapped to our stuffed packs, each of us has a snowboard, ax, avy shovel, and crampons. Under the weight of it all, we are beasts of our manufactured burden, surly and withdrawn into our own worlds, still not talking at, just getting on with it. Perfunctorily.

I almost run into Danny, stopped on the trail.

A few paces ahead of him, Aaron is adjusting gear.

Without saying anything, we decide to take a break and grab some water and calories.

We are two hours into the approach hike up the left side of The Lady, up a narrow canyon between her and Avalanche Peak, one of the few on the cirque we never hike because it terminates in a dry waterfall with no views. Unless you are climbing up and around to the right, which we are doing today.

"So."

"So."

"So."

We hoist the packs and start up the trail again.

When I go back to *Why bother* fifteen hard humping minutes later, I finally get confirmation that this is exactly what's on Danny's mind too. We are crawling with our heavy packs and protruding boards and axes under a huge downfall of lodgepole pine when he mumbles Aaron's closing words from last night, over root beers in Ullar's: "Because we said we would."

Because we said we would was always reason enough for me to do anything at work, no matter how difficult, if it was for Tom or Becky or one of my own people.

I dig in harder and decide that it will have to be reason enough today.

Even though I am terrified, truly terrified, for the first time up here.

Stay in the aerobic box, I tell myself. Breathe in, breathe out, and just keep climbing. *Because we said we would.*

I fall back on those words, and on the other thing Aaron said last night while we were not saying what we were really thinking.

"Based on everything we know," he rattled it off with the same coolness of his rescue clinics, "about the mountain, the couloir, and our skills, we have no rational reason not to. Unless," he turned to

Danny, "your irrational reason – your 'bad juju,' which is totally cool, if it's real for you – is an actual performance factor."

"It's not real," Danny says. "Because I know that's what it is. Witness consciousness conquers all."

"You sure?" Aaron searched his eyes.

"Fuck yeah, dude. All good over here."

For Aaron, *because we said we would* is also an obligation to everyone else who might ever try this same thing. Because someone will try – especially if we don't do it first – and they most likely will not have his skills or training or cautiousness.

I suppose *Because we said we would* has driven me up here today too, and not because I'm as public-minded as Aaron but because I am selfish. I want to bag a first snowboard descent of The Lady because I can; because most people are too weak or too old or too cowardly and cannot; and because there are some people who are so weak or old or cowardly that they would ridicule me for trying, for the simple reason that they cannot. (This would include my father, whose drunken malice never saw someone's ambition or aspiration as not worthy of minimizing, ridiculing, or tearing down altogether.) And for reasons I can't fathom, or at least beyond my control, I have to prove them all wrong – even if the thing itself is completely pointless.

Since I first started working it in the mountains, off the grid, up on the roof, I've become addicted: to the risks going up and the rush coming down; to the focus, stakes, and adrenaline; to the heady triumph and visceral power blast that always comes with facing down fear, making it to the top, and making it back to the bottom without killing myself. And aside from bad luck, from the shit-happens factor – i.e., the mountain killing me because it can – this really is all about killing myself or not, when I work it right to the edge and don't fall over but somehow manage to come back in one piece.

This is the great head-fuck that is the essence of all mountaineering. The mountain may or may not be welcoming on any particular day. And it may or may not beat you because of who it is and who you are. But you can always beat yourself on what is a perfectly fine and welcoming mountain. Which is exactly what is freaking me out today: that I may be set up to beat myself. And if I do, I will end up dragging the two of them down with me. But not if I un-beat myself.

Which is more or less what Danny said about witness-consciousness (I think).

He is right; I will shake it off.

This is why the three of us work as a team. And that is how I will answer this terror today: these guys. There is a solid foothold in the working fact of this team, and a solid handhold in the thousands of hours we have been up here practicing, and one solid foothold and handhold is all you need to pull your own shit together and get up the mountain.

And yet, and yet, I am not feeling it. I am spooked, an irrational reason I know, but addled by something real, and maybe something I should have told these guys about last night when I had the chance.

Last week, when I was up in Idaho and blown off by weather just short of the top of Borah (the extent of what I told them when I got back), bad luck struck and shit finally did happen, after all these years up here.

I was up in Sun Valley for a music festival I'd always heard about, and decided to drive a rental car all the way back here, if only because the Treehouse was starting to feel a little lonely and I thought some new mountains would re-ignite me for today. And even if they wouldn't, I still needed a long, tough training hike for today.

And there it was: Borah Peak, Idaho's biggest, which often means most dangerous, if not technically, then for how crowded it might get. Borah turned out to have both: the last 5,200 of its 12,662 feet are compressed into less than four miles, all of it straight up; the weather was unstable; and it was crowded, for a big mountain. A near perfect formula for how shit happens up here.

At the trailhead the night before the climb, I didn't get much sleep. There were a couple college dudes camping next to me, partying hard and wanting to hang out, their live recordings of one jam band after another going all night. And they had a nice old guitar neither of them could play.

If only to get them to turn the music off for the night, I made the mistake of picking it up and playing something quiet. But when they saw that I could play, all that old blues and blues-rock stuff, they kept at me, with their beers and their bong, "oh come on, dude, just one more song!"

The next morning, I got a late start, well past sunrise and into the day. I knew it was going to be a solid ten hours to the summit and back, with a knife edge along the top, and massive exposures; and I could see the first little cotton balls of cumulus cloud off to the west as I was leaving the trailhead; and I started up the trail anyway with all my gear.

I'd read and heard that Borah was a great place for practice, and it certainly proved to be, with steady ice ax work along the last harrowing ridge below the final summit. In one stretch, the ridge was maybe three feet wide and dropped 2,000 feet in either direction, inspiring the steadiest steps of your life if you're working without a rope like I was.

But aside from those electrifying minutes, the whole climb felt like a big long chore. Just get up, get down, and get back to Dudeville. No Presence, no Nothing. Perfunctory.

Actually, just a Nothing would have been better than the thunderheads forming and building to the west, right after I'd cleared the last of those knife-edge crossings up top. I saw them coming and calculated my way to the summit and kept going, the thunderhead still 40 or more miles to the northwest, if building from the valley floor to twice the height of the mountain.

I moved along the widening ridge and open face of the summit as fast as I could, my ice ax sticking up from my backpack like a lightning rod. The wind picked up and the darkening front of the thunderhead unfurled a sheet of rain that would turn into *virga* – rain that never reaches the ground. *Virga* is usually a sweet thing to see, sometimes shot through with rainbow and lightning; that afternoon, it was a cold, indifferent signal flag as big as the mountain to get the hell down. The whole colossus of the thunderhead was growing, moving straight at the range, straight for that summit, and I had those knife-edge crossings to navigate before I could start back down.

So I called it – because of course I had to call it – and turned around and hurried back as fast as I dared on that exposed, unstable rockpile of a summit face.

And then, shit happened.

I was moving a little too fast, faster than the two people also hiking back toward the ridge, a couple hundred feet below me.

So I had to wait.

But they kept stopping.

So I had to wait some more.

And they kept stopping and futzing with their gear.

Which reminded me of the ice ax poking up from my pack, as the thunderhead rolled toward us, building, darkening, and throwing off lightning.

So I started to pick my way across the rockpile carefully, staying (I was sure) well west of the fall-line down to them.

Then, in the worst possible series of events – where Murphy's Law meets Chaos Theory – my foot dislodged a rock the size of my boot.

The rock slid and tumbled and launched and bounced, dislodging a rock the size of a really big boot.

Which bounced, and then bounced left, and then bounced left again.

I just stared at it, thinking *Well that can't just keep going left.*

But it did, bouncing left again, and again, each time gaining speed and altitude, until it was spinning like a whirring sawblade.

Time stopped and everything stopped, as I watched the floating buzzsaw launch left again and I had time to articulate the entire thought *Well that can't possibly be happening but it is happening* and I finally remembered that you always scream "Rock! Rock! Rock!" and when I finally started screaming "Rock! Rock! Rock!" it was into a howling wind and they didn't hear me and it landed and bounced left again and I screamed louder into the wind "Rock! Rock! Rock!" and just as they heard me he turned and the rock launched to the exact height of his head...

...whirring like an airplane propeller...

...ZING!...

...right by his face, missing it by maybe a foot and a half...

...and down into the void below.

"Crrawww!" he screamed out – just like that bird in the wolf's mouth – as his reflexes caught up and he shot to the rockpile at his feet, covering his head.

I stood bolted to the spot, paralyzed by the terror of moving and dislodging another rock.

She rushed over to him as he crawled onto all fours, shaking and retching and finally throwing up. Then she turned up the mountain and screamed at me. I couldn't hear her for the wind, but it couldn't have been worse than what I was screaming at myself.

I am screaming at myself for it still. And Aaron and Danny would be too, if they'd been there to see. And Scott, and Tyler, and Kelly, and Leese, and Maggie, and everybody else I've ever climbed with and who has ever counted on me up here. And of course dear sweet Jill. *Crrrawww!* on me, for nearly killing someone, because I'd done everything wrong on the mountain that day: started late, turned around late, hiked too fast across a steep rockpile with people below.

I'm not some tourist hiker, some idiot out in blue jeans and sneakers trying to bag a resort summit; I should know better. And I do. But I didn't. And I nearly killed or at least horribly disfigured a guy, all because I was bored and lonely and in a hurry to get up and down a huge and dangerous mountain I never really wanted to be on in the first place. Whatever karma I earned when I bailed out Sean and Angie back on Sunrise Peak, I pissed away on Borah Peak, and maybe with huge negative interest yet to pay.

I am snapped back by Aaron's voice.

I look up and see them a dozen paces ahead, stopped by another huge downfall.

"No wonder no one ever comes up here," Danny says.

Another stand of trees has been blown down over the narrow and steep trail from an avalanche last winter, twisted and snapped at the height of our heads. The whole avalanche path above and below us smells like a woodworking shop, like good pine sawed into lumber.

We struggle to hike half bent over, stooping to get our packs, boards and ice axes under the downfall.

After we finally clear it, they push ahead, but I stop for a moment to look down the slide path into the gulch. There is a perfect parabola of freshly shorn stumps, all our height, reaching all the way down, its apex at the bottom where the slide path meets the main gulch. From up here, the enormous pile of trees looks like a little pile of broken matchsticks.

"Half an hour 'til treeline, Jack," Aaron calls back to me from fifty or so feet up ahead, where the trail ducks back into the woods.

I take a deep breath and try to think about something else, anything else, Jill even; but all I can think about is that terrible night in Idaho.

The white-knuckle drive out of that range and south toward Colorado tore at my already raw nerves, as one thunderstorm after another railroaded across that great sweep of agricultural valley, the little rental car flagging around in the wind and hail and screaming rain.

I pulled into the first motel I could find, got a room, and went straight to the bar.

As the storm was finally clearing and the sun coming out just in time to set, I was back in my room, as drunk or maybe even more drunker than I'd gotten in the Sacramento airport two weeks before. But this time, I was the exact opposite of elated and euphoric and blank: I was sodden, heavy, pathetic, scared, and all alone in the world. And so of course I drunk-dialed Jill's cell phone.

When I heard her new voicemail greeting in that old familiar voice – cocky but self-conscious, goofy but serious, strong but still with a little bit of that purr in it – something broke apart inside my chest. I blurted out a bunch of drunken babble about having just made a huge mistake on the mountain and almost killing a guy, and how I know I wasn't abiding by our agreement not to call or email or anything until we're well clear of each other six months at least, but it was all some huge mistake and I was sorry. Then I realized she can't help but take it all the wrong way: she will think I mean I made a mistake about her and I was trying to rescind our agreement. So I tried to backpedal it by saying I was just a little messed up about a near accident on a big mountain and I'm sorry.

She called me back a couple hours later, after I'd passed out.

"Are you alright? What accident? Are you hurt?"

"No, I'm fine," I said. "I was just climbing Borah in Idaho, when a storm came in. And this guy –"

"Good," she cut me off. "I just needed to know that you're not injured up there or dead."

"No, I'm ok, I just –"

"Good," she cut me off. "Now – please don't call me – ever again. Like we agreed."

But she didn't hang up. There was a long pause, and just as I started to say something, she cut me off again.

"I loved you," she snapped at me. "Just so we're clear on that. Ok? I fucking LOVED you. And you broke my heart. So please – don't ever – call me – again." Then she hung up.

The echo of her voice fills this steep, narrow gulch, the weight of her words latched onto my backpack and heavier than any of this gear.

And the only thing I can say comes out as screaming "Rock! Rock! Rock!" and "I'm sorry!"

I finally have to stop, completely out of breath now, the aerobic box trampled somewhere back in that avalanche debris.

Breathe in, breathe out.

No Presence, no Nothing.

I don't think I can hike another step up a mountain that feels worse than the usual indifferent today. I know the notion is absurd, but it feels angry. It feels like it knows what I did back on Borah Peak. Maybe everything in my body just hurts, which doesn't happen anymore up here, so I'm making it about the mountain.

But I have to keep going, because Aaron and Danny are counting on me.

Half an hour later, we finally get to treeline and find a good place to camp, a rocky ridge with a few dozen square feet of flat.

We set up the tent and kitchen in silence, cook in silence, eat in silence. Aaron and Danny and I are a machine when we need to be, and for this, we need to be. This evening, more than most, being part of that machine is good medicine for me.

After we eat, and the sun starts to drop behind us and over the back of Powell Peak and Mount Opal, we keep ourselves busy and don't say much. No whiskey and no weed for anyone tonight, just quiet, preoccupation, purposefulness.

Aaron stands over the mound of climbing gear, sorting hardware, then sits on a rock and practices knots.

Danny scrambles down and around the ridge, then up onto another slab facing west, sitting cross-legged and still, bathed in the last of the setting sun.

I wander off by myself onto a long flat rock. I sit and face the setting sun, watch, wait, listen.

And there it is, the Presence, but just barely.

I breathe in and out, reaching a little further out across the darkening mountains and a little deeper inside.

But the Presence seems as quiet and withdrawn as Aaron and Danny this evening, waiting too, it seems.

The moon rises over the mountains, just past full, the same moon that was new when Jill and I were in the Sierras.

But I am trying not to think about that trip, because I am trying not to think about Jill. Ever since I got back from dropping her off in California, the whole thing feels like one big, sad, stupid loss. And while I've endured my share of big, sad, stupid losses over the years, I am clueless about how to push through this one. I have no idea what to do with this sudden, aching emptiness welling up in my body, if only because I've always coped with my losses by pretending they wasn't there: by losing myself in childhood fantasies about running away; by drowning myself in work, ambition, and the ambitions of others; by heading to the nearest bar at the end of the day, and stumbling home to dreams of one day running west.

Of one day running out here, and up here. And now where?

I sit back and watch the moon work its way into the great vault of the sky, blotting out a few sputtering stars and washing the whole canyon in cold white light. The last of the warm air has risen out of the gulch below, and cold dry air crawls down into its place from the mountain behind us. It feels good after the long hot day, like cold water when you've been sweating all day and are thirsty.

Maybe I'm still just freaked out by what happened up on Borah Peak, but I'm starting to re-think my own little ghost dance out on the deck of the Treehouse last March. It sounded all wrong the moment I tried explaining any of it to Jill. But who can tell anything as personal and profound as all that to another human being?

Or maybe I am full of shit, as has been suggested on occasion by everyone from Becky to Amy the Rebound Girl to Jill herself. Maybe I can't just will my own stoical end, die alone, be no one's bother. Guy Waterman's friends had to climb up his beloved mountain after all, and recover his body and bring it back – in treacherous terrain and terrible weather – mourning their loss as they picked their way down with that awkward, heavy load. One of them could have slipped under the weight, fallen, pulled them all down.

Yes, death is inevitable, sooner or later, etc. And up here on this mountain – hanging from a rope, or flying off on skis or a snowboard – I can surely calibrate myself right to the edge of my own death in ways no one down there in the world can. I can in fact will it closer, or further away, with the twitch of a few muscles, like I did out on my deck, drunk and staring down the freezing cold.

But really: who am I to pretend toward death? Because I've climbed maybe 50 big mountains, thrown myself off half of them on skis or a snowboard? And when will I run out of chances, like Tyler, and not die, but end up badly hurt instead? Would I really welcome death then, rather than grovel and grope for help and hope, like everyone does when they crash, or fail, or start to fade? Is that what I really want – to find any of that out?

Maybe this is the skeleton key that unlocks the whole weird death cult bound up in the apex of mountaineering. Lots of those guys (and it's always the guys, not the Betties) who go really big – climbing up and skiing off the world's truly great mountains – do actually die, sooner or later, despite all they know, all they have to lose, all they leave behind. What were Alex Lowe, Doug Combs, or Shane Conkley really after? Aaron knew some of them, and has climbed with many who have climbed and skied with many more of them, and he always just shrugs off questions about it with one simple answer.

"They were junkies," he always says. "Addicted to risk, addicted to adrenaline, and they eventually overdosed." Then he changes the subject back to gear, and manageable risk, and getting back to the trailhead.

Because "summiting is optional, and getting back down is mandatory," which is what we all always say.

Behind me, I hear zippers opening and closing and opening again. Aaron and Danny are crawling into the tent and their sleeping bags in silence, a shadowdance of silhouettes in headlamp light.

I sit out on the edge of the rock a couple more minutes, watching the moon, listening to the woods below us creak and stir.

The Presence looms up from the gully, comforting but completely silent, seemingly as preoccupied as the three of us.

When I stand and head over toward the darkened tent, Danny murmuring something and Aaron laughing, I hear those words again – not Danny's voice or Aaron's voice or even my own voice, but the still small voice, the Presence, reminding me: *Summiting is optional.*

Getting back down is mandatory. You have no choice but to live through this.

We are up before five, two solid hours before the sun, a streak of light just breaking on the eastern ridge of the canyon. We do not talk; we are a machine. Water, flame, coffee, gear.

In the harsh gray-blue glow of Aaron's lantern, I wax our snowboards while Danny makes breakfast and Aaron sorts the ropes and gear for the rappel one more time.

"I wonder how much good this shit really does," Danny finally breaks the silence, as he rubs a glob of white sunscreen into his cheeks. "Even when you put it on all the time."

"It works," Aaron says, "if you re-apply it enough times. And it can't hurt, because at least you're still moisturizing." He stands up from the gear pile and stretches his back with a long sigh. "Either way," he lets out another long, weary sigh, then mutters, "you don't want to end up like Kelly."

"Fuck no, dude," Danny says. "All that sun damage? Makes the poor girl look twenty years older than she is."

"Which may be as old as she's ever going to look."

Danny and I stop and glance over at him. "What?"

"You guys didn't hear?"

We just stare at him.

"She has melanoma, stage three."

"That's the bad one?" Danny asks.

"That's the bad one."

Kelly and her faceful of sun. Skin cancer. There is nothing else to say, so we work on in silence.

The news about Kelly wipes out whatever tentative resolve I've mustered since the gloom of yesterday's start; gleaned from the tough silence and parting words of the Presence after dark last night; clung to during all the tossing and turning in the tent last night. I want only to get off this mountain as fast as possible.

Maybe Danny is thinking the same thing, because he catches my eye and looks away quickly, and smears another blob of sunscreen onto his nose.

Because we are going straight up, over, and down the summit of The Lady on a very one-way course, we pack and stow our camping gear under the ledge for a quick retrieval hike a few days from now.

Then, finally, we head up.

The moon is down, everything around us a black void. Our headlamps trace blue-white ovals on the rock, show handholds and footholds in its seams, sketch a long, steady, silent scramble up through the dark.

One hour and maybe 300 vertical feet in, I look up from the eerie puzzle and see long streaks of light orange breaking behind us and backlighting the eastern sky. A few morning stars I hadn't seen come out are flickering off.

We climb on in a steady hum, more machine than ever, toward the summit of The Lady. I've been up here before – with Aaron, Tyler and Scott that time – in full daylight and all in one day. We simply had to climb it, tag it, and go back down. It's not technically hard, just wildly exposed and dangerous down the front. Our route spiders up one of the tendons of her long graceful neck, along the ridge that rises over the upper couloir, a hundred rocky feet suspended over that forbidden snowfield.

Then our first obstacle: The Lady's necklace of round granite boulders, blown clean in the wind around the front of the summit.

There's enough ambient light now to see what we are doing, so we kill our headlamps. Aaron fixes protection and ropes in, and leads us up and over in one pitch.

Down below, in the hollow of The Lady's throat, I can see the top of the snowfield, surrounded by great piles of rock. It is another roughly drawn parabola, bisected by a fall-line that points the way for thousands of tons of snow and ice to gather, freeze and thaw, freeze and thaw again, and finally collapse with mini-avalanches ten months out of the year. Our ears are wide open to the rattle of any ice or rock, every exposed skin cell tuned to any sign of the temperature rising too fast, every handhold and foothold tuned in to any sensation of the mountain letting go, searching and scanning for any reason to bail...

And the altitude finally kicks in. It is a familiar buzz, one I know how to negotiate and sometimes groove on. But today, it's one more red light blinking in the visual chatter of my imagination.

Breathe in, breathe out, climb on.

Back in the box, breathe in, breathe out, then back in the machine.

And then finally...

Summit.

I mean: Summit!

But I don't really. There is no exclamation point on this one, no joy, just wary relief.

We climb up and onto the messy rockpile that is the summit of The Lady – "so she's a pinhead!" Danny yells over the wind – in maybe two hours from last night's camp. But each of us is so lost in his own thoughts, we don't do the usual high-fives and just go right to work on our gear.

Perfunctory, I think.

You have no choice but to live through this, I hear the words again.

Aaron threads the rappel ropes around anchors we will come get in a few days with the stashed camping gear. He drops their two ends down onto the top of the snowfield. Danny and I watch as they land on the rock at the uppermost end of that narrow bulge of snow, and spill onto the icy wellspring of that frozen river falling off The Lady, falling off the entire mountain, falling down into the canyon below still enshrouded in dark mist.

We check helmets and harnesses and beacons one more time, and start to pack up our gear.

Before I finish, I pull out my camera and take a few quick pictures – the most perfunctory thing of all about this whole perfunctory trip, it seems. The usual pictures of the view, which this morning is a sea of mountaintops, silhouetted against the wet blue pre-dawn sky, like whitecaps on the ocean. Then, with the last frame on this roll of film,

I take a picture of Danny and Aaron, who seem a little annoyed but pause anyway to look up from their gear, their faces deadly serious.

As I'm putting the camera away, there's a weird buzzing in Danny's pack.

"What the hell is that?" Aaron asks. "Is that – a cell phone?"

Danny digs his phone from the bottom of the pack. "That's weird," he says. "I guess I left it on." He studies the tiny gray screen. "And somebody's calling me. And the signal is actually reaching up here."

"That *is* weird," Aaron and I say in unison.

A cell phone signal all the way up here? That's impossible. The first cell signal just hit the middle of Dudeville two years ago, and has barely spread outside of town. And now up here?

"That feels like really bad luck," Danny says. "Like it's way too easy to call for help up here now."

"Yes," Aaron says, as we all look down at the screen lighting up *Incoming Call.* "But I guess that was bound to happen. And right behind it, tourists on every summit calling people –"

And Danny finishes his thought: "Just to say 'Look at me, I'm so awesome, I summited!'" He turns the phone off and stuffs it down into his pack. "Sorry, you guys."

Aaron leans down to check the ropes one more time. "Though it *will* make it easier to get help up here," he says. "For all of us."

Before we drop down on the rappel, we stand in a tight circle, take a few long breaths, scan each other's eyes.

"We all good?" Aaron asks.

"We're good," Danny says.

"Yes," I say.

"Good," Aaron says. "Let's do this."

Danny rappels down first. Right off the top, the end of his snowboard knocks a rock the size of basketball loose from the ragged summit seam.

Danny pauses and we all wait, and watch, for the sound of it hitting bottom.

And we wait.

And we wait.

Finally, there is no *Boom!* – only a small, distant cracking sound, like a much smaller rock, small as a billiard ball, landing not on rocks but on what sounds like a pile of dried bones.

Danny takes a deep breath and slips down the rest of the rappel.

I tie in and slip down the rappel, not looking around at the view awakening with the rising sun, but looking straight down past my dangling feet at Danny. The drop takes maybe 60 seconds, but it feels like a solid half hour, the adrenaline surging as I swing loose from the mountain into all that empty space.

When I finally land, Danny unhooks me and we high-five and he signals up for Aaron.

Aaron starts down.

And then stops.

He is most of the way down when both ropes pull tight and bounce him with a creaky heave.

"What's up?" Danny yells.

"Down rope is stuck," he yells back.

"Oh shit," Danny says to me. Then he yells back to Aaron, "Ok, man. You know the drill. We're down here."

We stand and watch him for several minutes. Light from the rising sun fills the walls all around us, and soon it will hit the snowfield below us, and this high, suspended tongue of snow will soften, start to melt, start to drip down into the void below.

Aaron struggles with the ropes, but he can't swing the down rope free of whatever it has caught itself on coming down. He has to get down soon, on the rappel or by re-ascending and freeing the rope.

Danny and I stand and watch him struggle for a few more minutes, hear him grunting, talking to himself.

"To hell with it, boys," he finally yells, and switches out to his ascenders, two big handle-clamps used to climb up, not rappel down, a rope.

It takes Aaron a half hour or so to shimmy all the way back up the two ropes to free up the jam, twisting and turning on them like a flustered marionette trying to claw its way up and smack the guy working the strings. His weight and struggle pull Danny back and forth against the anchor. Though it's not necessary – and if only because I am nervous and have nothing else to do – I tie into Danny's harness and anchor him, and we both pull back and try to straighten the ropes for Aaron as much as we can.

Aaron finally makes it back to the top and straightens out whatever was wrong with the ropes.

"All good," he yells down to us. "On rappel."

He rappels down in one good clean minute, a straight even drop, his eyes fixed on us.

And that's it, and there we are, finally: standing with our snowboards at the top end of this elusive, impossible snowfield, looking down on the slumbering streets of Dudeville. This is the real summit for us today, worthy of joyful high-fives all the way around.

"Here we are, boys," Aaron says.

"Here's where you should take a picture, Jack."

"Ha," I snort. "That was my last shot. I'm out of film."

"Just as well, man," Danny says. "You're not supposed to be taking pictures of something sacred." He gestures down the snowfield. "And this feels pretty fuckin' sacred to me."

"Yes," Aaron says, staring down the mountain. "It is."

We pack the ropes and cinch our backpacks as tight as they will go, then strap into our snowboards.

We sit there in silence for a good minute on that precious snow, breathing it all in.

Finally, Aaron looks at us. We both nod to him at the same time, and he stands to drop in first. We've never talked about who goes first; but I guess we've known without saying anything that he would go first, as our way of honoring him for having led us this far and on so many trips.

Aaron's turns spool out in slow motion: tight, measured, and even, the fifty forbidden turns we'd all always imagined, perfectly executed.

And because our scale when we look to the mountains is always off, it turns out to be more like 36 turns, but who's counting?

Danny stands, waves all-clear, lets out a big holler, and drops in. His turns are wider and longer and deeper than Aaron's, with sharper cutbacks and flowing tai chi arms, a surfer's dance down the snowfield.

He pulls up alongside Aaron and they high-ten.

Then it's my turn.

I stand on my snowboard and wave all-clear. But before I drop in, I take one long, last look around at the rock ridges and forested gulches and side creeks tumbling down off the cirque, down toward Dudeville along the bottom of this big, beautiful canyon. The town and everything around it looks beyond possible, beyond real, like an HO-scale model of reality.

From up here, I can see how and why this ramshackle little mountain town is a place borne of and fully beholden to its landscape, where gravity and timber and water and rock all converge at the bottom, everything with any mass finding its angle of repose. The town sits at the focal point of all those convergences, if only because something had to assemble itself at the bottom where two creeks came together: Dudeville, on the ruins of an old mining camp, on the remnants of an old native village, at the confluence of those creeks where game congregated, a sunny grassy little clearing that any native, or mountain man, or miner could see when he was up here and looked back down.

"All good?" I hear Aaron yell up to me.

"All good," I yell back and wave the all-clear again.

I breathe in, and breathe out, and feel the sudden cooling flush of good adrenaline as I turn my board and point it straight down the fall line, submitting to the will of gravity and dissolving into my own forbidden turns. I can feel through my board that the snow is perfect, a million microscopic crystalline beads, like the top of a giant snow cone just soft enough to eat but not so soft it might fall apart.

I am surfing off the roof of the world again, just as the sun breaks over the wall and spills across the snow, and for just a moment, the Presence is everywhere around and within me, and time stops.

Then it starts again, triggered by the cheering of Aaron and Danny at the bottom, who high-five me as I curve around them with my last turn.

On a normal day, this hike out would be hell. Everything below the snowfield is boulderfield, a great three-dimensional maze to navigate on our way down the rest of the mountain. But we don't care. Adrenaline is still the best drug ever, if the most dangerous drug sometimes.

We are finally animated and chatty, as we pick our way down, up, across, and around boulder after boulder, until the field finally spills like a raging river of granite into the woods.

With no trail out of these woods, this is like nothing we've ever hiked before. But we mapped out the route, from the draw below the boulderfield, over to an old mining road that crosses the whole drainage down at the bottom. I've been up that abandoned road a dozen times on my mountain bike, and reveled in the way the forest is taking it back. Its steep eroded banks collapse onto the rutted roadbed, and little white pines and blue spruces pop up in the middle like defiant pine-elves, reclaiming the road from beneath and on both sides.

Down at the bottom of the drainage, we bushwhack our way up and out, our boards catching in trees and legs tangling up in willows. But we push on, the last of the adrenaline driving us as we fan out across the drainage.

"This way!" Danny yells from down and left.

He's found a route through the trees and boulders that line the ridge above the drainage, and Aaron and I scramble over and follow him out along the ridge in silence for several minutes.

"That was some pretty good old snow," Danny finally says, "but nothing like those very first turns we ever made, hey Jack?"

I smile with the memory. "Wrong end of the season."

"Yeah, that was something," he says. "Turns that weren't turns, just one crazy ride straight down on all that blue light."

We hike on in silence, and I remember that great plate of fresh snow and the blue light shooting through it, electrifying it from within, the day I met Danny up in Steamboat. It was a cold January day, after an enormous storm had dropped two feet of powder on the whole Northern Rockies. They'd just opened the gates off the highest chair, a short hike to the summit of the whole place, and then a big drop down into the backcountry. Danny and I got there first.

We dropped in, side by side, between massive trees draped in sparkling snow, down a chute of sparkling virgin powder. With our first turn, we broke the plate of snow loose, just enough for it to start to move but not avalanche, and the whole of it rumbled down the chute with us riding on top. It was like riding a wave on the ocean except that it was a wave of snow, releasing all of its energy and all that blue light, trapped and diffused from the sun, cut loose and gleaming out from under our boards. We didn't make another turn, just held our edge and our balance, screaming with the sheer impossible joy of it.

We rode that wave of snow down between those great snow-encrusted trees, all the way to the bottom, where it broke into tumbling blocks and released still more light, a geometry of snow backlit with electric blue.

I am jolted – alarm – Aaron's voice.

"You guys hear that?"

I listen. There is a faint humming sound somewhere below us in the woods.

"I hear it," Danny says.

The humming deepens as we hike lower, then it divides into two, then three buzzings, like a beehive. Like ATVs. Like chainsaws.

We make our way down a steep embankment, and the buzzing is loud now, just up ahead. They back off to an idle, a couple guys shout over the rumbling, and the chainsaws roar up again, just as we stumble out of the woods onto the old fire road.

Coming up the road on a big ATV, a guy in a hardhat stops, jumps out, and spraypaints orange *Xs* on three big trees, then remounts and works his way up toward us.

Two more guys in hard hats are coming up the road behind him, chainsawing through the downfall around each marked tree, buzzing off its lowest branches, swiping through all the little trees growing around it and out into the road.

They stop and look over at us, but don't kill the engines.

"What are you guys doing?" Aaron yells over the idling roar.

"Clearing this road," the ATV driver yells back. "To get the crane up in here."

"Crane? For what?"

"For the new chairlift."

"Chairlift?"

"From Prosperity Resort, over to the top of Ten-Seventy."

He holds up a clipboard with a folded-up topo map, and points to the summit, a crisp red *X* marked over the brown isoline oval and brown *X* marked *10070*.

The guys with the chainsaws work their way closer.

"That's Powell Peak," Aaron yells over the roar.

"If you say so," he yells back. "The company calls it Ten-Seventy."

Aaron's face turns to iron, and without saying anything to the guy or to us, he turns and starts down the road.

Danny and I look at each other, shrug, and start after him.

The three of us hike in a silent, sudden hurry to a trail we know will cross back over the ridge to the main trail.

As we scramble off the road and down the trail, Aaron finally mumbles something about the chairlift, the resort spreading like a cancer further up the canyon.

"Sounds like it's time for a little monkeywrenching," Danny says, in what I know he wants to sound like his *FTW* voice. But it sounds more forced than anything.

"Yeah, right," Aaron mutters. "Glen Canyon is dead. Long live Glen Canyon. In your dreams."

The adrenaline from the descent has finally worn off and exhaustion set it, and we hike in our own gloomy silences from yesterday, a dull, steady march down the big cutoff trail back to town.

When we bottom out at the trailhead and instantly drop our heavy packs next to Danny's Non-Hippie Bus, I finally just blurt it out, as startled by my own words as they seem to be.

"What's up with you guys?" I hear myself say. "We just did it! We just snowboarded off The Lady."

Danny is pulling out his bowl and bag of weed, and Aaron is futzing with his pack, neither saying anything, both avoiding my eyes.

"First snowboard descent ever! Aren't you guys psyched?"

Neither of them look up at me, or at each other.

"What? What's up?"

"I don't know, man," Danny finally says, packing the bowl. "I didn't want to say anything about this before the climb. 'Cuz I thought – I don't know – maybe I'd change my mind up there."

"Change your mind about what?"

"I think I'm taking off," he says. "For Portland."

"Really?"

"Yeah."

"When?"

"Like – pretty soon."

Aaron snorts from over at his pack, but doesn't look up. "I knew that was coming."

Danny holds the bowl up a moment, but he doesn't light it, then finally puts it down.

"I know it sounds weird," he says, "but I just miss her. And like – I figured I'd get over it. But it's just getting worse, not better. And I kinda can't stand it. So I'm gonna go check it out. Just to see what that's all about."

I know this is supposed to sound weird to me, but I don't really know how it sounds at all. Maybe because I don't really know much about anything that goes on inside another man's head, especially when it's really about his heart. Starting with my own, I suppose.

"When are you going?" is the only thing I can think to ask.

"In a few days," he says. "After I wrap up some shit at the shop."

Aaron comes over, looks at the ground, and lets out a long sigh. "Well, boys," he says, and sighs again. "As long as we're sharing." He picks up the bowl and lighter next to Danny's pack, stares into it, goes to light it, then doesn't. "I'm uh – taking off too."

"Really?" Danny and I say in unison.

"Yes. My mom isn't getting better, and my dad needs my help."

"Wow," I say. "You're going Back East. To stay?"

"For now – yeah."

"Plus, it's time I started getting my shit together," he says. "Figure out the grad school thing, or more likely the med school thing." He nods at me. "Like your girl – I mean, like Jill – did. It just feels like it's time."

The sound of Jill's name triggers a sharp little pain somewhere inside me, so I clench my stomach to make it go away, and keep talking.

"Med school," I say to him, trying to sound psyched. "That's an option?"

"Yeah," he says. "Always has been. I just don't like talking about it, unless I'm sure."

"Huh. Med school. I can see that."

"Fuck yeah, dude," Danny says. "You'd be a kick-ass doctor."

"Yeah, maybe," Aaron says, handing the unlit bowl back to Danny. "For now, it's all about my folks. They really need my help."

"I hear you, man, "Danny says and puts the bowl back in the Non-Hippie Bus.

"This has all been great," Aaron says, looking up at the mountains and letting out a long, sweet sigh. "But I can't mess around out here forever. I'm turning 30 next year. It's time to get on with it."

The End of Summer

It's the first week of September, and the snow is falling, a sugar-dusting along the cirque. From down here in Dudeville, I can just make out the ghostly ridgelines, a veil of cloud enveloping the mountains, a cold veil over everything, a shroud.

I started up the trail toward Sunset Peak alone this morning. But the woods were dark with fog and what I knew would be an all-day dusk, the trail wet and slippery, so I bailed.

Back at the trailhead, I realized I was hungry but didn't feel like any of the calories in my pack, and knew there was nothing for me at the Treehouse but leftovers and email; but I also didn't feel like going into Dudeville, which I knew would be a ghost town at this hour, especially with this weather and this time of year.

After sitting in my idling truck for a few minutes, fighting the urge, I watch as my truck turns on its own toward town, rolls slowly down an empty Main Street, and pulls up in front of Ullar's.

The place is deserted, but for Maggie behind the bar, reading from a chunky new black laptop she has wedged between the last bottles and the phone. Her black lab Buddy is asleep over by the fireplace. The sultry lament of a singer-songwriter hangs in the dusty air.

"I was just thinking about you," Maggie says when I sit at the bar. "And that wolf you think you dreamed up, a couple years back up in Steamboat." She points at the computer. "Turns out you weren't imagining it."

"What's that?" I ask, trying to make out what she's looking at in the middle of a scrambled mess on the computer.

"*The Denver Post*," she says, pouring each of us a beer. "You can get the whole newspaper on the Internet now."

"I guess that was going to happen sooner or later. And there's some story about wolves up there?"

"Top story," she says, putting a beer down in front of me.

She goes back to the computer. "'Wildlife biologists have confirmed the presence and sighting of several gray wolves in wilderness areas straddling the Colorado and Wyoming border,'" she reads, "'following several independent reports by hikers over the past eighteen months. They believe the wolves have migrated down from the Yellowstone re-introduction, several years ahead of earliest projections. Visitors to the area are advised not to venture into those wilderness areas alone and should use extreme caution, until further information is available.'"

"Huh," I say.

"I guess you got lucky," she says, looking at me over the top of reading glasses I'd never seen her wearing before.

"I guess so."

Maggie goes back to the newspaper on the computer, and I see the old familiar logo along the top, columns and pictures just like the front page. So, it has finally really happened, after all the chatter about it: the print media has gone cyber.

I swivel around on my barstool and take a good hard look at what has been like my living room these past few years. The old wooden skis and snowshoes and ice axes lining the walls. The long heavy tabletops carved with hundreds of names, initials, and dates, all worn into the beer-stained wood by thousands of elbows. The enormous blackened fireplace, Buddy asleep on its great slab hearth, his white-whiskered snout splayed out on his oversized, trail-hardened paws.

A commotion catches my eye out in the street, and I swivel all the way around and look out through the smudged window. But whatever it was – a flock of birds? A couple people on bikes? – is come and gone.

I swivel back to the bar and look up at the TV, its screen blank and dusty, and take a long swallow of beer.

The tourists are all come and gone too – like a flock of birds or couple of people riding by on bikes – just like they do after every Labor Day. But this year, so has everyone else, just like that. One big farewell party in here the other night, and now Aaron is Back East, and Danny is off to Portland.

Portland, man, Danny emailed me, *Funkytown on the west coast, the end of the Oregon Trail, you gotta check it out! Big rivers and rainforest and waterfalls and green green green everywhere. It's one big rinse-off from dry and dusty Dudeville, man. And the people, they're a little chubs and a little pale, but they are all cool and everybody plays music. It's like a big college town for grown-ups. You gotta come check it out!*

"People?" Seriously, Danny? Wasn't that the reason to go the *other* way, to the rivers and rainforest, waterfalls and woods? *FTW!!!* Right?

FTW always used to be right, long before I ever set foot in the West, or saw a real mountain, or met Danny. The woods were where I always went, no matter how good or bad it got with work back east, because it was where I learned to go no matter how ugly it got when I was a kid. Twenty feet through that curtain of leaves and there was no drunken, enraged father, no sick and angry and aggrieved mother, no taunting bullies, no petty teachers, no idiotic rules – just a quiet path through a break in the trees and into the woods. And then more and more woods, and a waterfall on the creek running through it all, always there, spilling into a little pool, all of it a million miles from the world.

I would run off and scheme and dream in those woods, and always about how I would one day run off for good. But I was never out there alone. I was out there with Daniel Boone, Davy Crockett, Jim Bridger, Kit Carson, the Last of the Mohicans, Eagle Feather, Ishi, The Last of his Tribe, and Huck Finn. And I was out there with all the cool kids I "met" in the pages of *Boys' Life* magazine, every issue of which I devoured the first day it showed up in the school library. They showed me how to build shelters, start fires, dig pits for food, how to keep warm and dry and fed out there when the snow started falling. Huck in particular helped me figure out how to survive on the run: how the next year, when I ran away for good, I could wander into town in the middle of the night for food and supplies, steal what I needed and sneak back out, and no one would ever know. I always knew that a year or two after that, when I grew up a little more and had stashed enough food, I would be big enough and strong enough to keep going, all the way to wherever the woods ended. Which I knew had to be Out West, because everyone and everything in the books I'd read over and over – even if a great river might pull them south – ran off to the west as soon as they could.

Then, one day when I was big enough and strong enough to hike all the way to where the woods ended, I discovered that the furthest west they ran was that little ski area west of town. I knew by then that it was as far west as I could go without a truck and money for gas; but I also knew a kid who had started working out there for his big brother.

That dingy little ski hill was my first taste of the freedom. It too was surrounded by woods, and they paid me three bucks an hour for shoveling snow around the lodge, hauling wood, digging out cars. By the time I was 16, they put me on the lifts and gave me a fifty-cent raise, and I was working every night and all weekend to save up for that first truck.

But the guys I worked with, all still into their 20s, were already broken old men: all married with kids, hooked on cheap whiskey, two packs a day, and the lottery. That wasn't any kind of future I wanted, so maybe west wasn't the best idea right then, but east to the nearest city, to get a job that didn't change with the seasons, make better money, maybe find a way to pay for college so I would never run aground like those guys.

The door slams.

I look up from my beer and see Tyler trying to hobble in, on crutches, kicking at the door with his working leg.

He is just back from another surgery and rehab down in Denver. He stumbles over to a bench along the nearest table, Deputy Dog waddling in behind him.

"How you doing, man?" I ask.

"How do I look, *man*? I'm fucked up, that's how I am, *man*."

"I guess happy hour starts a little early when you're laid up, huh?"

"No, *man* – not just that fucked up. I mean, I am – fucked – up. For good. *Man*."

Maggie comes around the bar with a mug and pot. "How about a little coffee, Tyler?"

"But you're going to walk again," I say to him.

"That's what I heard," Maggie says in her mama-bear voice.

"Never like I did," he mumbles. "Never do anything like I did."

"You don't know that," I say. "You never know."

"Aww," he waves me off. "I don't know shit, actually."

I can't think of something to say, until I think of something Aaron always says.

"People heal," I tell him. "Look at all the great skiers who came back from nasty crashes."

"I don't know, dude," he mumbles. "Maybe. Who knows. Sorry for being such a dick. I'm just wasted." He looks at the coffee sitting in front of him, starts laughing, then he bursts into tears.

Maggie is back behind the bar, and we look at each other and shrug.

Tyler's sobbing slows, and he stretches his cast leg out under the table.

A moment later, his head drops onto his chest as he passes out.

"Wow," Maggie says, and goes back to reading on the computer.

I go back to my beer and remember something else Aaron always says: "Junkies addicted to risk and adrenaline are like any other junkies: they can't ever get enough."

He is exactly right, and things don't usually work out for junkies. They die in big ugly ways, or they slowly liquify, and die in small ugly ways. I have no idea anymore what I want with my life, but I know that I don't want either of those endings.

But for a long while, I think I did. The first one anyway. I wanted to put myself as close to the edge as my body and head could handle, to take on as much risk as I could without freaking out. And why? To prove something? What? And to whom? Maybe just to prove, to myself, that I could save myself, over and over and over? And for what? More time out there at the edge? More time out there with the Presence, risking my own private martyrdom for my own private religion?

Madness! Or so it all seems to me on this dreary day.

Or maybe I've just spent too many hours thinking about it this summer. Maybe it was just that horrible near-miss on Borah Peak. But the Presence has been more and more absent these past few weeks.

And I miss it.

Or maybe I just miss Aaron and Danny. And Jill.

So now what am I supposed to do?

I always used to have an escape plan: as a kid, then as a young married scrounge, then as a young divorced business guy. So what now? In every one of my forty years, I never once had a vision for being somewhere, only a fantasy about running off to somewhere else.

"Huh," Maggie says.

"What?"

"Says they're running a chairlift all the way up Deer Canyon."

"*Over* to Deer Canyon, yeah," I say. "We saw a crew clearing trees along the old fire road when we were coming down from The Lady."

"No," she reads on, "it says *up* Deer Canyon. Two chairlifts. There's another coming over from the resort. They're developing the whole thing."

"But that means it'll top out – somewhere up on the right side of The Lady."

"That's what it means. Check it out," she points at the screen. "There's a map."

I go around the bar and look at the article on the screen as Maggie clicks on the little map. But it takes too long and only half-loads, then the whole thing crashes.

"Oh well," Maggie shrugs. She turns to me, pulls off her new reading glasses, and gives me an odd half-smile.

"What?"

"I'm thinking about closing up for the day. Weather sucks and the town's dead." She glances over at Tyler, passed out and slumped over on the bench. "Help me get him home first?"

I notice her smell, maybe for the first time ever: like the woods, after a good cleansing rain, with a hint of cinnamon and clove.

I walk back over to my barstool and beer and try to avoid her eyes. But I can see past my beer that she is still smiling at me, and I realize what she means.

"Make a good pot of coffee," she says, "maybe smoke a bowl. I'm sure we can find a way to kill the rest of the day."

"I'm sure," I say.

She smiles at me again and turns back to the computer.

I stare down into what's left of my beer and remember what Danny had said about her: about how she made great coffee in a French press, stirred it with a chopstick, stood over the bed with her big red nipples poking out of her bathrobe. I know I'm supposed to get all excited about it, and maybe there's a little tickle of all that down there.

I look up at Maggie, at the waterfall of chestnut hair over her broad shoulders, her strong jawline and full lips, and steady, thoughtful gaze. She is sturdy, capable, funny, and smart, and she still goes pretty big. And she's halfway to my age from Jill. So how has this not come up until now?

She turns and catches me staring at her.

"You thinking about it?"

"I am," I say.

She smiles one more time and turns back to the computer.

I know she means an afternoon of wild sex and nothing more, and I know it would be a great way to fend off this weird, looming dread. But then what? Ski dates and road trips and promises? Or then nothing? And then weirdness every time I come back in here?

Maybe if I were on Ecstacy, like with Jill those couple of times, I could see all of it unfurl like any one of half a dozen perfect mountain town love stories: the lost boy and the girl next door, who was right there the whole time; the two old kids in the crowd, finally getting together, and turning into everybody's cool aunt and uncle; the grande dame and her aging mountain man, holding court in here twenty years from now about we bought Ullar's and saved it from the developers. Or would that last one take a sharp turn as I went to work for those same developers – rationalizing that I could help them minimize the damage they were going to do to the mountains anyway – because Maggie was suddenly pregnant, and glowing even brighter than she is right now, all thanks to some drug-induced psychosis one afternoon when the weather sucked and we were both bored.

Or maybe it really would just be sex, because the weather sucks and we're both bored.

"Still thinking about it?" she says to me, without turning to look.

"I am."

"Lemme know what you come up with."

But all I can come up with are stories that wind down in Dudeville, in a place we once loved and guarded so jealously as our own, before it was overrun by people who have no idea why we don't call it "Columbine." And I don't like how any of those stories end.

In their wake, all I can think is what a perfect arrangement it all would have been three years ago, when I first rolled into Dudeville, and I couldn't imagine ever turning 40, or ever leaving.

But I don't think I want to be here anymore.

Maggie turns and studies my face, the half-smile starting to crack at the edges.

"Well?" she asks.

"That sounds like fun," I say, trying to avoid her suddenly hard eyes. "But I have to get back to my house and deal with some stuff."

Her smile disappears, like I'd just slapped it off her mouth.

"Suit yourself," she says, sputtering a bit. Then she sighs and her eyes go soft again, and she cracks another smile. "You know what they say. 'You don't lose your girlfriend –'"

But she sees that I can see that she is forcing it, and doesn't finish the joke.

"That's what they say."

"But it never hurts to ask," she sighs again, then squints at the computer and puts her reading glasses back on.

I down the last of the beer and slip off the barstool. "See you around, Maggie."

"Yeah," she says, not looking up from the computer. "See you around."

I walk out into the empty street, and lift my eyes to the mountains, and feel completely, utterly alone. I think I've always felt this way, but it never bothered me until now. Maybe I should spin around on my heels and head straight back into Ullar's before Maggie takes off. Help her get Tyler home, then we hurry up to The Treehouse for a good, long, meaningless romp.

And then what?

I stand in the middle of the street, wishing I could pretend for just a little bit longer, but I can't.

The snow is falling again, up on the cirque and all the way down here in town. Little stinging crystals of it have turned the air cold and damp, muffling the town with the sudden hush of early winter.

It is only the first week of September, but it feels like the world is ending, before we ever had a chance to finish the harvest. We may have survived the end of civilization that Y2K was going to bring; but maybe the math was wrong, and it's just coming a year or two later.

I start down the empty street and think about Danny's email: *Portland, man! Funkytown on the west coast, the end of the Oregon Trail, you gotta come check it out!*

So maybe I'll go to Portland, just to check it out, and make sure they're doing ok. *Mountain Gazette* says *When in Doubt Go Higher.* But maybe that's true only on the eastern side of the Great Continental Divide, and what it really means is, when in doubt, keep going west.

Lots of people – great, Danny – and I'm sure they're all cool. But I have to go somewhere, and he and Julie are there, so why not? Lots of people, and they all play music. Ok.

I climb into my old truck, turn the wipers on to blow off the dusting of snow, and head out of town.

*   *   *   *

*Kleinke * 360*

REFERENCES & INSPIRATION

FICTION

The Adventures of Huckleberry Finn, Mark Twain
Angel of Repose, Wallace Stegner
Animal Dreams, Barbara Kingsolver
The Big Rock Candy Mountain, Wallace Stegner
Dharma Bums, Jack Kerouac
Looking for Mo, Daniel Duane
The Monkeywrench Gang, Edward Abbey
The Way West, A.B. Guthrie

MEMOIR

Desert Solitaire, Edward Abbey
Forget Me Not, Jenny Lowe-Anker
Lighting Out: A Vision of California and the Mountains,
   Daniel Duane
The Mountains of California, John Muir
Roughing It, Mark Twain
The Yosemite, John Muir

NON-FICTION

*Blood and Thunder: The Epic Story of Kit Carson and the Conquest
   of the American West*, Hampton Sides
*Bury My Heart at Wounded Knee: An Indian History of the
   American West*, Dee Brown
Cadillac Desert, Marc Reisner
Eiger Dreams: Ventures Among Men and Mountains, Jon Krakauer
The Emerald Mile, Kevin Fedarko
I Will Fight No More Forever: Chief Joseph and The Nez Perce War,
   Merrill D. Beal
Into Thin Air, Jon Krakauer

REFERENCES & INSPIRATION

NON-FICTION (cont'd)

Mountaineering: The Freedom of the Hills, 6th Edition,
  Don Graydon & Kurt Hanson, editors.
The Open Space of Democracy, Terry Tempest Williams
Wilderness and Rescue Medicine, 4th Edition, Jeffrey Isaac &
  David Johnson

FILM
The films of Warren Miller
Meru, Jimmy Chin & Elizabeth Chai Vasarhalyi
Scrapple, Christopher Hansen
Steep, Mark Obenhaus

POETRY
Leaves of Grass, Walt Whitman
Selected Poetry, Robinson Jeffers

ACKNOWLEDGMENTS

Dudeville was informed and inspired by everyone along for the limb up and ride down, especially: Rob, Josh, Jody, Leonard, Rachel, -Tabs, Chris & Karen, Fuckindrew, Tim, Sarah, Sean, Kevin, Becky, tan, The Big Girl, and Fuck Yeah Dude. And, of course, the dogs, ettle, Buddy, Sampson, Lucy and Simon, who always summited first.

Huge high-fives to George Pillari, a reincarnation from the era of ne great editor, who traffics in the nitty-gritty but still sees in books; o Mindee Thyrring, gifted designer and consummate Betty on snow nd surf, who jumped right in and saw *Dudeville* from the inside out; o Ryan Fleming, fellow seeker and word junkie, for reminding me ot to apologize for the *real* love story in here; to Mimi Patterson for er sharp eyes and good cheer; and to Rabbi Ariel Stone, checker of he Big Facts, and my music partner and sister from another mother.

Heartfelt thanks for the close reads and unvarnished feedback rom my dear friends Mia Birk, Rob & Tara Bodner, Brian Buchanan, iteve & Kalyn Cohen, Tasha Danner, Adam Elstein, Kathy Goodman, Craig Havighurst, Miles Hochstein, Sarah Krakauer, Sarah Loughran, Tim Madden, and Matt Snook.

And ... the last word goes to my beloved wife and best friend, Sara Radcliffe. *Dudeville* exists because she would not let me *not* write it. ihe endured multiple drafts, countless dinner table rants, and untold nonths of a husband in zombie-author mode. Her incisive mind, oaring heart, and sweet grace inspired and sustained this book from onception to completion, as they do me, every day.

*Kleinke * 364*

ABOUT THE AUTHOR

J.D. Kleinke has worked in the US health care "system" since 1989. He is the author of three books about medicine in America, including *Catching Babies*, a novel about the culture of maternity care and childbirth. He has also been involved in the formation, management, and governance of several health care companies and non-profit organizations. His work has appeared in *The New York Times, The Wall Street Journal*, and dozens of medical and business publications. He and his wife live in Portland, Oregon, and Half Moon Bay, California.

*Kleinke * 366*

*DUDEVILLE * 367*

*Kleinke * 368*

CPSIA information can be obtained
at www.ICGtesting.com
Printed in the USA
BVOW08s1552121217

502601BV00002B/140/P

9 780692 977767